Dancing
WITH
THE Wind

A TRUE STORY OF ZEN IN THE ART OF WINDSURFING

Other books by LAURIE NADEL

Corazon Aquino: Journey to Power

The Great Stream of History: A Biography of Richard Nixon

The Kremlin Coup

Sixth Sense

Intuition at Work
(anthology edited by Roger Franz and Alex Pattakos)

Dancing
WITH THE *Wind*

A TRUE STORY OF ZEN IN THE ART OF WINDSURFING

Laurie Nadel

PARAVIEW PRESS

NEW YORK

Dancing with the Wind

Permission to quote from CBS News broadcasts has been given by CBS News, 524 West 57th Street, New York, NY 10019

Permission to quote from "Honey, They Shrank My Head," *Maxim*, July 1996, Dennis Publishing, Bolsover Street, London W2, England.

Permission to quote from *Zen and the Art of Motorcycle Maintenance* by Robert Pirsig granted by HarperCollins Publishers, 10 East 53 Street, New York, NY 10022

A percentage of royalties from print and electronic versions of *Dancing with the Wind* are donated to the The Ocean Conservancy and the Tricycle Exchange for Buddhist Studies.

Book and cover design by Smythtype

ISBN: 1931044317

Library of Congress Catalog Card Number: 2001093731

*For my teachers
in all the worlds*

The events in this book are real. Many of the names have been changed to protect the privacy of those individuals.

Contents

Foreword
From Tattoos to Mt. Fuji
to the Flow and Back

TATTOOS
Have you ever felt so strongly about something that you've considered tattooing it to your body? All stylistic motives aside, look around and under clothes. Find hearts with names, symbols of nationality and religious icons. These prickly inkings are marks of permanency. All but the most drunken can understand the levity of the tattoo parlor chair. I've often wondered whether I would ever feel the need to permanently adorn myself.

MT. FUJI
If there was a single image that typified my love for windsurfing it would be The Great Wave Over Mt. Fuji. In this print a surging dark blue wave towers over a dwarfed mountain. The water encompasses the entire work as if showing its dominance over the land. Outstretched fingers pass through the air like a child's hand in a candy shop display. It almost pauses, daintily picking at the scared fishermen. Some have called the men in the fishing skiffs insignificant. The fishermen hide in the gunwales, cowering from the wave's greedy fingers.

Last winter while at University, I found myself in the tattoo parlor chair. This is a metaphor "for almost doing it." It became quite clear that my appreciation for the Japanese wood block print would have to be shown by a nice frame and some prominent wall space.

THE FLOW

When windsurfing, I feel like the fishermen–insignificant. Like in the print, the ocean is bigger than a mountain and yet seems dainty and graceful as it looms above me. I flow down the face of a wave, not hapless as often described, but insignificant nonetheless.

AND BACK

Laurie Nadel has binded years of life into these pages. I choose the word binded carefully, as some of these memories were locked deeply away. Encompassed in these memories are daily accounts of her successes and failures. You might feel a twinge of intrusion–do not. These are your experiences also.

My relationship with Laurie started early in the summer of 1997. She appeared in Windsurfing Hamptons for a lesson. The short drive to the Peconic Bay found water as still as a bathtub. We started the lesson anyhow, but ended up talking more about our shared fondness of the sport.

Throughout the summer, which brought us many nonwindy days, I realized Laurie and I were mirror images of each other. Our involvements with windsurfing started as a thrilling challenge. It has transcended to a way of life. For me, it brought a meager livelihood from contest winnings and sponsorships, and for both of us a way to reach a heightened yet meditative state, referred to in these pages as The Flow.

I am now in my fourth month living on Maui as a professional windurfer. Each day during these four months I have trained at Ho'okipa Beach Park in Paia, Hawaii. On this one reef, winter swells break in perfect conjunction with strong trade winds giving the ultimate proving ground for the world's best windsurfers. I took to this place immediately, if not confidently, and have taken my share of beatings.

On the sixteenth of February, 1998, a heavy north swell battered the Northern shoreline, particularly Ho'okipa beach park. I waited on the beach for the right moment to launch, watching as the waves marched like corduroy soldiers to the beach.

The events that followed are not particularly clear in my mind. I remember punching through the first sets of white water. Underneath my board the water started to become the deeper green that signifies deep water, and in this case safety. I knew that if I could reach the outside I would not be crushed by the rearing waves that break on the inside reef.

I knew that something was wrong when my momentum was not strong enough to push me forward against the current. This did not bode well for my chances of clearing the largest set wave, just seconds away. I remember feeling the wave suck water out as it inhaled before breaking. I was halfway up the twenty-foot wave's face before I chose to jump and swim for the bottom.

The trouncing that incurred was vicious at best. I was flipped, turned, twisted, torn and finally pinned against the reef and forced to swim five strokes to the surface. The first breath was joyous if not short-lived, as the next monster took its turn flogging me. The next time I surfaced, I saw my gear over a hundred yards away, and drifting fast! I swam quickly and waited for the succession of waves to surge behind me and force me through the cycle again and again.

Once tumbled to the inside where my gear first traveled, I saw the current taking it out again into the Pacific. At this point and a few more deep dives I was questioning my will to swim further. The thought of death was stark. I watched as my equipment took a heavy beating and luckily floated within swimming distance. I got myself together and limped my way back to the beach.

My troubles were not over as I got washed against the reef's shelf and its prickly urchin inhabitants. This injury added to the insult and I whimpered a bit once on the coral sand. It was in that moment I felt most in The Flow state. Bruised, beaten and meek, I understood Nature's power, my will, and how a life without risk is not really a life at all.

Interesting how you can feel most alive after almost dying. I went windsurfing an hour later at a slightly calmer beach down the road. Test your mind, body and soul, and you will discover what it means to find The Flow. That is what this book is about.

Jace Panebianco
January 1998

Prologue
United Nations headquarters, NY
November 1974

"Is that you?" He asks the same question each time he calls. "Of course it's me. Where are you?" I answer the same way each time. I know that he is calling me once again from a pay phone because he believes his phone is tapped. This is 1974, after all. Nixon. Watergate. J. Edgar Hoover. More essential to this story, however, 1974 is B.W. Before Windsurfing.

"He" is a diplomat from a Middle Eastern country and I am an American reporter working for the United Nations news service. Come to think of it, my phone is probably tapped, too. But then, maybe it isn't. Maybe this is just part of the intrigue of international politics, along with the love affair that he and I are having here between the shadows of the Chrysler building and U.N. headquarters. Anyway, we are developing a telephone ritual.

"I am between the earth and the sky. Where are you?" he asks.

I smile. "Between the light and the water."

I'm joking, of course, but something seems to tug at me whenever I say this, as though my spirit is pulling at a wet-suit zipper, wanting to get out. Lately, I have been sitting at the window, staring as sunlight catches the East River, chasing the current in silvery ripples, downstream. Somewhere, the background seems to hold a thoughtform from a Joni Mitchell song about wishing she had a river she could sail away on.

In the meantime, he and I are in a kind of suspended time zone. I feel as if he is my twin, my shadow. We are about the same height. We have the same smile. Similar facial structure. We walk and breathe in the same rhythm.

One evening, I notice with curiosity that people seem to be staring at us as we walk through the East Side of Manhattan holding hands. When we stop to kiss under a streetlight, for the first time, I notice he is dark coffee brown. Since I tend to see people from the inside out, it has never occurred to me that he is different.

"I just noticed why people stare at us." It's hard not to feel a little foolish.

"That's not it," he says. "They see our light."

One night, after we have made love, and before he is getting ready to return to his country, I ask him why he always says that he is between the earth and the sky. "Because I am, silly. Why do you always say that you are between the light and the water?"

The truth hits me. "Because that is where I'd like to be."

Part One
1981–1986

It furthers one to cross the great water.
−I CHING, HEXAGRAM #5[1]

Volendam, The Netherlands
May 1981

Springtime in Holland. Wall-to-wall tulips, just like the postcards except it's very cold, about forty-five degrees Fahrenheit with floor-to-ceiling Eurofog. My husband and I are on our honeymoon, biking along the Dutch coast.

"Look!" I point to three men, off the coast, standing on the water, holding on to sails. I hold my breath as they ride, suspended between two mutable elements, their physical shapes dissolving into an etheric mist.

"I don't believe...they're doing it!"

"Doing what?" asks my husband, Pete.

"They are between light and water." Almost lightheaded at seeing physical proof of a daydream from long ago, the image of the three sailors is awakening some primal DNA code.

"What's the big deal? They're windsurfing," he shrugs.

"Is that what it's called?"

I like to think that Pete grew up in the Pacific Ocean. He was a lifeguard in Australia before we met in the middle of the Ambrose Channel, the shipping lane for New York City. We were sailing a friend's twenty-eight foot Triton that afternoon. (A lot of people are surprised to hear about a sailing community in New York City, but before there were roads, Dutch and English explorers and tradesmen sailed wooden boats through the same excellent system of bays and rivers.) Blessed with fearlessness and impeccable coordination, Pete was the one soul onboard that day, who actually enjoyed being hoisted in a canvas harness, forty feet up to the top of the aluminum mast, where he untangled the halyard lines. I can't even stand on a chair without getting dizzy.

"Windsurfing."[2] Spoken softly, for the first time, the

sound of the word contains all the mystery of a solitary buoy in the fog, echoing across the water at the end of the day. Saying it brings back that tug, from here to somewhere between the light and the water. A feeling, something like tears, is forming at the back of my eyelids. "I *have* to do that."

Pete's expression goes long and strange: amazement, concern, and amusement mix with just a hint of mockery. After all, I am the clumsiest, least athletic woman he has ever ever met. On our first date, I set fire to our table by putting my linen napkin over the little candle. It was an accident, but he was pretty angry. By way of apology, I blurted out a confession: the time my cousin took me to see *Lawrence of Arabia*, and I slipped on my high heels, and slid on my butt all the way down the steps of the packed balcony of the Ziegfield theater. When Pete didn't laugh, I merely compounded my own discomfort. "...and I once stretched out my legs and knocked a table clear across an Italian restaurant in the Bronx."

What I haven't told him yet, is how I was five feet eight inches tall when I was eleven years old. At summer camp, where everyone else my age was age-appropriately petite, the other girls called me "Dumbo" and "Freak." When it turned out that I was inept at sports, they put toothpaste in my sheets as punishment. At sixteen, when I started working as a waitress in the Poconos, the cooks regularly placed bets on how many trays I would drop during a meal.

"Windsurfing?" Pete laughs. Now, he is looking at me as if I have just announced that I intend to flap my arms and fly off the top of the World Trade Center. "You? You want to windsurf? Why?"

Okay, I think to myself. *Maybe I'm the world's least likely candidate for this, but...*

"So I can know what it's like to hang out between the light and the water," I say.

Inside, my spirit is sparkling like foam on the crest of a

wave at high tide under a full moon. Like Archimedes in the bathtub, discovering the principles of displacement, I have Eureka'ed. I have found it. I am going home.

Port Washington, New York
July 10, 1982

I should have known better than to take this up. After all, one is supposed to learn from experience, isn't one? By now, you would have thought I would have realized my own limitations.

It looks so deceptively easy. Like that bumper sticker: "Happiness is a hand-held sail." And me, unfazed by the prospect of falling into the water a few times. Ha! All it takes is a flash of that black and white image of three windsurfers off the Dutch coast to conjure up sureness in the solar plexus.

Although I welcome the Unknown, there is an aspect to all this that I hadn't taken into account: the pain. Physical and emotional. To be truthful, I have no natural ability for windsurfing. Or any other sport, for that matter. After nine months of diligent weight training three times a week in order to build upper body strength for hoisting the sail, I'm still unprepared.

Even with today's light wind, I am unable to stand and hoist the sail. Two hours and more than fifty attempts later, I'm a failure. Of the three students in the beginners' class, I am far and away the worst. By worst, I mean the klutziest, most ineffective, and incompetent. Even the fat, fifty-year old doctor does better than me. Adding to my humiliation is a small crowd of people standing on shore, laughing as my legs and arms pretzel into Chaplinesque tangles, flipping me ungraciously off the board. By force of will, I drag myself back onto the board again and again, while the young woman instructor calls out across the water:

"Straighten the mast, don't grab it! Hold the uphaul! Not the mast!" In my mind's eye, she's a two-dimensional cartoon, with her thoughts floating in a bubble over her head:

"Not the mast, dummy!"

"Pull with your shoulders, not your back!" It is way too much to remember when simply standing up takes all my energy. It's hot, about eighty-five degrees, and I'm getting dizzy. Finally, I heave myself onto the board, stand up with shaky legs, put my left foot just in front of the mast and pull–yank–pull the sail up, using my shoulders not my lower back, and grab hold. A minor puff of wind carries me about twelve feet towards a seawall.

"Drop the uphaul! Drop the uphaul!" the instructor yells in time for me to avoid smashing into the wall. Now I have to get back. No matter how hard I try, I can't change course and end up banging into the seawall. Basic beginner's mistake number one: Allowing yourself to be carried downwind.

The instructor swims out to retrieve the board. She stands up easily, hoisting the sail, skimming back to shore, as I swim behind her like a disgruntled seal pup following its mother. "You did well," she says, as I wade ashore.

"You don't have to lie to me." I grab my towel, wiping away embarrassed tears which I hope she doesn't notice.

"No, really," she says, gently. "Most people can't even stand on the board their first time out."

Now, lying on the sand at Manorhaven Beach, about half a mile from the site of my first lesson, that part of me that does a really good job of putting me in my place, is having a field day. *You could hardly stand up. You were terrible. So clumsy. It's too hard. Damn.* My back and leg muscles contract in spasms. My arms feel like I've been hanging from them for hours. My knees burn, somewhat bloody, from rubbing against the board. "Beginners' knees," I think they're called.

Various aches throb in their own distinct rhythms, disappointment being the hardest to take. I had no idea it would be so difficult. Not to mention the unexpected, bottomless surge of fear as I slammed into that seawall, out of control.

This is pathetic. Surely I'm wasting my time. I'll never even master the basics.

Port Washington, NY
August 15, 1982

Every Tuesday, my day off, I drive to Olympic Windsurfing in Port Washington and get a portable, tie-on roofrack for my 1978 Oldsmobile. Then I help whoever's working in the shop to carry a Windsurfer to the car, where we tie it to the rack. The Windsurfer is a cumbersome twelve and a half feet long sailboard weighing in at about fifty-five pounds. Getting it on and off the roof of the car is an ordeal in itself.

After driving two miles to the bay, I struggle with the rig, which seems to have a will of its own. The cloth sail is wound, like a flag, around the fifteen-foot long mast. I have to unroll it, then attach a teak wishbone contraption called a boom. The boom is what you hold onto when you are actually windsurfing. Not that I have actually windsurfed yet. The boom ties onto the mast and to the outside tip of the sail, called a clew. Everything hangs together, or not, depending on how well you can tie a half-hitch. You'd think after five years of earning Girl Scout merit badges, I'd have this skill down, but half-hitches were never required for those little round merit badges: "First Aid to Animals," "Swimmer," and "Cook."

After the rig thing is tied together, I jam it into a contraption called a universal joint, which then gets jammed into a narrow slot in the middle of the sailboard. The universal holds it all together. Hopefully. Sometimes, universal, sail, boom, and mast all come off in the water, but I'm learning how to slam the rig back into the slot. One of the kids in the store tells me if you wrap some aluminum foil around the mast base, it holds better, so now I'm driving around New York with a roll of aluminum foil in the trunk, just for Tuesdays.

Eventually, I push off, maneuver the Windsurfer into

position, and attempt to hoist the sail. It's usually around now that I begin my regular routine of falling off, crawling back onto the board, and smashing into moored sailboats. In the background, I hear howls of laughter from my fans, about a half-dozen locals who come to the bridge every Tuesday to watch me make a total fool of myself. Funny, no one else is windsurfing.

Back home, Pete jokes that I look like a tomcat after a fight. My knees are perpetually skinned, like a kid learning how to rollerskate. My shins are black and blue. My finger-tips are scraped raw from getting caught in the rig, my palms are blistered, and my back feels like it was hit by a truck. In the CBS newsroom, people give me strange looks.

"Are you having trouble at home?" Ernestine, the news-room manager, whispers, one Wednesday as I walk past her desk.

"No, why?"

"Well, dear, you're looking a little bruised. Your cowork-ers are worried."

This makes me laugh. "I'm learning to windsurf!"

She now looks even more concerned. "What's...what did you call it, dear?"

I start to describe the surfboard and the sail, moving my arms to demonstrate holding onto the boom. Ernestine is trying to look cool but I know she thinks I'm weird.

"Are you sure it's worth all this, dear?" She scans my bruised shins up to the cuts on my knees, looking into my eyes for signs of dementia.

"Nice lats." Jack, our weekend producer and newsroom bodybuilder grins as he he walks past my demonstration of how to hold onto a boom.

Jack's the man. A few months ago, when I told him about wanting to windsurf, he brought in all these maga-zines with pictures of guys like Arnold Schwarznegger and Lou Ferrigno using metallic torture devices. Spreading the pages all over the newsdesk, he pointed out upper body muscles with bizarre names. Delts. Tris. Lats. (*Ugh.*) "You're going to have to train," he said, firmly. (*Double ugh.*) "Where do you live? I'll find you a gym."

Jack's research leads us to a no-frills weightlifters' gym five miles from my home, in a converted supermarket, right under the same elevated subway where they filmed the car chase scene in *The French Connection*. In another sign of friendship, he and his wife trekked to Brooklyn from the Bronx–an hour and a half on the subway–one freezing afternoon in February to check on my training routine. Now I know: "Never do abs first. Save them for the end." Personally, I think maybe they just wanted the thrill of doing French curls and lat pulls underneath a giant poster of The Incredible Hulk.

The owners of the gym and their relatives wander in and out, carrying new babies, making jokes to each other and laughing. A warm, traditional Brooklyn family, they are each, in their own way, encouraging and interested in how I'm making progress. I'm not sure whether or not I am–I still don't know a lat from a delt–but I'm quietly persistent. And I'm learning some important tips, like how to get sweat stains out of workout clothes.[3] A few weeks ago, the Incredible Hulk came to work out, twirling two forty-five pound weights in his fingers as if they were frisbees. If I even tried to lift one of those things, it would mean a one-way ticket to Walter B. Cooke.[4]

The gym is a serious place. I go through my training routines in silence, nodding hello to bench-pressing firemen and police officers just off the night shift. No one flirts. Well, hardly anyone. For me, the workout gives me time to stop thinking about the lists: tasks, projects, assignments, people to call, and stories–as many as one hundred, between thirty seconds and two minutes apiece–that will stack up on my desk later in the day.

The news syndication department where I work is a kind of news factory that broadcasts footage on closed circuit feeds to more than two hundred network affiliates as well as to overseas clients, including Japanese TV, every day. People think it's a glamour job, but like all writing, it's grunt work. Perhaps it's where I trained for the inner strength to take up something as difficult as windsurfing. Every day, our department scrambles for scraps of footage and outtakes that the evening news rejects, which we recut and freshen up. In addition to the day's hard news, we specialize in oddball feature stories, like talking squirrels, chainsaw sculptors, and trailer park artists (my favorite being the man who makes lamps out of washing machine agitators), watermelon spitting contests, and bizarre events, such as rattlesnake festivals. These "slice of life" stories are supposed to give people overseas a look at lifestyles in America, but my partner Sal and I often wonder what a family sitting down to breakfast in Seoul must think of us, when they see this stuff on their morning news programs. A writer and news editor here for the past twenty years, Sal is my Siamese twin. Our desks are joined so that we can pitch ideas, copy, jokes, and frustrations back and forth, throughout the day. I don't know how I would handle the load without Sal's laid- back sense of humor.

The high volume of material that we turn around for broadcast, between the peak hours of three and seven PM, makes me feel like I'm a cross between a short order cook and a canner in a sardine factory. How many words can you pack into a thirty–second can? How many cans can you fill up every fifteen minutes, while simultaneously taking "orders," about incoming stories over the phone? Multitasking, I think it's called. It takes tremendous concentration. Learning how to zone into the quiet spaces between so many different sounds in order to write, must be excellent training for something–I'm just not sure what. I tell myself this is like practicing Hannon scales on the piano, and that someday, when my wrists are really strong,

I'll be able to write longer pieces, maybe even books.

Writing TV news in cramped, noisy rooms with no windows is not what I pictured when I studied writing in college and a one-semester flying leap, in and out of grad school. In the thirteen years since I graduated from Sarah Lawrence, I've had more writing jobs than are good for me and some excellent adventures and opportunities: writing TV news in London, writing and producing for another network in New York, working as a foreign correspondent for *Newsweek* during the state of siege in Chile and reporting on the Amazon oil boom for United Press International. A subject whom I was interviewing tried to turn me into the general in charge of the Chilean air force, so I left the country in a hurry. Having learned the hard way that I don't have the nerves of steel required for being a war correspondent, I do a fair amount of volunteer work as a human rights advocate for journalists around the world who are not as fortunate as I was. There must be an angel watching over me. He or she must have pulled some strings up there to get me here so I could begin to settle down. It was my intention to stay six months, save some money, then work my way around the world with Pete but there's a lot to be said for getting grounded and working hard with a great group of people so it's been four years and counting. "God help you when you start counting those years," Sal laughs.

In contrast to the good-natured chaos of a newsroom in the afternoon, the repetitive rhythm of ten reps, four sets of exercises, pushes out thoughts of work so that I lose track of time and place. I imagine this is similar to walking meditation, where with each movement, conscious focus dissolves, taking you into a zone where you no longer think.

After one Saturday morning workout, while I'm grabbing a cup of coffee, I have a chance to indulge one of my favorite vices, listening in on strangers' conversations in places where I don't belong. Until now, the top two nuggets in my collection have come from the New York subways: "Yeah, he got boined. You know how it is in a fire" and "'Ja hear about the moidah in 3c? The cops sealed off everything and now I can't get no hot water in 2c." Leaning my head over my coffee cup to make it seem as if I have no interest in anything else, I can hear two young, local gentlemen in the next booth talking about the going price of a "contract". Their dialogue sounds like something from a bad de Niro movie. It's hard to believe they aren't acting. In Brooklyn these days, it costs more than three hundred dollars to make a car "disappear." At low tide, you can see them rusting away in a marsh near Kennedy Airport.

I'm about to tell Jack about that conversation, when he asks, "You're really doing that thing with the surfboard and the sail?"

"Of course," I smile.

He and Ernestine exchange looks. They think I'm not playing with a full deck.

"Ain't you afraid of them sharks?" The homeboy accent is burlesque, the question, half-serious.

Should I clue him in to reality? "Brooklyn Girl Eaten By Shark" is not a viable lead. I should know. I spent a year writing the Saturday night news for a local station, a program so bad that our inhouse nickname for it was "News for the Hard of Thinking." I got laid off after I refused to participate in the Gary Mark Gilmore Execution Sweepstakes. It was in poor taste, I said, to bet on the exact minute someone was going to be put to death, even if that someone was a convicted killer. On the other hand, the question of what constitutes "poor taste" is fairly flexible when, on a nightly basis, your lead is likely to be random shooting, a corpse dredged out of the Gowanus Canal on a giant meathook, or a headless torso found in a dumpster. That job gave me nightmares.

"The only sharks I'm afraid of are the ones that wear

three-piece suits and write memos," I smile while Jack and Ernestine say, "Amen" with high-fives all around. I figure, in the end, one of them is more likely to get me than any of those sharks in the water.

Port Washington, NY
August 22, 1982

Did you ever think about what happened when you were learning how to walk? With each new step, your parents cheered. Now, think back: When you fell down, did anyone applaud? Yet, if you didn't fall down, you would never have learned how to pick yourself up. That's because falling down, which we perceive as failure, is a built-in part of learning how to walk.

Maybe I should congratulate myself whenever I fall. Or fail, for that matter. Then again, isn't there some Japanese CEO who defines success is ninety-nine percent failure?

Today, I finally stand up, take sight of a buoy about four meters away, mentally set a course, and windsurf all the way there, without falling!

Then turn and sail back in one smooth tack.

That might not seem like a big deal to you, but to a klutz like me, it is simply one of the most elegant moments of my entire life.

Port Washington, NY
September 15, 1982

I have my own sailboard now, a three-piece German-made Shark. The trail to the Shark started on a railway platform in London twelve years ago, when I sat on my suitcase next to a young Dutch woman who was sitting on her suitcase in Euston station. Anne-Mieke had just spent a year working as an au pair in Chicago and she was on her way home. Would I like to come with her? A train and a boat and a train later, we arrived in a village with a windmill on the river. Not only was she great company, her parents were almost as happy to see me as they were to have her home again. My family would not have been so thrilled had I arrived home with a stranger after a year's absence.

Last week, she and her fiance, Leo, brought this sailboard over from Amsterdam. It's ideal for anyone living in a narrow, Victorian townhouse, without a garage or storage shed. Rather than one twelve-foot long plank of polyethylene, the Shark breaks down into three, four-foot planks.

Before I can get out on the water, I have to put it together with a few dozen metal rods, screws, washers, and other unidentifiable alien metal thingies. It comes with a 5.0 meter, yellow Neil Pryde sail but I now have acquired a black and white Neil Pryde 4.0 meter sail, which is what I am sailing with today, even though the wind is out of the northwest at 10 knots. Sailing with a 4.0 meter sail in 10 knots is ridiculous, but I want to succeed. With a beginner's sail and beginner's wind, I might have half a chance.

Today's triumph is launching off the shore at Manorhaven and floating through sailboats anchored in the bay without hitting any of them!

Hovering smoothly along the surface of the water, I head across the point where an abandoned beach club

looks like a cross between a ghost town and a scene from
The Great Gatsby. As I round the tip of Sands Point, a squeaky
door on one of the abandoned cabanas echoes across the
bay, a haunting sound carried by the wind, blending with
the harmonics of halyards clinking against the sailboats'
aluminum masts, and the sad crying of seagulls. A herring
gull crosses my wake, dive bombs for food and sweeps back
in front of me as I balance, repositioning against the swell
of the open bay. There is no one else around. The feeling of
freedom and scent of sea air are intoxicating. As the wind
picks up, I gain speed, holding on to life with a capital L.

> *"Drunk with turpentine and long kisses,*
> *like summer I steer the fast sail*
> *   of the roses,*
> *bent towards the death of the thin day,*
> *stuck into my solid marine madness."*
>
> –Pablo Neruda[5]

Plumb Beach. Brooklyn, NY
May 22, 1983

...the way of the 'artless art' is not easy to follow...
—Eugen Herrigel[6]

Zen in the Art of Stubbornness. Or is it a fine line between stubbornness and determination?

In windsurfing, there are rituals of assembly and disassembly. Patience and focus when assembling equipment is an art in itself. In *Zen in the Art of Archery*, published in 1953, the author describes how he spent his first year of Zen training just holding the bow. No arrows. No shooting. We Americans would consider that year wasted. But there's a reason for this: A master archer's arrows seem to release themselves, traveling straight to the center of a bulls-eye. Blindfolded, the masters' arrows will split the center of those arrows that have found the target. Wanting to find that zone of excellence that takes you beyond everyday mind keeps pulling me to the water.

Like Herrigel learning to hold his bow, I am training myself to see the process of rigging a sail as essential preparation for the mental focus needed on the water. I am paying attention to details, the way a skydiver does when packing her parachute. Mistakes can be fatal since your life hangs on the connections between boom and mast, mast and board. This is pretty scary, considering how mechanically challenged I am. To me, the three most dreaded words in the English language are, "take a screwdriver." As in, "Lady, this is easy to fix. You just take a screwdriver..."

After "take a screwdriver," my three least favorite words are "easy to assemble." Or disassemble. Disassembled, the Shark fits into the trunk, along with the sail, the collapsed mast, aluminum boom, clunky teak daggerboard, and the world's most complicated metric tool kit. Each time I open the trunk, it feels like I'm staring into the heart of my deepest lunacy. Zen in the art of...what was I thinking?

Today, it takes me half an hour under overcast skies to rig. By the time I am finished, it is raining. Having done all this work, I can't stand the prospect of having to take it all apart, so I shimmy into the black wetsuit with its long, red neoprene stripe that makes me look like Wonder Woman on drugs and lug the board about one hundred and fifty meters–a meter is a long yard–through the muck of low tide. As I head out, four guys beach their boards, grumbling about no wind.

New York harbor is famous for its patchy fog. On summer afternoons when my friends and I have gone out for a short sail we have, at times, found ourselves becalmed somewhere in the middle of the harbor, navigating slowly home by flashlight, trying to coordinate markings on the marine map with the shallows that could bring us aground. One Memorial Day, as we tacked across the Upper Bay at dusk, the entire skyline of Manhattan disappeared to starboard! We had been heading toward the Statue of Liberty but the Lady was now invisible, as well. Grey mist, thick as cotton candy, matted our hair and eyelashes. We were poring over a damp navigation chart when a bank of lights whipped past us, setting up so much wake that we almost capsized. It was the Staten Island ferry! One other afternoon, the rest of the world vanished into a circle of white as we disappeared into a solid patch of fog in the middle of the Ambrose channel. Every tanker, cargo, and passenger ship that comes through New York harbor–including the QE2–has to pass through the Ambrose channel and here we were, invisible, as the deep horn of a giant tanker let us know we were about to be run over. We managed to jump start the engine and motor out of there in time but it was close. Sailing in New York harbor must be as crazy as riding a bicycle on Broadway, which I can relate to since an altercation with an angry bus driver in midtown made me realize how tiny is a human being on a bicycle.

Today, I'm within sight of the Ambrose Light and nothing can stop me. I trudge past the mud, get on the 'Shark' and uphaul. Nothing moves. I am standing alone in the middle of nowhere. I am standing still, wondering if this is a metaphor for something else. As in, "I feel stuck in my life and now I'm stuck in the fog." As in, "I was going nowhere and now I'm going crazy." Or maybe it's the other way around. Then I realize the daggerboard is stuck in the mud–a simple mechanical problem–so I tug it loose and walk the board a few meters further south. It looks as if I'm halfway across Dead Horse Bay, so named because of the horses killed and shipped to the glue factories along these shores during the nineteenth century. Then I am up, moving slowly but steadily, picking up breeze from the east. Downwind, a green and orange spinnaker puffs out.

From Breezy Point across the bay, Plumb Beach is nothing more than an exit off the Belt Parkway, which hugs the coastline of Brooklyn. Famous as a primo spot for watching submarine races, spotting Coney Island whitefish, which seem to proliferate the morning after those "submarine races", and an occasional drive-by shooting,[7] this thin crescent of sand is the only windsurfing beach within the city limits. Because it gets prevailing southwesterlies from spring through fall, it attracts a loyal contingent of local sailors and floating population of transient Eurosailors and Israelis. Windsurfing this close to the city line can save hours spent sitting in traffic.

You can catch some neat urban scenery from the water, starting with commercial fishing boats heading in and out of Sheepshead Bay. Sailing around the point into a clearing, I can make out the hazy outlines of the World Trade Center, the Verrazzano Bridge, and Coney Island's parachute jump. I spent the entire fifth grade looking out the window at that parachute jump. Fortunately, I don't remember anything else about fifth grade. On a really bad day when nothing goes right, it's helpful to remember that I can't be locked up again in Public School 193.

On Friday afternoons, in the middle of winter, my dad would take me to visit Aunt Sadie, who lived in a Victorian mansion that had been converted into a boardinghouse in Sea Gate, a gated community at the western tip of Coney Island. Four years of Fridays, I watched the copper-colored Verrazzano Bridge go up, pillar by pillar, cable by cable. When it was finished, they painted it battleship-gray. God knows why and She's not telling, but even now, in the middle of Dead Horse Bay, I can't help thinking that the Verrazzano would look a lot prettier if someone would paint it back to its original orange. I never dreamed I'd be revisiting landmarks of my childhood on a sailboard in Sheepshead Bay, which goes to show that life is altogether different than what I thought it was going to be. Reality 101 is turning out to be very different than fifth grade.

Out here on the water, it's a fine line between feeling in control and losing it altogether. Heading southwest, the openness becomes unnerving. If I get into trouble, I am alone. A flash of anxiety interrupts my focus, so that I start to fall, reclaiming balance just in time. Another important lesson: Don't allow the board to get parallel to the angle of the waves. Keep it at an angle.

A speedboat passes, cutting as close as it can. There aren't very many women windsurfing around here. Some of those motorboat captains like to see if they can kick up enough wake to knock me over. I'm learning. Today, I drop sail and wait for the wake to pass but end up drifting into the anchor line of a small fishing boat.

"Sorry," I apologize, paddling—*it's cold!*—out of the way.

"Not enough wind for that," a fisherman calls out to me.

"Well, it got me this far."

Now it has to get me back as the tide starts coming in.

Port Washington, NY
May 23, 1983

Peter and I argued last night, and he fell asleep. He tells me he doesn't like being tied to me, that he doesn't find me attractive any more. Besides, sex with the same person is boring. We have been together for about five years. I don't know what to say.

Driving today, I'm fighting a fuzzy cloud of heaviness in my head, and a harsh tightness in my heart and throat. High tide was at 10:30 this morning; hopefully, there'll be enough wind to get out. I buy some grapefruit juice at a deli in Port Washington, rubbing sadness from the corners of my eyes.

At the launch ramp, it is humid and cloying. I sweat while putting the board together. The tide is sucking out quickly. When I get in the car to move it off the launch ramp, the battery is dead.

A young man with a moustache who is eating his lunch near the shore says, "Sounds like your battery's dead." I ask for a boost, the car starts, and I move it off the ramp. Just to check, I turn off the ignition then switch it back on. The car starts, so I suit up, fasten the mast to the board, and push off. There is no wind at all. I stand on the board for about fifteen minutes, sweating. Since I am worried about the car, I tack and catch a tiny fluff of breeze back to shore where I take the board apart. When I try to move the car back to the ramp, it's dead again. This time, I get a boost from another man who is putting his motorboat into the water.

En route to the mechanic, it occurs to me that the whole day is a disaster. I miss the turnoff for the Van Wyck Expressway and end up at the exit for the Triboro Bridge, heading north instead of south. I find a turnaround, and manage to get the car back safely to the garage where it promptly dies. Apparently the battery has slipped off its casing and gotten punctured when I went over a bump.

A sudden, cool fog moves in from the bay. Now, I'm shivering in my shorts and bathing suit so I walk to the gym where I have some sweatpants and a sweatshirt in my locker.

"All's well that end's well," I think, but not really. I slam the glove compartment door on my finger.

Plumb Beach, NY
May 30, 1983

Wind 15 knots, southwest. High tide, 11:30 AM

Joan and Ben are boardheads. They each own several sailboards, a bunch of masts, a quiver of sails and several wetsuits. Joan gets the wetsuits from the shop where she works, although to call it a shop would be to glorify it. Actually, it's a grungy wholesale warehouse in the equally grungy garment district, but they have great prices. Joan's two Israeli bosses yell at her a lot. I don't know how she stands it. I would have quit by now.

Joan and Ben hang out in an old post office truck that he won in a poker game, cooking vegetarian hot dogs on a little burner. On the weekends, they drive out East, looking for beaches with good to excellent launch conditions.

Hanging out in the van, today, studying the waves, we talk about mushrooms and the wind. Joan tells me her last boyfriend was "almost perfect," except that he had a mushroom phobia. That's not "almost perfect" in my book. Image: Woody Allen freaking out at the sight of a mushroom mistakenly hiding in a pepperoni pizza.

The mushroom conversation is distracting me from worrying about the wind getting too strong. *It is. No, it's not. Yes, it is. Just get out there.* After an hour of debating with myself, it's time. As I'm putting the Shark together and rigging, a bearded Eurosailor walks over to observe the mini-rituals. In an accent like Arnold Schwarznegger, he tells me that my three-part Shark is no longer being manufactured. Does this mean I could be holding onto a collector's item or a potentially useless relic? Or both?

Under gray sky, in slight fog, I head out on a reach into whitecaps and waves that look pretty high. A clear run in stiff wind. My right hand and left foot start to cramp. I direct the muscles to relax. Surprisingly, they obey. Heading back is trickier, with waves foaming around the tip of the board. My foot slips on the daggerboard and gusting wind tugs the sail out of my hand. I sheet in, expecting to get dumped.

Instead of falling off, I am dancing with the wind.

Exhilaration: Swiveling, second-by-second, feeling my way along the edge of the swell. Eventually, after falling in and coming up face-to-face with some oncoming boats, I'm stretched to elation by all this open sky and water.

"You did really well, kid." How rare to talk to myself out loud. It sounds good, out here. So I say it again. "Back there. You did real well. Adroit!" One of those words nobody uses. Especially not me since it means skillful and graceful.

Back to the wind, shuffling onto the board, I uphaul, heading southwest on a broad reach until I fall backwards, twisting an ankle and clonking myself in the head, with the boom. Adroit, my ass.

It starts to rain, a slight drizzle at first, then larger, sloppier drops. It's almost sleeting, in fact. Wet on wet on wet. I head back, nervously watching the sky. It looks like it's clearing. Then there's thunder. I hightail back to shore. Fifteen minutes later, the sun comes out but the tide is getting very low. "If I go out now, coming back will be a bitch," I'm thinking, as a patch of fog envelops Plumb Beach and the wind picks up. Joan heads out, a terrific run, disappearing into the fog and reemerging. A sudden thunderstorm, a quick downpour, more majestic thunder, and jungle-like sheets of rain commence for twenty minutes while I'm derigging. Nearby, a couple huddles under the aluminum rain gutter of the round, concrete New York City Department of Parks restroom building.

"The clouds travel like white handkerchiefs of goodbye,
the wind, traveling, waving them in its hands."

–Pablo Neruda[8]

Port Washington, NY
July 9, 1983

Windsurfing dreams: I am windsurfing on a Mistral near the Battery, at the tip of Manhattan.

Dissolve to: windsurfing in Indian Harbor, a waterfront community in Greenwich, Connecticut.

Dissolve again to Seattle. My father tells me that I am a spiritual hitchhiker... "That's why you are so restless," he says.

But, hey, aren't we all spiritual hitchhikers in some way?

Oak Beach, New York
July 11, 1983

About fifty miles southeast of New York City, Oak Beach is little more than a strip of stubby grass and rocky sand, scattered picnic tables, a parking lot, and a bikers' hangout called The Oak Beach Inn.

Crowded on weekends, hardly anyone is here this afternoon. Now, at low tide, a wide sandbar forms a channel about fifty meters to the south of where I stand. At high tide this evening, the sandbar will be filled in and the bay, wide-open.

A minor rigging accident: I smash headfirst into a telephone pole while carrying the sail to the water. A southwest wind, about 10–12 knots, is coming off the ocean. Happily pointing into a sandbar, I tack back to shore. A gust pushes me into a rocky point. I tack back to the sandbar. The third time, as I'm heading east/southeast, one small fish wriggles over the sandbar. If she can do it, I can, too. Picking up energy from the incoming tide, I glide over the sandbar into deceptively calm, shimmering cobalt water. A man in a skiff, pulling a girl kneeling on a wakeboard, motors by.

"Good windsurfer," he says. I'm not sure if he means the Shark or me, but I'm pleased.

The current feels stronger now and the wind is picking up. Hanging on, whipping along on a reach, I seem to be speeding southeast toward a landmark obelisk at Robert Moses State Park that marks the western end of Fire Island. Suddenly, instead of placid bay, I'm running into whitecaps! That hospitable blue is now greenish gray, the color of a threatening sea in November. On the next tack, the wind tears the sail out of my grip. Waves pitch me off the board, into the air. Coming down, I feel like a pancake in search of a pan. The Shark is floating away, downstream. Flopping into the water, I swim quickly, grabbing its tail, counseling myself to stay calm as I climb back up, grateful for the wetsuit's insulation. Incoming tidewaters are freezing cold around here, even in the middle of July.

Now, I'm talking to myself as windsound wraps around my head, causing auditory whiplash. "You can do it!" I'm hauling the sail into position, grabbing the boom, whizzing along a starboard tack, feeling the pull through the right side of my body, every set of ten reps for the past two years now paying off because my life is hanging here, taut against the wind, bracing to ride this heaving, curling, foaming edge of water underneath me. I'm hanging on with everything I've got. My knees are bent, my weight pulling on the boom. I inwardly reason, *If I don't make it all the way across, I can ditch the board on the other side of the bay, hitchhike across the Robert Moses bridge, walk along the Ocean Parkway to Oak Beach, pick up my car and drive across the bridge to the other side to rescue the gear.* Contingency plans are in full gear as dark clouds scud across the horizon from the southeast. Heading for the sandbar on a port tack, I foul as the wind yanks the sail away. In the water again, I hang onto the board, coaching myself not to be scared, to get back up on the board, when a fragment of dialogue resurfaces: "Ain't you afraid of them sharks?"

"Sharks," I say the dreaded word out loud, as if anyone could hear me. "Oh shit. There are sharks at Jones Beach." Images from late summer newscasts of shark fishermen flash across the screen of my conscious mind, as I scramble back on the board, reassuring myself that there are no sharks here, there's nothing to worry about, don't panic. I tell myself to remember what I told Jack—"Brooklyn Girl Eaten By Shark" doesn't cut it as a headline. Besides, God didn't bring me out here to get eaten by a shark. Did She?

Getting up again. Knees bent. Hanging out on a port tack, through greenish waves. This time, I last about thirty seconds before wind grabs the sail. It has been about an hour since I launched and I'm getting tired, which is not great, considering that my neoprene-covered legs are dangling in potentially sharky water. Imagining something taking a swipe at my toes, I lecture myself on the danger of panic. *And what about them sharks? They live near the bottom of the sea, don't they? Maybe I'd better swim over to that sandbar.* Holding onto the board and kicking as the current carries me to the sandbar, I find it ironic that I should be using a sailboard called a Shark as a flotation device while my lower appendages are vulnerable to Jaws.

A small motorboat with two fishermen heads toward me. One of them shouts over the sound of the engine, "Do you need help?" When they get closer, I see two potbellied characters. The one with a St. Christopher medal around his neck leans over to grab the tip of the mast, while the other one pulls me up, gasping for breath like a dying fish, flapping on the tiny deck of the boat. "Rest, rest," one of my rescuers says, giving me some water to drink. Sitting up, surveying the whitecaps around us, I'm beginning to understand that, like Zen archery, windsurfing "...is not a pastime, not a purposeless game, but a matter of life and death!" [9]

Together, we grab the rig and haul it up to the deck. The Shark is tethered to the stern as we motor back to Oak Beach. "Thank you, thank you, thank you," I repeat over and over again, explaining how the wind got too strong for me.

"It's the law of the sea," says the St. Christopher character. "My father once fell off a fishing boat and no one stopped to help him. In Joisy, remember Oinee?"

Apparently Oinee is the other guy, since he answers St. Christopher with "yes."

"You go out alone?" St. Christopher asks me. "No one

would know where you was."

"They would know tomorrow when I didn't show up for work," I say. Pete's out of town, and I can't help wondering if Jack and Ernestine would say it serves me right, and whether my disappearance would rate even a paragraph on United Press International, or fifteen seconds on the "CBS Evening News."

Not that it would make any difference to me. At least, I wouldn't have to write the obituary.

Heckscher State Park, NY
July 24, 1983

Wind, 15 knots. Southwest.

I was kind of half-joking about not having to write my own obituary. The other day, a producer joked, "We're going to start calling you the Obit Queen."

It is now my job to research, write and produce obituaries of famous people, preferably before they die. Sounds ghoulish but someone has to do it. Besides, when a celebrity dies, don't you think he or she would like a mini-documentary, about two and a half minutes long, with highlights of his or her career, ready to air that very same day? Wouldn't you? If you were really famous and you died two hours before the evening news, and no obit producer like me had squirreled away a special reel of your best soundbites or photo opps, wouldn't you be disappointed? Wouldn't you wish you were "in the can," ready to go on the air on the day of your death? Well, almost ready. If you were a movie star, I would be on the phone with frantic, last-minute calls to the studios asking for permission to broadcast your clips?[10]

If you were a just-dead celebrity, wouldn't you rather there was someone like me, keeping a "Ghoul Pool," a list of famous people considered "most likely to die in the near future." So, who's in the Pool? In the past six months, I've updated Yasser Arafat's obituary three times. I've done Henry Kissinger's and former President Richard Nixon's and former First Lady Pat Nixon's, and right now, I'm looking for good, early pictures of Haffez Assad, the ruler of Syria. Updating Rose Kennedy's obituary every year is becoming an obligatory annual, like the world's longest electric train at Christmastime. The other day, a producer joked that "when Laurie does someone's obituary, it's a guarantee that he or she will live at least another five years, or until the obituary is outdated at least twice." That's not a bad thing, especially if it's your obituary.

Obituary writing is a quirky tradition in American journalism. I understand there is even an obituary writer on staff at the Pentagon, whose job is similar to mine, except that she also coordinates plans for the top brass' military funerals. Douglas Edwards, something of a tradition in his own right, narrates most of my obituaries in that measured, rich baritone that was, for many years, the "Voice of CBS News."[11]

Writing a script that is paced for a particular announcer's speech patterns is something of an art in and of itself. We write the announcer's copy on the right half of an eight by eleven sheet of paper, estimating every two lines of copy will equal about five seconds of airtime. The problem is that every announcer reads at a different pace. Some are faster, while others read slowly. Juggling syllables along with facts so that the script matches the image, while simultaneously gauging how someone else's inflection, tempo, and tone of voice will sound so that the viewer gets a powerful impression of the subject, is the heart of producing a relevant obituary. I'm very fortunate to write for Douglas Edwards and it's a privilege whenever he lets me know, with a word and a smile, that he likes the script.

Producing obituaries is a way of creating a legacy to remember important people of our times and their contribution. No matter whose obituary it is–Sir Lawrence Olivier, Count Basie, or Ansel Adams come to mind–I look for something inspirational about each person. Perhaps it's how he or she approaches adversity. Rose Kennedy: "Early on in life I decided that I would not be vanquished." Count Basie: "I haven't ever felt discouraged." Sir Laurence Olivier: "Use your weaknesses. Aspire to your strengths." Or, photographer Ansel Adams, quoting Alfred Stieglitz, on the perfect epitaph: "Here lies Ansel Adams. He lived his life for better or worse, but he's dead for good."

Historically, obituaries "offer clues to our cultural values."[12] While nineteenth century obituaries described the deceased person's character, today's obituaries concentrate on his or her career accomplishments, status, and wealth. Women's obituaries used to focus more on their relationships with prestigious or notorious men, rather than on their own life journeys. Blacks and Native Americans did not have obituaries written about them, unless they died in unusual ways. Between 1910 and 1930, newspapers published dozens of obituaries of people who claimed to have witnessed President Abraham Lincoln's assassination. Nowadays, we write similar stories about people who survived the sinking of the Titanic.

Somewhere in the next century, when sixty-five million of us baby boomers get to somewhere between the ages of seventy-two and eighty-five, we'll probably be watching "The Obituary Hour" after the evening news. By the year 2050, more than 834,000 Americans will be at least a hundred years old.[13] Along with the demographic bonanza for the nation's funeral industry, the years between 2020 and 2035 – the "golden age of death,"[14] as some funeral directors call it, should make obit producing a transferable skill.

Producing obituaries relieves me from writing explosions, train wrecks, and natural disasters but there have been a few conversations which have given me pause:

"Why, exactly, do you need this footage, now?" the Vatican's public relations priest wants to know.

"It's for...it's for...well, we do these profiles for world leaders on a regular basis...in case... I mean, it's for if..."

"I understand." Something in that cold tone of voice makes me feel as if I should be kneeling in one of those little wooden booths, saying, "Bless me, Father. Someone. Anyone."

"It's for when he dies. That's what you tell 'em," barks the Executive Producer, who happens to be standing behind me. A tough little cigar-chomping angel, he's allegedly the prototype for the TV character, Lou Grant, although I'm not convinced.

"It's for if he dies," I repeat.

"Not if. When. Holy Father's gonna die. President's gonna die. You're gonna die. I'm gonna die, sweetheart. Say 'When, not if.'"

"When. It's for when he dies."

"Good. You're learning."

"Too bad you don't have that conversation on tape," Sal says later. "You could use it in his obituary. Or yours."

Even as we watch people getting killed on TV every night, death is up there, near the top of a list of topics which people hate to discuss.[15] It's not my own personal favorite, by any means. On the other hand, I cover my eyes whenever there's a medical story with pictures of injections or bloody surgery. Sal, who also covers his eyes, sometimes jokes that this job is making us so weird that we can look at the most gory pictures of death without flinching, but we can't watch a human life being saved. When we're on overload, we compete to see who can write the blackest humor:

"The death team...gravity and concrete...claimed two more lives in Chicago today, when a couple of construction workers fell off a scaffold..."

"Twenty-eight people in a McDonald's in Omaha failed to get the break they deserved today when a homicidal maniac carrying an Uzi gunned them down before killing himself...but not before he downed three big Macs..."

"Florida is known for its juice...and convicted killer Mark Ansom got a real taste of it today when the Sunshine State turned it on for him..."

Overload. "Our minds are so warped we'd probably get booed off the set of Johnny Carson," Sal laughs, chucking a script into a tall wastebasket overflowing with wire copy and scripts.

Flip a coin. Life or death. Heads or tails. You never

know. If there's one takeaway from working here, it's an understanding that, as bioorganisms, we are, each of us, a walking time bomb, programmed for cellular self-destruction. Not if, when. Which is why windsurfing is becoming a necessary counterbalance to the constant ringing of telephones, walls of monitors cranked up to high volume, and the occasional telex tantrum. The Tokyo bureau chief has an annoying habit of banging on the bell in Japan, so that it goes off in a fury, a few feet from my desk, whenever he wants our immediate attention.

Like windsurfing, newswriting is a continual exercise in focus and concentration as news rolls in continually in waves, like the ocean.

Speaking of ocean...

"Get here early and we'll save you a space." Joan and Ben call the newsroom from a pay phone at a new beach, an hour's drive from the city.

A parking lot the size of an airfield in a third world country extends from a four-lane road to a strip of shoreline, ideal for launching a windsurfer on a southwesterly. The Great South Bay reflects a five-mile stretch of shimmering gray sky. On the far shore lies Fire Island.

I have decided to sell the Shark and get a one piece sailboard, even though that will mean lifting it off and on to a roofrack. Today, I am fixing the bruises and nicks, called "dings," with a file and "Liquisole." In the meantime, I sail Ben's Alpha Competition board, leaning way back and sitting in mid-air. It flies through the water, confirmation it is time to sell the Shark and move on.

Heckscher
July 25, 1983

Wind: 8–12 knots. Southwest.

Dancing on the water, smiling at the sky. My worries—job, marriage, fires, bombings, earthquakes, building collapses, assassinations, obituaries, news conferences, and assorted daily mayhem—seem to dissolve on land, where I left them. Sometimes, when I'm out on the water, I wish I never had to go back. Fantasy: Pack the sailboard on the roof of the car, continue driving east and become a waitress in Montauk.

The uncertainty I feel about life is reflected in how I move on the water. Grabbing onto the mast below the boom, my legs go wobbly, dumping me into the clean saltwater as the sail falls on my head. The underwater tack maneuver: swimming underneath the sail, popping up alongside the clew. Back in position, I find myself on a reach, about a mile southeast, for a visit to a clam boat. The clammer talks about his work, dredging up little necks and cherrystones. We exchange small talk about the wind as it picks up. Another tack: across the ridge of the swell, under a fearless sky.

Whenever I fall, I am thinking about
a) how well I am doing
b) whether people on shore can see me
c) how hard it is to balance
d) something other than what I'm doing at that very moment

Mindfulness means simply paying attention. Or perhaps paying simple attention. Or maybe paying attention to simple things like where you put your hands and feet. My mistakes on the water come from not focusing on that place that knows from within, how to adjust to fluctuations

of sea and wind.
Clearing and emptying the mind are the keys.

Heckscher State Park, NY
September 23, 1983

The HiFly 343 has arrived. It looks huge, probably because it's one solid piece instead of three. At twelve feet, six inches long, it's not much bigger than the Shark. It looks fast and solid, like a Lincoln Continental compared to a Volkswagen. Naturally, the first thing I do is misplace the mast attachment that locks onto the boom.

Although Pete is naturally athletic, he has refused to try windsurfing, on the grounds that it's "not fast enough." Over the summer, he has made friends with a group of Hobie Cat sailors who launch near our windsurfers' section of the beach. (A Hobie Cat is a catamaran, meaning a sailboat with two hulls. Hobie Cats have no cabins or engines and are designed for flat-out speed in high-wind conditions). The Hobie crowd is fun to hang with and Pete adores flying the hull of the catamaran during small craft warnings.

Along with the HiFly, we have managed to acquire an eighteen-foot Hobie Cat, a trailer to tow it to the water, a $5,000 loan, and a new circle of friends. After a weekend of windsurfing and flying hulls, we talk back and forth on the phone, all week. On Monday, we talk aches and sprains, rehashing tacks, gibes, and best maneuvers. On Tuesday, we're depressed because it's only Tuesday. By Wednesday, we focus on the weekend weather outlook. On Thursday, we plan menus. By Friday, some people are already sailing, having gotten off work early. I take breaks between writing stories to call the weather lady for the wind reports, repeating with a grin, "Southwest 15 to 20!"

"She's talking to the weather lady again," someone says.

"Must be nuts," someone else says, patting my shoulder.

"What do you mean, 'must be?'" laughs Sal, tossing a crumpled 'bombing in Belfast' script at my head.

Friday evening, we shop, cook, and pack for the weekend. A lot of effort goes into making this fun.

Today, with 15 knots spilling out of the northwest, an offshore wind takes me to Fire Island in less than an hour, without using a daggerboard to stabilize the sailboard. When it's time to head back, the wind shifts to southwest, picking up to 20, with whitecaps. My arms give out as the swell keeps pitching me off. A grayhaired fisherman in a brown, wooden fishing boat motors over to ask if I need help. Flashback: St. Christopher and Oinee. "The law of the sea."

"No thanks, I'm waiting for my husband." I sound like Alice in Wonderland speaking to the hookah-smoking caterpillar while seated on her mushroom, making it seem perfectly normal to be stranded on a bank of whitecaps, perched on a twelve-foot long plank of polyethylene. With wind howling cold around my ears, this is no longer fun.

When my "ride" shows up, we tie the HiFly to the Hobie through the hole in its upturned nose, lash boom and mast to the trampoline, and scream out of there. How suddenly the sea is out of control!

"Don't be afraid," someone shouts as we start flying the hull. Slipping down the trampoline, hanging by a hook, suspended eight feet off the water on a Hobie cat captained by a maniac is my idea of terror. Especially when the maniac is my own husband and he's annoyed because I'm such a wimp.

"Everyone's scared of Hobies at first," Hobie veterans Scott and Pam reassure me while I settle down by taking the rig apart, letting everything dry out. No screws, nuts and bolts. So much easier than the Shark.

Changing in the car, I wrap myself under two sleeping bags, lying on the grass in the sun. "Cats get to lie in the sun like this. Maybe in my next life, I can be a cat," I'm thinking, as a seagull walks straight up to where my head peeks out to look at orange shafts of light fanning down from a screen of dark clouds over the Captree Bridge.

"Here." I offer small pieces of cheddar cheese, sopresata, and wheat crackers to the seagull.

"Who's your buddy?" Pete asks, touching my hair.

We laugh, lying together in the sun.

Heckscher State Park, NY
September 25, 1983

Towing a Hobie Cat and a HiFly down Sunrise Highway in a red 1972 Chevy Malibu: flat, six lanes wide, whooshing with cars. Passing BJ's Jungle, Divers' Way, Exotic Adult Entertainment. Gas, gas, gas. Almost one hundred miles long, running from Kennedy Airport all the way past the Shinnecock Canal to Southampton, Sunrise is to Long Island what Ventura Boulevard is to L.A., without the palm trees. Maybe someday, I can write a Hunter S. Thompson chronicle about Sunrise Highway and an emerging wind worshipping subculture.

Lucid dreams, where you are participating in the dream as well as aware that you are dreaming, often feel like this—as if you are observing yourself from a point over your shoulder—arms flexed, hands curving around the boom, breathing, in three dimensional silence. Like those multidimensional dreams remembered, years later, details along the horizon stand out: the black silhouette of a clamboat, a ferryboat's flashing wake, one cedar house on stilts, and a water tower, backlit, in flaming, late afternoon sun.

We are very much aware of winter coming on. One friend says he gets depressed when he sees little kids wearing coats at night because it means that our summer is over. I will miss the smell of mildewed wetsuits drying above the bathtub after these end-of-summer weekends.

Heckscher State Park, NY
October 2, 1983

Heckscher's Law:

The wind shall blow until you get your sail rigged and board in water.

Then the wind shall stop blowing until you get your board out of the water, put it against the car, derigged, with the sail drying out.

Then the wind shall blow again.

Just my luck. I almost get mugged walking out of Macy's on Thursday night but reach the car and escape before my pursuers can catch up. The Chevy refuses to start on Friday. I drop a heavy thermos on my toe on Saturday and now there is no wind at all. "Here, wind, come on, come on." Talking to the wind makes as much sense as calling a cat.

First a hint, then a tickle. Dune grass ripples and "it's picking up," we tell each other. Seduced, I pull on a wetsuit, rig, and I'm off. One gust later, it dies. I should have known. Any sport that requires you to encase yourself in neoprene is probably of questionable merit.

Nonetheless, there is always something to learn out here on the water. "The beginner's mind is good for trying a new approach," writes Herrigel, who might just as well be writing about writing. Or windsurfing, for that matter.

Tacking, I head up into the wind and let the board do the work instead of yanking the sail. It isn't all about picking up speed. Today is a lesson in the art of effortless motion.

Indian Harbor, Connecticut
October 10, 1983

"Windsurfing looks like a great sport if you have servants!" Charlene observes with a wry smile as she watches me wrestle this fifty-five pound clunker down a rickety set of wooden stairs.

We are visiting a couple who are moonlighting as groundskeepers on an estate. The owners, emergency room surgeons who have emigrated from Eastern Europe, have decorated their halls and balconies with smuggled Bulgarian icons and red velvet wallpaper. The neoDracula school of decorating. Not that I would ever say anything like that.

Out in the channel, it's just a few brown ducks, a handful of dinghies, and me, on a private tour of the most massive homes I have ever seen: one after the other, after the other, spreading across the waterfront. What would I do with thirteen bedrooms?

Floating toward a stone seawall that juts out past the point, a comparatively modest eight-bedroom colonial perches on top of a hill. But around the point, this "modest eight-room colonial" turns out to be merely one side of a house so big, I can't see its full span!

Surprise spills me into the water.

I come up laughing, face to face with a duck.

Heckscher State Park, NY
November 13, 1983

People die all the time.

– Chairman Mao's *Little Red Book*

The news god must be having fun. It's raining death.

It feels like I live in the control room: "Go to 5837. Give me a three second close-up of a bloody face. Forward to 8973. Let's take five seconds of rescue workers in debris. Bring the sound up till the end of the shot. Now back to 4595. Pick up the slow pan of the bombed-out embassy. Forward to 7864. Zoom into body bags being carried out and bring up the siren sounds till the end of the shot."

"Why are you being such an asshole?" Less than an elbow away, another producer is starting to lose it with the senior tape editor.

"I went to asshole school," the editor smirks.

"Really? On a scholarship, I bet." I wonder whether they are laughing or getting ready to kill each other. Regardless, we've got two minutes to check our edit of the U.S. Embassy bombing in Beirut and cue it up for the five o'clock feed.

"That looks great. Thanks...and could you cue it up, please..."

But the editor who is supposed to be feeding to the net is not at the control panel. "Walking is not in my IBEW contract," he's hollering, as another producer wheels him in to the control panel, in an office chair.

"Pushing buttons is in your contract," she says, patting his bald head. "Now, I wouldn't want you to strain yourself, honey..."

October 25: We're still cutting aftermath of the Beirut bombing when the Marines invade Grenada, two days later. By the end of the day, all anyone thinks about is going home. At least, that's what I'm thinking, on my way through that last set of doors to the hall, when the new Executive Producer calls out, "How's that JFK special going?"

It seems like a strange time to ask about a special that isn't going to air for another two weeks. "Coming along."

"Good. We just got a call that Philippine leader Ferdinand Marcos is dead. Get your butt up to the library."

Obit Alert! If only I had a police siren for these mad, last-minute chases through the building.

Hours later, having combed through numerous card catalogues, ordering cans of film from the archives across town, there is still no bulletin about Marcos on any of the wire services. Maybe he's not dead and I can go home. Funny thing about being an obit queen. You start to take it personally when anyone newsworthy kicks the bucket on your shift. It's like they do it to you, personally. It's bizarre, how some little dictator on the far side of the planet, whom you've never even met, can impact whether you eat or sleep.

If he is dead, we'll need his obituary for the early morning feed.

Picking up the phone, I identify myself to the foreign editor of United Press International before asking the key question: "Have you heard the rumor that Marcos is dead?"

A few seconds of shocked silence later: "Marcos, dead? Did you say, 'Ferdinand Marcos is dead?'"

"No. I didn't say that. I asked whether you had heard the rumor that Marcos is dead."

"Rumor? What rumor?"

"The rumor that Marcos is dead. I guess you haven't heard it. If you're not running a bulletin on the wires, my guess is that it's only a rumor...What's your guess?"

"Probably just a rumor," he sighs. "And if you get any other details, could you please call me right away?"

"Of course," I lie because I'm going home.

There are two kinds of special events: planned and unplanned. Marcos' death would have fallen in the "uplanned" box, if it hadn't turned out to be a rumor that came from a Japanese cameraman in Washington, D.C., who got it from someone who heard it on the radio in Tokyo. It's been a great week for unplanned special events, if you include the American embassy bombing in Beirut and the Marines' invasion of Grenada. We know the invasion must have been planned by someone–maybe the Invasion Planners Service–but as far as we're concerned, it falls into the unplanned category.

Planned special events would include the upcoming twentieth anniversary of President John F. Kennedy's assassination. For the past month, I've been working all hours, producing a one-hour special on the anniversary with Walter Cronkite and Dan Rather. Everyone old enough to remember is talking about where we were when we first heard that the President had been shot. (Ms. Signorella's art class on the fourth floor of Midwood High School...) Immersed in research: Hour upon hour, frame by frame of the original black and white footage gets logged, seen, again, as if for the first time. In Bettman Archives, dozens of manila folders, each one as thick as a Manhattan phone book, crammed with black and white stills of those four days in Dallas...looking for images that have not been shown on TV. Was it two or three mornings later...there it was: a black and white picture from United Press International...in the limo, Jackie and J.F.K., right after the first shot was fired. Her head is turned away from the camera, but the President is smiling into the lens. The picture jumps out, making me catch my breath. It's his last smile.

After the still image is transferred to videotape, and the rest of the black and white footage has been cranked, by hand, through a moviola, or squawk box, by a film editor old enough to remember how, there remains the logging of shots, then the cutting and scripting of various versions, including a five minute package, narrated by Douglas Edwards:

"November 22, 1963…a day of awesome tragedy, which, even now, twenty years later, has the power to shock and horrify, and to fill us with a sense of tremendous loss. On that day, President John F. Kennedy was assassinated in Dallas…

"It started innocently and happily enough, on a Friday…

"At 1:40 in the afternoon, CBS News interrupted the network program, "As The World Turns." Walter Cronkite announced, "…A bulletin from CBS News…President Kennedy has been shot by a would-be assassin in Dallas, Texas. Stay tuned to CBS News for further details."

Sitting across from him, twenty years later, I can see Cronkite's expressive, sharp, light blue eyes tear up again, when he talks about that day. "In the news business, two things happen. First, you're struck by the enormity of the story, whatever it is. And right away, on top of that, you turn professional, and your thoughts are on how you approach the story and how you get it out. There's underlying emotion, of course. And I think that's what happened in my reaction to each of these bulletins. I couldn't help thinking, 'How terrible!' But then, 'How will we get the story told in the best possible fashion?' The point where emotion is really hard to suppress, is when I have to say, 'He's dead.' It was tough."

It wasn't long before Cronkite's next bulletin: "From Dallas, Texas, the flash, apparently official…President John F. Kennedy died at 1 PM Central Standard Time, 2 PM Eastern Standard Time. Some thirty-eight minutes ago…."

As much a part of history as the assassination itself are those next few seconds, in which Cronkite removes his glasses to wipe his tears. Clearing his throat now, to describe the images that evoke all the sadness of those three days, he talks almost as if thinking out loud, about "…the doctor at Parkland Hospital, who was trying to avoid saying there was no hope for the President, but who obviously couldn't disguise it…Jackie Kennedy in the airplane, in her bloodstained suit, standing there while President Johnson took the oath...the riderless horse always gives me a gulp, and the reaction of people along the cortege...and the picture of Charles de Gaulle and the other heads of state, all of them looking like midgets compared to de Gaulle's lanky form as they came down through a long lens, out of the White House and down the East Driveway of the White House...all these heads of state coming down through a misty haze that you get through a long lens...it was quite an effective shot..."

Despite the zoning out after nights of reviewing old footage, frame by frame, the pictures from the Kennedy assassination continue to have a haunting effect on me. In the second half of the special, it's Dan Rather, with his large, intense eyes and precise use of language, who puts words to the feelings that I'm sure millions of Americans must have whenever they watch any of those scenes. "It was a special time. I happen to believe that for television journalism, we had gone through our childhood and were entering our adolescence. And during those four dark days in Dallas, we grew into adulthood. From that time forward, television journalism moved with a confidence that it had not had before. It moved with an assurance, not always for the better, that it had not had before. I think that we had learned a great deal about ourselves, and I think the country learned a good deal about ourselves. I think before those four days...television journalism and television journalists, whether we would admit it or not, had a deepseated inferiority complex as compared to print. We came out of that day, not feeling superior, but feeling parity, saying, 'There are some things that we can do better than print.' Like cover an assassination of a President."

Apparently, our one-hour special has made television history, as well. On Thursday, when the network carried the Cronkite-Rather interview, an engineer at KHOU-TV in Houston jumped into action when he heard "This is a CBS

News bulletin." Not realizing it was file tape from twenty years earlier, he punched it, live, so that the daytime program was interrupted with the "news flash" that President John F. Kennedy had been assassinated in Dallas![16]

Today, my first day off in more than three weeks, I can't seem to come down from the news high. Juxtaposed against flashing mindframes of cutaways and medium close ups, panning across to those classic wide shots of Presidential coffins and bodies loaded onto stretchers and all that debris are lower key montages of pastel afternoons like this, floating between space and time. Today's fading, gentle waltz on slow water, shimmering against a backdrop of rainbow tinted clouds will be filed in my own private archive, to be retrieved and savored during the long, icy months ahead.

Tacking back to shore, on this, the last day of my windsurfing season, it's hard not to zoom in to a superfat man, like Jabba the Hutt, who is smoking a mammoth cigar and walking his chubby little dachshund on shore. Pumping the regatta sail to keep from getting becalmed, a giggly thought breezes by:

He should have walked the cigar and smoked the dog.

Auckland, New Zealand
February 21, 1984

Mokoia Island rises, forested and green, from the middle of Lake Rotorua on New Zealand's North Island. This island-within-an-island is the setting for a legend that could be considered the Maori equivalent of Romeo and Juliet, about four-hundred years ago.

Tutanekei, the illegitimate son of a Maori chief, was living on this island when Princess Hinemos appeared "like a white heron in the water." Forbidden from ever meeting because their fathers were sworn enemies, when the Princess heard Tutanekei playing the flute, she swam to Mokoia. In the morning, when Tutanekai's slave went to wake his master, he saw their four feet and ran to get the Maori elders. Unlike the Montagues and Capulets, the elders blessed them and declared them married.

A sixteen foot, five and a half inch-tall wooden gateway representing Tutanekei, carved in 1836, will soon be flown to New York's Metropolitan Museum of Art as the centerpiece of a traveling exhibit of 174 Maori art objects.[17] The question—whether to allow Tutanekei and the other carvings out of the country—is extremely controversial to the 227,000 Maoris who make up New Zealand's indigenous population. They believe that these carvings are not merely wooden statues; rather, that each person's spiritual essence lives its respective statue. As one Maori professor explains, "A cynic may argue that it's just a piece of wood, but you cannot convince a Maori that it is so."

As Pete and I are learning from the curators whom I am interviewing for a series of magazine articles about the exhibit, it has taken ten years for the Maori elders to let themselves be persuaded that the artwork will be safe if it leaves New Zealand. The Maori professor has pointed out that "the American public takes art for granted but it has taken us a lot of soul-searching to decide."[18]

As it has taken both of us a lot of soul-searching to decide to spend a big chunk of our life's savings on this one-month trip to Australia and New Zealand. We have been talking about leaving New York and relocating to this part of the world. I have a tentative job offer with a TV station in Sydney, which seems ideal, except for a feeling I can't explain, that keeps saying no. "Australia is very far away," our friends said, sadly, the night before we left. Far away from what? The F-train?

Now, after twenty-six hours of flying, with a middle of the night pit stop at Honolulu airport, "far away" has a whole new meaning. It feels as if we've been dropped on an island underneath an invisible dome that seals it off from contact with the rest of the world. Withdrawal from TV news set in on Day Two. There are only two, ten minute world news programs, broadcast on BBC radio. If you miss those ten-minute newscasts, you miss out on information about the rest of the world. *So what? Isn't that what you want?* a part of me asks. As for the other part, well, coming down a steep mountainside, a crackly voice, so faraway that it could barely be heard, was announcing, "Thousands of people lined up outside the Kremlin to pay their respects to Yuri Andropov..."

"I hope they remember where I left his obit." An automatic reflex strikes–pick up a phone!–just as a few hundred sheep begin to wander across the road. There are sheep everywhere you go in New Zealand, sixty million of them and three million of us, as in, people. We've been hearing the casual warning, "Watch out for the sheep shit," ever since we stepped off the plane and into one of those genuine Monty Python moments when culture shock and jet lag collide, in my first visit to a Kiwi grocery store, with floor-to-ceiling wall shelves stacked with round, white cans: SHEEP TONGUES SHEEP TONGUES SHEEP

TONGUES SHEEP TONGUES SHEEP TONGUES, SHEEP TONGUES. Bold font. Bright blue capital letters. SHEEP TONGUES SHEEP TONGUES SHEEP TONGUES SHEEP TONGUES... Just thinking about it makes me laugh, which annoys my husband no end. "What's so funny about sheep tongues? They happen to be delicious."[19]

Twenty minutes later, only half the sheep have made it across the road and I really, really want to call the newsroom. Knowing that there are no phones for a hundred miles only makes it worse. Five hours later, we have driven only fifty miles, and it feels as if we're time-traveling backwards. Who needs phones in the nineteenth century, anyway?

Like Salvador Dali's painting of watches melting in the sand, time wanders at its own curious pace whenever you're on vacation in a foreign country. Like those airports in the third world, where you ask, "What time does the plane leave?" And the man at the ticket counter shrugs, "It leaves when it gets here." Anyway, isn't time more valuable when counted as sunsets reflecting in streams, or mystical, balsa-colored hills dissolving into white mist, the cries of curlews in forests of the night, or the most poignant of personal reunions?

The juxtaposition of differences in geography and culture with the familiar makes this an extraordinary journey for us, as we reconnect with old friends and meet various members of our extended family. My in-laws, who emigrated from the Netherlands, after the Second World War, to a town of 30,000 people on the east coast of New Zealand's North Island, have retained their language, love of classical music, and old world gentility. My father-in-law, now seventy, dresses in a bowler hat, crisp, starched white shirt, necktie, and cardigan, with his umbrella or newspaper rolled up under his arm, for his morning walk to the wooden sidewalks of the town's main street, with its hitching posts, for the shepherds who ride in from the hills, on horseback, for haircuts and beer. Against the frontier town backdrop, he resembles an endearing character from a short story by du Maupassant, not so much out of place, as out of time.

Pete is having fun, driving the rented van through winding, rugged mountains that resemble Scotland's, in the north, and Colorado's, in the south. "The beaches back home are clean," he had often complained. To prove his point, we detour to "the most beautiful beach in New Zealand." At least, that's the pitch. Climbing down a bluff, past a gnarled pine, to a wide strand of silver–white sand, past a couple of ubiquitous sheep, I trip over something that turns out to be a rotting, yellow, sheep carcass, covered with maggots.

"Very clean." I can't help myself.

"It's not that bad."

"How can you complain about a few beer cans and used condoms, when this is totally gross?"

"It's biodegradable, isn't it?" he shrugs, as a downpour chases us back to the van. The weather is suspiciously English, considering it's the middle of summer. The Maori name for New Zealand is Aoteoroa, which means "The Land of the Long White Cloud." What they don't tell you is that the long white cloud rains a lot. And, as we newswriters like to write over those Sunday parades, "The weatherman failed to cooperate today..."

With an assignment to write about windsurfing in New Zealand for *Boardsailor* magazine, I'm delighted by the 5,700 miles of coastline, and steady wind, but the cool, damp weather is bringing me down.[20] Good thing I insisted on the wetsuits for Pete and myself, even though he tried to persuade me that we wouldn't need them, because, "after all, it is summer." But New Zealand is relatively close to Antarctica, and the wind from the south is assertive, even in summertime.

I had assumed that because New Zealanders are water

sports addicts, sailboards would be as common and as easy to find as sheep; however the first three letters of the word *assume* are a.s.s., and I should have brought my own gear. As it is, we've scoured both islands, from the Bay of Islands in the north, to Lake Wakatipu in Queenstown, on the south island. Just when I thought I would go into wind-surfing withdrawal, we discovered Wakatip Windsurfing on the Frankton Arm of Lake Wakatipu in Queenstown. Queenstown is the jumping-off point for organized wilder-ness adventures–rafting, jetboating through the Shotover Gorge, glass bottom boat and hair-raising plane trips to the fjords of Milford Sound, trout fishing, and ski trips to the Southern Alps. "Four years ago there were no sails on this lake, but each year, there are more and more, " Lake Wakatipu's manager Harry Rankin commented as he rigged up a New Zealand-made Superstar–a twelve-footer, with fiberglass over foam construction. The wind soon picked up to a steady, onshore 25 knots, whisking me to the middle of the glacier lake with an unobstructed three-hundred and sixty degree view of the craggy brown mountains.

Barely ten years old, windsurfing will become an Olympic event for the first time, during the 1984 games in Los Angeles. Thanks to a newsstand magazine called *New Zealand Windsurfing*, Linda Stent of the New Zealand Windsurfing Association introduced us to Bruce Kendall and Grant Beck, contenders for New Zealand's Olympic team. Grant is encouraging me to go the next step and get into that padded vest-with-hook contraption called a windsurfing harness. "You have to try," he says almost reproachfully, as if it would personally bother him if I did-n't attempt it. Interviewing Olympic level athletes as part of a story on windsurfing conditions in New Zealand has started me wondering about the personality traits that make someone a world-class athlete. Both men display supreme discipline, dedication to practice, and focus on winning. Windsurfing with Grant in Takapuna Bay is as awesome to me as practicing serves with Martina Navratilova would be to a novice tennis player who had only been on the courts for a couple of years.

Breezy Point, NY
Easter Sunday, 1984

The first launch of the season: a photo shoot for a wind-surfing magazine.[21]

The assignment: a look at the best windsurfing sites in the New York metropolitan area with professional photos of someone windsurfing in front of the skyline.

The guinea pigs: Ben and I have volunteered to rig up and float around in our new $400 drysuits. I can't speak for him, but mine makes me feel like the Michelin man. Since the booties attached to the one-piece suit have no traction, I'm slipping off the board more than I'm on it. But, hey, anything that doesn't kill me builds my character. Or something like that.

There are logistical problems – a combination of Mike the photographer's Wednesday deadline, our respective work schedules, and the fact that we can't find an accessible launch site with skyscrapers in the background. Mike's 300mm telephoto lens pulls in the skyline so that it appears closer than twentysomething miles away and it's a dicey shot, at best. Here, down a sloping jetty of rocks, alongside the Breezy Point Coast Guard station, we brace against wind gusting off the pylons of the Marine Parkway Bridge. My first fall brings on an "ice cream headache," that sudden-onset pain which shoots between your eyes into the back of your brain. The water temperature is about as close to ice as anything I've ever experienced, and it occurs to me that my life is protected by these thin rubber gasket seals around my neck and wrists. This suit would fill up with frigid water in no time. A break in the neck seal could be lethal.

After shooting one roll of film, Mike suggests that we drive to New Jersey, where the skyscrapers are closer and more photogenic. I balk at spending hours in Easter traffic, but Mike insists the background isn't "strong enough" for the magazine. We compromise on Staten Island, where, one hour later, we are checking out a crumbly old pier. Two rednecks in a pickup truck follow Ben's post office truck all the way to the pier, where they park a few feet away so they can stare at us. It's not as if there's a hardcore community of windsurfers in this part of the world. To these guys, we must look like spacemen.

The wind is howling from the Upper Bay to the north, through the midspan of the Verrazzano–Narrows Bridge. In order to get a shot of the skyline, we will have to windsurf across the harbor, on a reach, perpendicular to the dock, then run downwind towards the skyline, past tankers queuing in the Ambrose Channel. Eight to ten feet below the pier, the swirling water glows an iridescent green. You could get shivery and clammy just looking at it. Right up there with headless bodies in dumpsters are those TV stories about toxic waste sites, and I've probably written more of them than I can count, or remember. Not to mention that five miles to the west, lies "Cancer Alley," the most polluted section of northern New Jersey. (Q: Why does California have the most lawyers in the country, while New Jersey has the most toxic waste sites? A: New Jersey got first choice.)

"No way."

Ben and Mike glare at me. "I know we drove all this way and it's cold and you're going to be mad at me and tell everyone I chickened out..."

"I thought you were a pro." Clearly, the photographer is disappointed. There are a lot of things I'll do for a story. A lot of things I have done. But...

"No way."

"Don't think about it," says Ben. "Just jump!"

"Are you kidding? Look at the current!"

"We could drive to New Jersey," Mike suggests.

"No way!" Ben and I chorus. Like the Marx brothers,

interrupting each other, we fill in each other's lines: it's late, it's getting dark, we're cold, plus there's all that Easter traffic. Just before we lose the sun, we fake a few shots. With the rednecks looking on, amazed, we rig up, with the skyline in the background, as if we're planning to jump into that slime and windsurf, anyway.

Heckscher State Park, NY
June 24, 1984

Small craft warnings. Hard to believe, but I make it out and back a few times, before my arms feel like their being pulled out of their sockets.

"Just getting the sail up and standing in these conditions is pretty good," someone comments when I get back to shore. "You definitely need to get a harness."

Heckscher State Park, NY
July 14, 1984

No doubt, this rainslicker-yellow personal flotation device with its chest harness hook has got to be the ugliest one in the world, but the extra length gives back support. It's a thickly padded life jacket with a metal hook that attaches to lines tied on each side of the boom, close to the mast. The theory is that when this hook grabs one of the lines, your body can lean back and take the weight of the wind-filled sail. It's supposed to relieve pressure on the arms and shoulders. At least, that's the theory.

I plot a strategy. At 15 knots, I rig down to a 4.0 and adjust the boom lines but nose dive into the sail again and again, scraping my legs. (Beginner's knees! Not again!) I'm told it takes about a summer to get used to it.

Windsurfing with Ken Winner [22] says to try hooking in, on flat water, in eight to twelve knots. The southwesterlies kick up quite a bit of chop at 12 knots, but after six attempts, I hook in and ride, for twenty seconds, before catapulting forward, face first, into the boom. The next time, I go longer, maybe about thirty seconds, but as my body takes the weight of the sail, it releases strain in the shoulders. What a relief!

A longer run, southeast, to the "NO SHELLFISHING" buoy; I unhook for the return tack. Hooking in again, riding the crest of the swells. Definitely an improvement! This contraption could change windsurfing forever.

Heckscher
July 29, 1984

Southeast, 10 knots. I am rigging with a still mind, and each phase of assembly is falling into its own rhythm: threading the sleeve of the cloth sail through the fifteen-foot fiberglass mast, pulling the downhaul, fastening the downhaul cleat on the mast foot, snapping the boom, tying the outhaul, checking the cleat, and attaching the rig to the board. All one fluid movement.

Maintaining flow. Windsurfing five miles across the Great South Bay to Fire Island. All one fluid movement.

Landfall is perfectly still, a shallow marsh. The only sounds: clams gurgling in the mud and seawater lapping against the hull of the board. Quite a contrast to the frenzy of the newsroom. The other day, as I looked up from my desk at the freeflowing montage of bombings, plane crashes, train derailments, toxic waste spills, and assorted murders on various monitors, sounds and images swirled into a blank and time itself collapsed, then telescoped, as if everything happening in the planet was happening right there, right now. And that was all there was. A scary question: Is this is what God sees when He looks at planet Earth?

Out here, wrapped in the rolling swell and emptiness of the sea, I begin to unwind.

Heading back around four PM, a gust pulls the 6.4 Neil Pryde out of my arms. The massive HiFly pitches, nose first, over the swell. I start falling in. Crawl back up. Fall in. Again and again. Defeat. This is usually where I begin to panic, but I've been here before and recognize fear. "You know what to do, you can handle this," I coach my fearful, klutzy self. "You can. You did. You will."

Heckscher
Labor Day, 1984

Wind, gusty as hell, whooshes around the western point. The ocean is all whitecaps and foaming current. I use a 5.5 meter sail and the harness. I'm flying over the chop. Windrush! Swirling around my ears, the wind and I whooping at the sea, picking up speed, breathing it all in. An act of loving life.

Coming in, tears take me by surprise.

Maybe it's work. Or that recurring dream that started after August 28th: the Israeli invasion of southern Lebanon. A slow motion close-up of a child getting his face blown up. Last Sunday, too tired to make the trip out here, the same dream, five times in a row. Waking up in a sweat.

A few days ago, during an incoming satellite feed: a zoom-in to close-up of a curlyhaired teenage boy, lying, wounded, on the tarmac of some airport, makes me want to throw up. "I must be losing it," I apologize after walking out of the control room. When I go back, I have trouble looking at the screen. That boy is somebody's child.

Wrapped in a blanket, I try to sleep on the dunes. Maybe a nap will get rid of the nausea. For three weeks now, off and on, a chronic upset stomach. Stress? More like grinding glass in the intestines. For the past few weekends, I've been too weak to rig even a small sail.

Irresistible, the friendly scent and sound of a southeasterly in the high trees. Tingling behind the ears. On the water, it's hard to hook in. The HiFly is too big for the chop and she heads up, into the wind, faster than I can sheet in. Time to rig down. A shorter board would help, I'm told.

Pete calls for me to help hold the catamaran mast as he locks in the steel pin that keeps it upright. Normally, I like to help by staying out of the way. While holding it, I turn my head to say hello to a friend and Pete snaps, "Pay attention." Nothing unusual here, except I burst into tears, crying, "Don't yell at me!" Sensing trouble–and what could be more troublesome than a woman crying while her husband is holding a heavy, teetering, aluminum mast–two of Pete's friends run over to help. Standing back, relief mixes with embarrassment. I feel like even more of an idiot when, carrying the rig, I trip over my own uphaul and fall onto the concrete.

Begin at the beginning: Outhaul release. Flip the boom clamp. Remove boom. Release downhaul. There is a kind of sorcerer's logic to these steps, each pull magically releasing a bit more of my own tension as well as the sail's. Eventually, the black and white 4.0 meter sail gets unrolled and the mysterious formula is executed again, this time, backwards.

Finally, hard, pure windsurfing.

In the middle of jibe, a huge, black cloud advances across a field from the north. It looks personal, with its forked branches of lightning. Like it's coming to get me. Panicked, I lose coordination. No matter what I do, I keep sliding off the board, bucking in the swell, shit-scared, when Pete and Warren come screaming across the bay, hauling me onto the Hobie. We get back to shore just as a stormcloud so huge that the first one looks like *nothing* rolls in from the north. The wind whips around to the northeast. Within twenty minutes, the temperature drops fifteen degrees, as cold rain whips across the field.

Quick curtain. Summer exits, stage left.

"The sky is a net crammed with shadowy fish.
Here all the winds let go sooner or later, all of them.
The rain takes off her clothes."[23]

Heckscher State Park, NY
May 26, 1985

Wind: southwest, 5–10 knots.

Another birthday.

I think I'll dye my hair red and buy a pair of green sneakers. I'll become "the red-headed lady in the green sneakers," which will solve any fashion problems. Assuming that I have any fashion problems. It's hard to worry about anything except the baby.

Baby?

"How did that happen?" Two months' pregnant by the week after Labor Day? The obstetrician raises a skeptical eyebrow at my question. "You don't know how it happened?"

"Oh. Right. "

How could I not have known? Isn't your period supposed to stop? Not always, as it turns out. If nothing else, being pregnant has shown me God is really a man. If She were female, She would have figured out a kinder, more efficient way for humans to reproduce. And, forget about labor. Only a male deity from Celestial Engineering could have come up with that.

Twelve hours. They say we forget, but I think we turn off the sound and black out the images, until the part where they hand you the baby. I'd never held a baby that didn't start wailing right away, so I must be living proof that "maternal instinct" is real. Within seconds of holding this five pound, eighteen inch, football–sized creature who arrived six weeks early, everything else in the universe seemed to give way. If, as some ancient teachings say, a mother sees her baby's soul at the moment of birth, then soul-to-soul contact sweeps through, like a tsunami, leaving in its wake just this: unconditional surrender and overwhelming gentleness.

Wiped out, in the force of that wave, are pre-birth anxieties: How will I talk to her? What if I don't know what to do? Why can't babies be born toilet trained and speaking English? Roaming around, in the middle of the night, opening the Bible at random to Corinthians 13,11: "When I was a child, I spoke as a child, I understood as a child, I thought as a child: but when I became a (wo)man, I put away childish things."[24]

"Remember, worse people than me have been mothers and everyone has survived," I whisper on our way out of the hospital room, having changed her first diaper, backwards. After a few days, apprehension gives way to complete amazement: Intuitively, I know what to do, even waking up, minutes before she does, knowing that she's about to cry. What could be more sacred than the silence of sitting in a rocking chair, in the middle of the night, nursing a baby back to sleep?

Physically, it feels somewhere between being in love and jet lag: very high and extremely tired. There's also the chaos of renovating and unpacking, along with settling into the new, three-bedroom apartment we bought when I was eight months pregnant, so that we wouldn't have to climb four flights of stairs after the baby came. Moving day brought on labor. ("Never fails," smiles the doctor, who forgot to tell me this before we moved.) The newsroom–where everyone took great care of us both, and the technicians placed bets on whether I would go into labor in the control room–feels like another planet. So do those flash frames: Six months pregnant, making an end run, behind the moving sets of "As the World Turns," to get an obituary into Studio 41 in time for air.

It's all I can do, these days, to get out of the house. No sooner do I dress the baby than she falls asleep again. Or we're on the way out the door, when there's a diaper emergency. If life is a movie, ours must be *The Princess and the Slave*.

In appropriation of this new ageless, timeless, mindless new identity, character and job description have merged completely: Slave is to clean up after, and do Princess' laundry. An endless proposition, rather like Sisyphus pushing a rock up the mountain. But isn't the last line of Camus' version of the Greek myth, "One must imagine Sisyphus, happy?"[25]

The first day of early spring, a familiar warm, sea-smell comes in through the window. I look up from the washing machine. The trees are starting to bud. A yearning to fly, once again, across the surface of the water begins to tug. The Spirit wants out, at least for an hour.

Carefully packing the baby, extra diapers, wipes, extra clothes, bottle, and her portable crib, a vinyl-covered shoebox padded with a New Zealand lambskin, the two of us head for the gym. Placing her next to me, on the floor, near the leg press machine, she manages to sleep, undisturbed, through the sound of barbells crashing on the rubber mat, across the room. The sight of a newborn asleep in the middle of so much activity must touch some universal, empathic gene. Who can resist smiling? Within the hour, just about everyone in the gym comes over to look, sharing pictures of their own babies, nieces, nephews, and grandchildren.

Today will tell if the effort to get back in shape has made any difference. Fine tuning the downhaul, the outhaul, and, once again, the downhaul, reassures me that the role of slave hasn't killed off all my brain cells. I can still tie a half-hitch! Gripping the boom, hooking in, negotiating swell, and tacking, all flow back naturally. Windsurfing enhances this new happiness. Maybe that passage from Corinthians doesn't mean I have to give up windsurfing.

In mid-afternoon, a Yuppie invasion: Toyotas, Subarus, and Isuzus, stacked with the latest windsurfing gear, pull into our parking field. Attack of the Club Med crowd. Where the hell did these people come from, anyway? (Oops! My fault.) *Wind Rider*, "Windsurfing in the Big Apple."

Mixed in with friends' congratulations—"Hey, you were out there windsurfing last summer and you were pregnant!" and "Can she jibe yet?"—are some snarly remarks like "Why did you have to write about our beach?" It seems like everyone is bothered by the impact of that one story.

Except for Warren. Wrapping a giant arm around Ben's shoulder, he's grinning like a sonofabitch. "They're predicting great wind for tomorrow," he says. "Whaddya say, we all stay up and listen to the weather radio all night?"

Heckscher
May 27, 1985

You should study not only that you become a mother when your child is born, but also that you become a child.

—Zen master Dogen [26]

Wind: southwest, 15 –25. Life is easy. Sitting in the sun.

Now five months' old, wrapped in a blanket, the baby sleeps in her Perago stroller, a most generous gift from our friends in the newsroom. My mind wanders: If the techs had won their bet, and she had been born in the control room, we would have called her Telstar.

Instead, we call her Mindy.

Gulping salty wind, reflecting on all those shades of blue merging into the horizon, I smile, thankful for this day, and all that has brought us here, together.

In time, perhaps I can learn to see the world, again, as she discovers it. For once, there is nothing making me feel as if I have to do anything. How strange and unexpected to feel so at home in the unlikelihood of becoming a mother. Dogen writes, "When a fish swims, it swims on and on, and there is no end to the water. When a bird flies, it flies on and on, and there is no end to the sky. There was never a fish that swam out of the water, or a bird that flew out of the sky." There is so much, and at the same time, nothing to be said about this, being in one's own element.

Without words, there is so much I want for her: safety, comfort, beauty, health, and love. Travel and adventure. Friends. A peaceful home. To be cool in the heat of summer and warm on the coldest nights. To know she is loved at all times. But of all the things I wish for her, above all, I want her to know and love the sea.

Heckscher
August 16, 1985

"Haven't we always had her?" Pete smiles. It is getting harder and harder to remember a time before...

We make a spontaneous decision to go sailing, followed by a packing ritual: food, diapers, baby gear, board, rig, Hobie tool kit, extra clothes, towels, and, oh yes, the baby. In the middle of the week, we have the Great South Bay all to ourselves, and it seems silly not to make the trip whenever the wind calls. How many times in our lives will we have an opportunity like this? In the end, what could be more important than our first summer as a new family?

As it happens, I've got six months of maternity leave, unpaid. Pete lost his job when the baby was six weeks old. At first, panic set in. What about the mortgage and all those bills that come with settling in to a new home? Corinthians was right. Time to give up childish things and go back to work. Then we look at each other and laugh. "It's summer."

"We can always go back to work in the fall."

"Isn't this our first summer as a family?"

Enchanting though it is here, on the edge of the Great South Bay, the bills are mounting up. It's scary, but we'll have enough to float us through the rest of summer. Floating has become my natural state. A cloud of peacefulness surrounds me almost all the time. Harmonious with each other, Pete and I take turns going out on the water while the baby sleeps in the tan Chevy van, her furry little portable crib tucked safely between the rolled-up sails. (Thank you, Neil Pryde.)

A languid, stretching starboard tack brings me back to shore, to my family. As he heads out, I sit on the floor of the van, watching her for the first sign of restlessness so that I can nurse. It's not my favorite thing in the world, but it's healthier for the baby. Seeing me in this new role, a lot of people seem to be in shock at the guerrilla raid that having a baby has staged on my old personality. From Dad, a mixed compliment, for sure: "I never expected that you would be such a wonderful mother."

This new, quieter rhythm brings up anxiety about going back to work. My leave is up in two weeks. When a producer called, yesterday, to ask what I want to do when I come back, I said, "I want to win the lottery so I can stay at home with the baby."

He has two daughters, so he laughed, "I understand."

Heckscher
August 17, 1985

Winds out of the northeast, shifting to southeast, 10 knots.

Today is the day.

Windsurfing, solo, across the Great South Bay. Forty-five minutes with the 6.4 sail. For a new mom, this much freedom feels like an act of rebellion.

Coming back, I fall twice. My hands get sharp cramps. My shins are sore, and a blister on the Achilles tendon, where the wetsuit seam chafes the skin, adds to the overall discomfort.

Barely halfway back, exhaustion sets in. *What if I don't make it?* An edge of panic gets intercepted by a calmer inner voice: *Look behind you.* This voice seems to speak from the center of silence. Maybe it has always been there but I've been too crazed to hear it. Turning to port—a wide-angle view of sails sparkling white against a cobalt sky as light dances, silver on the water. Like art, it soothes the edge, allowing you to see something simple from a different perspective.

Montauk, New York
September 12, 1985

Windsurfing in the Atlantic for the first time: Remember what it feels like in the wash cycle, flipped upside down and turned over, after catching a big one just wrong. I almost drowned a few miles from here. Maybe that's why all this wide-open water makes me nervous. Nothing between me and Brazil in a stiff northwest.

Back at work for the past two weeks. My heart's not in it, but we're fortunate in many ways. There are so many friends in the newsroom, it makes leaving Mindy less painful. She and I spend the morning together, even though a lot of our time is taken up with housework, grocery shopping, and laundry. Mom stuff. At noon, I take her to spend the rest of the day with Harlene, a longtime friend of the family who is also becoming our guardian angel. With five older children in the house, the baby gets plenty of love and attention. It's a great environment. There's one question that I have to ask her: "How could you stand being pregnant so many times?"

"It never felt any different, being pregnant," she laughs.

"I guess not. If you felt like I did, you wouldn't want to go through that again."

Pete, who comes from a large family, himself, says he wants four children, someday. I couldn't imagine having enough energy to take care of an infant, keep house, work full-time, and be pregnant, much less, take care of two babies. Not to mention the cost. We're financially over-whelmed as it is, even with both of us working, so all I can do is try to joke, "Think of me as your first wife, honey. I'll start you off. After this, you're on your own."

Maybe it's not a joke. Since we've gone back to work, we're both on edge alot more than we're calm. As journalism jobs go, mine is relatively stable. No sudden calls in the middle of the night ordering me to catch the next plane out. Journalists thrive on those last-minute changes, but it's been years since I got a charge from walking in front of a loaded machine gun to take a picture. I've also been on the receiving end. "Sorry I can't make it to dinner, love. I'm in Kansas City with the President," was the straw that broke one engagement,[27] and made me realize that I wouldn't want to be inflicting that lifestyle on anyone else down the road. Now, with a baby at home, having a stable schedule is even more important. Although I don't start work until one in the afternoon, I never know when I'm getting home at night. A late-breaking story, like an avalanche in Utah, can keep me in the newsroom till eleven, and arriving home at midnight just doesn't cut it. Like the other night, when Pete made it sound like the avalanche was all my fault, and I ended up crying in front of the microwave.

Lately, even our sailing weekends have been deteriorating into bickering, and I'm starting to wonder if maybe windsurfing is like life, in that you don't always enjoy it. Take the other day, watching a young woman learning how to waterstart:

Pete: "What's wrong with you? You've been windsurfing longer than her and you can't do that."

Me: "She's probably not working full time in a news job, taking care of a baby, and cleaning up a house."

Lurching from chore to chore, errand to errand, laundry pile to laundry pile and from story to story is really a drag. It never seems to be enough: what I do, how much I earn, or how hard I work. *What has happened to my life?* Spinning around in my head, like a crumbling autumn leaf, that question has been troubling me all weekend. Maybe this is "just a phase," like adolescence or blue jeans that you grow into, then out of, without trying. Or maybe this is "just life." No answers, only more questions.

As breeze fills in, later, to 20 knots, out of the northwest, my friend, Pam, and I decide to look for flat water. Driving through two crumbling stone pillars onto a crumbly macadam road we discover a wide, flat pebble beach, on the northern shore of a deserted lake. We can't believe our luck! No one else is around, as we rig and carry gear from the van, changing into our garish neoprene suits. Conditions on this lake are wildly beyond expectations: pure, driving wind, along silver water, shiny–flat as liquid mercury. In this exquisite, sparkling afternoon, we women are the only two souls chasing the edge of the wind across the shimmering, crystal flats.

Tonight, after building a fire on the beach, we stand around, roasting marshmallows and hot dogs, congratulating each other on finding what must be the best windsurfing and Hobie beach for a hundred miles, speculating on tomorrow's wind, enjoying the stars and promising to come back again, next year, and every year.

Linking arms, the others form a circle around me.

"If you ever write about this place, we'll have to kill you."

New York Harbor
July 2, 1986

Until this morning, the most interesting thing I had seen in New York harbor was the sight of three men having sex on the second floor of an abandoned pier. We had been running downwind in the Triton, wing-to-wing across the Hudson at dusk.

"Look, up there!" I pointed. Everyone on deck stared until someone yelled that we were about to hit the decrepit wooden pier. We managed to come about with seconds to spare. I still wonder why that man in the middle was wearing a plaid flannel shirt in the middle of August.

I also wonder why would anyone want to windsurf across the Atlantic Ocean. But from the top deck of the press boat, I bear witness to two young Frenchmen windsurfing in front of the Statue of Liberty who have done just that–windsurfing, unescorted on a tandem sailboard, thus, replacing that man in the plaid flannel shirt as "the most interesting sight in New York harbor."[28]

Stephane Peyrone, twenty-six, and Alain Pichavant, twenty-seven, enter the windsurfing record books today, after their historic five thousand-mile, voyage on a specially designed, thirty-one-foot tandem sailboard, the Liberté de Timex. They set sail from Dakar, Senegal, on June twenty-third. Twenty-four days, twelve hours, and five minutes later, they landed in Guadeloupe, breaking the 1984 record for a transatlantic crossing on a tandem sailboard set by fellow Frenchmen Fred Bauchene and Thierry Caroni, who took forty-eight days to windsurf across the ocean on a twenty-five-foot board that was more than six feet wide and four feet deep. Why in the world would anyone want to do this?

"For a seaman, it is very important to cross the Atlantic

Ocean one time in his life. It is like climbing Mount Everest for people who go up the mountain," Stephane says. "We wanted our arrival in New York to symbolize the historic relationship between France and the States in coordination with the rededication of the Statue of Liberty. Even if the restoration of the Statue is not entirely French."

It was not Stephane's first attempt to windsurf the Atlantic, his partner Alain Pichavant explains. "Four or five years ago, he tried to cross the Atlantic.[29] There were four guys on a regular board, changing shifts every six hours. Two or three days before they arrived, one of the guys got a burst appendix and the escort boat had to rush him to the hospital, so they never finished the crossing."

There were times when it looked like they might not finish this crossing either. On the second day of their journey, they hit a thunderstorm with 50-knot winds. "At the beginning, we lost a lot of time changing the sail," Alain says, adding that "on the second night, we were very tired. The board started in surf, very quick, and I couldn't control it with the sail."

During that storm, the sailors lost their sunglasses and all their fresh food. "We had fruit, fish, French cheese, many things like that. When the board flipped over, we lost everything," Alain remembers. "We were pretty upset for two or three days.

"Then we lost the radio. I used the radio two hours after we left Africa to see if it was working. I was supposed to call back the next morning at eight. We didn't sleep through the night, and I wouldn't go inside the board, where there was a hollow tube just large enough for one of us to sleep. We were seasick and not in very good shape. I tried to stay in the tube for fifteen minutes at a time, but I couldn't. At first, it wasn't a big problem because we had 25 knots of wind to deal with but when we began to feel better, it was very upsetting that we had no radio and we couldn't talk to land."

"Twenty four days without any contact," Stephane comments, "Well, that was exciting and dangerous, too!"

Having lost their fresh food, they consumed special food developed by The Knorr Factory specifically for their ocean expedition. "We worked with a team of doctors and tried many things before we got it right," says Stephane. "Our food was 3600 calories a day, dehydrated. It's easy to prepare in four minutes. You mix hot water or salt water and it explodes."

Living at sea, in a wetsuit, with no place to change, presented its own challenges, says Alain. "During the first ten days, we were wet all the time. And I had some skin problems. Fungus. After the first ten days, we were able to keep more things dry."

"We knew that we would be wet all the time. We brought a lot of cream to protect our skin but we had problems all the time. At the beginning it wasn't easy, because we didn't sleep, we didn't eat, we didn't have the rhythm of the board. We were always thinking about every possibility," Stephane adds.

Possibilities that included humungous waves! "In the Atlantic, the waves are always straight on. And they are big swells," Stephane says.

"Four hundred foot swells," says Alain, completing Stephane's sentence.

"So you have big, big, big, big surf. Sometimes we put the nose under the water. We had a little rudder near my foot at the back. We didn't use it across the Atlantic because we needed to go straight. We used it two or three times in the big crossing during a swell. The Liberte is designed to come as close as possible to a doubled version of a Division Two windsurfer, with a hollowed-out section inside the hull for sleeping, so it's slower to turn than a regular board," Stephane continues. "We put on a rudder because when we entered harbors in the United States, we needed to turn quickly."

Although the Liberte was designed with a hollow sleeping tube, neither sailor spent much time in there, preferring to sleep for ten or fifteen minutes at a stretch, standing up with his head on the boom, hooked in to the harness lines with an Interwind harness designed just for this trip. "After two weeks, we were used to staying up all the time," Stephane remembers. "We would stay up for three hours and lie down, inside, for three hours. The biggest problem was passing the time. We windsurfed at night, because during the day it's too long. When you start early in the morning, it's hot and it seems longer than at night. We had music, but it was always the same: Dire Straits, French singers, classical music. We would hear the same sixty-minute tape three times, during a three-hour shift."

As for sails, he notes that "we had a 7.5 meter which we never used until Guadelupe. We used the 5.5 and the 4.0. We didn't need a smaller sail because we were able to handle more sail on this board, more than usual. It was not a question of wind, though. It was a question of sea. Even if you have a smaller sail on, with a 4.0, it's difficult because it's not enough sail. The swells are too big."

How did they train to get the stamina for windsurfing across the ocean?

"I practiced long distance windsurfing a long time. I don't know how it came to me. I think it's sixty to seventy percent in the head. The other thirty percent is physical training," Stephane observes. For Carolyn, "it's important to train in jogging, running, and endurance swimming, as well as a lot of endurance windsurfing."

And when they reached the point where they were so tired that they couldn't go on, how did they make themselves continue?

"I don't know," Stephane concedes. "There's a mental aspect to it. You have to think of a lot of things. You have to keep your attention on the technical part of sailing. You have to stay on the board. During the world record distance event, two years ago, I learned to sleep one to two minutes on the booms. Every ten minutes. After sixty hours of sailing, of course, I fall down maybe ten times when I sleep. You have to be strong mentally. There is no training for that."

And when his hands were cut up and he was sunburned, seasick and hungry? What about those times when he thought, "I really want to go home. I don't want to be here?" Stephane replies, "It's not a question of your hands hurting or being hungry, because you will be able to eat every day for the next several years, but you will only be able to make this crossing once. You think of this and of all the people who were involved in organizing the expedition, for the past two years, all the people who are waiting for you. And most of all, for your own sake, you think of this like any job. If you have a problem, you have to solve it in order to succeed. You have to succeed or you're not going to be satisfied with yourself."

In the middle of the Atlantic on their windsurfer, what did they miss the most?

"My friends and home," says Alain, noting that he has been away for six months.

"French cheese," smiles Carolyn.

Stephane shrugs, the kind of shrug that only a French guy can do, accompanied by one of those equally French enigmatic smiles.

Would they do it again?

"No, it's enough," says Stephane.

Would Alain do it again?

"No."

Finally, what advice would they offer to anyone who wants to windsurf across the Atlantic?

"I don't advise you," laughs Carolyn, who is joined by Stephane, who adds, "If they want to do it, they have to be in good physical condition, first of all. Then they have to have a good head. But I wouldn't advise anyone to do this."

Which leaves the last laugh to Alain. "Non!"

[1] I Ching. Bollingen edition. Hexagram 5, Hsu, Waiting (Nourishment). New York, NY: Bollingen Foundation, 1950, p. 24. As Carl Jung writes in the forward, "Why not venture a dialogue with an ancient book that purports to be animated?"

[2] Windsurfing started in the mid-1970s. It took off in Europe, especially in Germany and the Netherlands. Obviously, it was a lot more popular in Maui and along the California coast, than on the East coast. The first windsurfer was designed and patented by Californians Jim Drake and Hoyle Schweitzer in 1969. The very first prototype, called a "Skate," was launched on May 23, 1967. (*American Windsurfer*, Volume 4, Issue 4, 1996; p. 38.)

[3] Okay, okay. It's Lestoil. The trick is to work Lestoil into the sweaty areas of the fabric, rubbing hard with a nailbrush. Then wash in warm water. Your laundry room will give off an industrial fume smell for a day, but your clothes won't have sweat stains.

[4] Walter B. Cooke is a New York family chain of funeral homes.

[5] Pablo Neruda, *Twenty Love Poems and a Song of Despair.* (London: Jonathan Cape, 1969), p. 29.

[6] Eugen Herrigel, *Zen in the Art of Archery* (New York: Pantheon Books, 1953) p. 17.

[7] In case you've never dated in Brooklyn, submarine races are a euphemism for make out spots. Coney Island whitefish (or Hudson River trout if you dated in the Bronx) are used condoms. Drive-by shootings are among the quaint local Saturday night rituals.

[8] Neruda, op.cit., p. 15

[9] Herrigel, op.cit., p.31.

[10] On the day of your death, there are no fees for using film clips in your obituary. But when an obituary is produced in advance, usage fees can be significant as I found out when a studio charged $1,000 for one minute of Sir

Lawrence Olivier as Richard II in the famous scene, "A horse! A horse! My kingdom for a horse!"

11 Douglas Edwards was the first CBS News anchorman, preceding Walter Cronkite.

12 Janice Hume, assistant journalism professor at Kansas State University, researched more than 8,000 obituaries as part of her doctoral dissertation at the University of Missouri. Her landmark study, *Obituaries in American Culture*, by University Press of Mississippi/Jackson was published in 1999.

13 U.S. Census Bureau report statistics published in *Time*, June 28, 1999, p. 21.

14 I did not make up this marketing concept. It has been floating around for the past few years. Erik Larson refers to "the golden era of death" in a column written for a bonus business section of *Time*, December 9, 1996, p. 63.

15 In a 1999 study conducted by the National Hospice Foundation, it was reported that 75 percent of Americans surveyed said they want their final wishes carried out, but won't take the time to articulate those wishes.

16 The "news flash" story was reported on page six of *The New York Post*, November 12, 1983.

17 Te Maori opened in the Metropolitan Museum of Art on September 11, 1984 and closed on January 6, 1985. From there, it traveled to the St. Louis Art Museum (February 22– May 26, 1985) and the M.H. de Young Memorial Museum in San Francisco (July 6 – December 1, 1985) before returning to New Zealand.

18 This Sidney Moko Mead quote appears in "Te Maori: The Spiritual Art of New Zealand" by Laurie Nadel. *Islands*, February 1985, p. 36.

19 This is a perfect example of cultural humor. As a gag gift, I brought home several cans (tins) of SHEEP TONGUES. Whenever an American friend unwrapped one, there would be immediate laughter. On those few occasions when a New Zealander would watch an American unwrapping the SHEEP TONGUES, and breaking into

laughter, he or she would look disapproving at our lack of culture. "What's so funny about SHEEP TONGUES? They happen to be delicious, especially when jellied," we have been told, seriously, by several New Zealanders. One night, when a group of Kiwis was visiting, and we ran out of food, I remembered the last can (tin) of SHEEP TONGUES. Grossed out, the Americans gathered in a knot to watch a friend gratefully digging into the contents and praising the taste. Well, I did say it was cultural...

[20] "New Zealand Odyssey: In Search of Sails" by Laurie Nadel, was published in *Boardsailor* magazine, May 1984, pp. 106–108.

[21] "Windsurfing in New York City," by Laurie Nadel, appeared in the May 1985 issue of *Wind Rider*.

[22] *Windsurfing with Ken Winner* was published by Personal Library Publishers, Toronto, Canada, 1980.

[23] Neruda, op cit., "Every Day You Play," p. 41

[24] The New Testament of Our Lord and Savoir Jesus Christ, King James Edition (The New York Bible Society, New York, 1957), p. 397.

[25] *The Myth of Sisyphus and other Essays*, by Albert Camus. Alfred A. Knopf, Inc., New York, 1955. page 91.

[26] Of all the Zen masters, it is Dogen (1200–1253) who is known for expressing the essence of Zen as moments of enlightenment that come when performing daily tasks, like cooking or washing rice. (*The Little Zen Companion*, edited by David Schiller. Workman Publishing, New York, 1994.) pp. 216, 298–299, and 316.

[27] Don't ask.

[28] "Transatlantic Crossing" was published in the September/October issue of *Wind Rider* (pp. 66–69); in "Board Briefs," same issue, "Liberte de Timex Wraps Up in New York," p. 15.

[29] Stephane Peyrone successfully windsurfed, solo, across the Atlantic in April, 1992.

Part Two
1987–1994

In the middle of winter,
I at last discovered
that there was in me
an invincible summer.
−ALBERT CAMUS[1]

Centerport, NY
July 23, 1994

> *It is necessary at the outset to know and to cultivate the three essentials of Zen practice: great faith... now matter how many obstacles, internal or external, we meet on the way; great doubt, and great determination.*
>
> —Thich Thien-An[2]

Wind: northwest, gusting to 25 knots. Almost a decade since the last time I noticed. Or, for that matter, cared. The past two hours, I've been standing here, studying sifting water patterns, like accent marks above French vowels that no longer make sense.

Underneath the sound of the wind, the doctor's warning: "Windsurf? You'll be lucky if you can walk up stairs..."

Heckscher State Park, NY
Flashback to September 4, 1987

No entries this summer. I have chronic fatigue syndrome. Even driving to the Great South Bay is exhausting. One August afternoon, wind barely pushing five knots, wiped me out. Besides, this is not why I took up windsurfing in the first place, to trek with a vanload of duffelbags, gear, and paraphernalia for a baby, to sail back and forth in the same place, like biking around the periphery of a playground. I took up windsurfing to explore my own courage.

Centerport, NY
July 23, 1994 (continued)

Whitecaps whip up, as thunderheads roll over Eatons Neck, two miles across the bay. Questions crash into each other, like heavy surf before a storm.

What if I can't?

What am I trying to prove?

How many years has it been, anyway?

By the spring of 1987, if Murphy Brown had married Crocodile Dundee, this would have been the outcome, after those initial, knife-between-the-teeth acts of daring became less and less endearing in the struggle to cope with everyday routine, while sinking in financial quicksand.

There is a bitter writers' strike during one of those periods when Pete is, once again, "between jobs." We have yet another argument about the bills. He goes back to splotching pink primer on the white plaster kitchen wall. When life gives you lemons, make lemonade. Or make a joke, and bolt.

"I'd better get out of here before we make headlines in the *Daily News*."

Relaxation: driving into the heart of the midtown rush hour. It's crazy to feel safer in a sea of yellow taxis than your own home. Two months later, after the strike. Remember that joke about sharks in three-piece suits? Corporate cutbacks, downsizing, and bean counters with their "sinister faces of boredom",[3] peering over people's shoulders. If anyone's having fun around here, it's gotta be an accident. Reality bites:

Q: Why are those people reading newspapers?

A: They're writers. They're supposed to read the news before they write.

Q: Make them stop. They're wasting time.

It's right around now when the baby comes down with a sore throat. Three days later, she's fine, but my throat starts getting scratchy. Three weeks later, I can barely push her stroller to the corner. Six weeks later, like Albert Camus:

"In bed. Fever. Only the mind works on, obstinately. Hideous thoughts. Unbearable feeling of advancing step by step toward an unknown catastrophe which will destroy everything around me and in me." [4]

As the Iran–Contra hearings get underway, the first doctor diagnoses the sickness as chronic fatigue syndrome. As bad as I feel, it seems worse not to show up, especially when the others are calling in sick. Some days, I'm the only one in that newsroom writing the Iran–Contra hearings. It's no longer funny to joke about coming to work so I can sit down. Stationed at the desk, I cover up for the weakness in my legs by asking friends to walk over to the printer, across the room. That way, no one will catch on that I'm too sick to get up and do it myself. After a few months, I start using vacation days for sleeping. When am I ever going on vacation, anyway? There's no money, and those days spent, hooked in, flying over the chop, must have been someone else's vacation. Or maybe someone else's life.

In an effort to control the fear that whatever this is, it's not going away, I decide to treat this sickness as if it were just another story. When the reporter's instinct to take notes in a crisis kicks in, it tends to soften that edge of panic that comes on when life around you gets out of control. It may, in the end, prove to be a delusion that writing down facts, ideas, and reactions makes any difference in a crisis. But, as I recognized one night in Santiago, during the state of siege in 1973, when a burst of machine guns after curfew scared the lions in the zoo across the street into a frenzy of terrified roaring, writing scary things down while they're happening can make you feel safe, especially when you're not. The more frightened you feel, the more notes you take. There's a certain comfort in a mundane ritual of doing what you know how to do when you find yourself on the edge of terror.

One phone call to the Center for Disease Control's public information office and seven pages of handwritten notes later confirms that, like most stories, there's good and bad news. The good news, such as it is–the illness is not "in my head." Not only is chronic fatigue syndrome not a psychosomatic condition, it qualifies as an epidemic, affecting somewhere between two and five million Americans.[5] The bad news: With its mysterious, viral base, chronic fatigue syndrome, usually caused by the Epstein–Barr (EBV) or cytomagelo virus (CMV) hits most people for around three years, and it cannot be treated with antibiotics or conventional medicine. The first line of attack, says Doctor Number One, a holistic M.D. with this own radio show, includes Vitamin B–12 shots, Vitamin C, and some herbs, rumored to be immune system boosters. Six months later, even he is stumped by the lack of progress in the bloodwork. "Take a week off and get into bed," he says. I feel guilty handing my boss the doctor's note, since I'm leaving her short–staffed. Is that my fault? "Talk to the bean counters if you don't have enough staff," something in me wants to say, but what's the point?

System failure notwithstanding, the mind persists in seeking explanations. Doctor Number Two explains that people in high–stress jobs often burn out their adrenal glands, the immune system's first line of defense. "The human body needs to keep producing adrenaline to keep you primed for creative challenge and deadlines. To manufacture adrenaline, your body needs rest. Over time, with a constant demand for adrenaline and not enough rest, your adrenal system will begin to shut down," she said, adding that scientific studies of animal behavior, such as John Christian's 1955 research on a population of Sika deer on James Island in Chesapeake Bay, have shown, repeatedly that decreased resistance to stress due to overactive adrenals can result in illness, or death.[6] By expecting to function, at high speed, indefinitely, I had ignored some simple warning signs. For eight years, I reported in to work with colds, and sore throats, and fevers. "We're short a writer. We'll pay you double time. Please, just come in and write the show." Rarely did I say no. I thought I was doing the right thing.

The next three months are pretty much a blank, with a few fragments of memory:

Waking up. Fighting through a black sea that pushes me down. By the time I open my eyes, I'm covered in sweat from the effort it takes to wake up. Somewhere, across a long, dark plain is the small light where I need to go to keep from wetting the bed. It's too hard to push through this black gel, so I lie here, in my own sliminess, asking for just enough strength to sit up. If I can sit up, I can shift my legs; gravity will help them to the floor. Then I can leverage my body against the headboard. Leaning forward helps, too. Somehow, eventually, I make it to the toilet. Most of the time.

I always shower. Wash my hair. Brush my teeth. Then, it's the Quasimodo Lurch, again. Because the room spins around so much, bed functions as the focal point. When I make it back, safely, the ceiling flattens out, swirling into moving checks and plaids, like one of those black and white prints by M.C. Escher that turn three-dimensional when you look at them. By now, I'm dizzy and nauseous, but I coach myself to keep my eyes open. If I can wait it out, the dizziness will go away.

When it's safe to begin movement again, I force myself to make the bed. Then, everything goes to black. Pete has been up for awhile, feeding the baby and playing with her. As difficult as our life as a couple has become, as a father, he's infinitely affectionate. They sound so happy, down the hall. Even though I can't make it into the kitchen, hearing them laugh together makes me smile. Sometimes he brings her into the bedroom before he leaves for a job interview, or she naps in her crib. Around noon, the main event becomes getting her dressed, then walking her two blocks, to Harlene's building. Our guardian angel, Harlene always offers to come pick her up, but there's a mental component to the daily drill. If you stick to the same routine you've followed for the past two years, maybe this little girl won't get scared because Mommy's really sick. The fact is, I can't stay awake for more than an hour, and I'm afraid. Which is why I force myself to make the bed, shower, and follow my old routine. If I give up making the effort, then the illness will win.

Getting a squirmy toddler into a snowsuit and boots, down a flight of stairs, into a Perago stroller, through a heavy glass door, down a flight of six, brick steps, and up a two-block long, sloping hill, never used to be a big deal. Now I can't even open a window! Pushing a stroller two blocks takes an hour, to an hour and a half, with frequent stops to sit down on various front stoops. By the time I ring Harlene's doorbell, I'm drenched in so much sweat that it feels like I've been trekking through the Himalayas.

Half an hour of rest. A few glasses of water or juice. Time for the reverse trek home before the inky blackness descends. Before giving in to it, there is one exercise that is part of my ongoing strategy to outsmart this disease. With symptoms that are identical to other illnesses, like mononucleosis, and depression, chronic fatigue syndrome is especially hard to diagnose accurately. "I'm depressed because I'm so fucking sick. How do you expect me to feel?" I've been known to snarl.[7] "Yuppie flu," Doctor Number Three calls it, patting my shoulder. "And you're a perfect candidate." Apparently, around eighty percent of C.F.S.D. patients are energetic, often athletic, "high achieving" women, in their thirties. Not that I identify with "high achieving," or "athletic," despite Judy Mahle Lutter's flattering description in Women's Sports and Fitness: "Laurie Nadel fits the profile of others reporting similar symptoms...A high-power newswriter...before getting sick, (she) wind-surfed three times per week."[8]

Practically overnight, I've changed from a woman who does everything, to someone who can do nothing. Worse than that is feeling useless. That is, when I'm awake enough to feel anything at all. Along with this pressing fatigue that never goes away, no matter how much I sleep, after a year and a half there's a deadening of hope that I will get all the way back to where I used to be when I could work and make love and cook and look after the baby and go to the gym and windsurf. Oh no. None of the eight doctors who reconfirm the diagnosis have spoken to me about the psychological impact of losing your sense of control with a concomitant loss of safety. When your body no longer functions, and no matter what you do, you can't make it do what you want it to, life itself gets pretty scary. If you don't get better, you feel that you're no longer the person whom you used to be. If, like me, you started working after school when you were twelve, your sense of identity as a productive human being is no longer viable. Disturbing questions won't leave you alone. Questions like, "Who am I, if I'm not able to work?"

Maybe I no longer know, but I refuse to think of myself as a "sick person," one of those killer phrases that can sabotage your sense of self by making you think that's who you are. I've got to believe I'm a healthy person with a long-running medical condition, a cognitive reframe that makes chronic fatigue seem like a bad play that's been running on Broadway for too long. Like all bad plays, it has to end at some point. But I don't know when.

Nor do I know how. If there was medication, I would be taking it. Since there isn't, I'm experimenting with Chinese herbs, nutritional supplements, various chiropractic approaches, and meditation. Every afternoon, when I get home, I force myself to sit up straight for twenty minutes while I go through a series of focusing exercises. The purpose of meditation is to quiet the mind through a repetitive, focusing technique that can be a sound (mantra), an image, or a combination of the two. Studies at Harvard Medical School have shown that meditation, which activates the parasympathetic nervous system, can help strengthen the immune system.[9] The vicious cycle of a long-running illness is that struggling with the symptomology creates more stress. Over the long haul, those negative emotions that develop when your body doesn't heal make you feel defeated, worthless, and depressed. Which, in turn, generate molecules of emotion that are harmful to your health. Meditation seems like the best weapon to counteract the downward, counterproductive inner process that seems to have become an inevitable side-effect of chronic fatigue.

While there are many systems of meditation, including transcendental meditation (TM) and yoga, my cousin, Randi, has given me a book, *The Psychology of Enlightenment*, by Gurudev Shree Chitrabanu, who has been her meditation teacher for years. The thin orange book contains a basic exercise program for building up the seven wheels of energy along the spine, called *chakras*. Each *chakra* represents a set of inner qualities: stability, creativity, will, love, communication, inner vision, and spiritual awareness. My first exposure to *chakra* meditation came when I was covering Shirley MacLaine's psychic awareness seminars for *Family Circle*. She teaches a system which moves through all seven *chakras*, from the root to the crown, in one session. Chitrabanu's system exercises only one at a time, for twenty minutes, every day for a week. Starting with the first chakra, stability, located at the base of the spine, you move up to the second chakra, creativity, for the following week, until, after seven weeks, you have strengthened on all seven. Then you begin again, at the base of the spine.[10]

My favorite meditation works the second chakra, whose

symbol is a silvery crescent moon that slides from the sky, onto its back, to form a silver canoe that floats me, gently and smoothly, into quieter waters. When I open my eyes, it feels as if I have been truly far, far away. The slower pace needed for this inner focusing has made me aware of what Carl Jung calls the "external" and "internal" worlds. Until I came down with chronic fatigue, most of my attention was focused outside myself, toward the external world of people, activities and things. Ironically, it took this horrible virus to open the door to this complex internal world of concepts and ideas. Before getting sick, I didn't even know that I had an inner world! Nor had it ever occurred to me that it's possible to navigate through an inner landscape that has depth, color, brightness, subtle fragrance, and sound.

Wind, snapping at a sail, pulls me back to the beach. With the sadness of someone who realizes that something, or someone she loved is now completely out of reach, I watch a handful of men, and one young woman, rig flapping, clear Mylar sails, smiling to themselves, as they step around their black, carbon masts to clamp the booms, tight. This is the first time in seven years that I have even looked at windsurfing equipment, and it's quite intimidating. Sail design has obviously changed since I owned my blue and green Neil Pryde 6.4 meter cloth sail with its small, clear plastic window. Not only are these new babies transparent, they have complicated systems of battens and cambers for stiffening. *Why would I choose to go through all this again?*

A profound sigh takes me by surprise, startling a young woman who has been rigging with perfect concentration. Gently tapping at her boom clamp with a rubber headed hammer, she nudges it a fraction of an inch higher on her carbon mast before looking up, to ask, "Do you windsurf?"

"I used to."

"Why did you stop?" Her expression clearly says, "How could you...?

"I was in jail for awhile." This is a much cooler line than,

"I was sick." When you tell people that you were "sick," they look revolted and afraid, as if they might catch something deadly, just from listening to you. But say that you were in jail, and they'll flash you a worried look, like they're not sure whether you're an escaped psychopath, or a garden-variety sociopath with a strange sense of humor. Whatever. It always gets a reaction. Like now. That young woman has just grabbed her board and bolted into the water without looking back.

"Too much wind for you." The short, blond boy, who must have been all of nine years old in 1987 when I wrote the last entry in this journal, shakes his head, no, in time with the clanking sound made by the roof rattling against the thin aluminum walls of the windsurfing shed. Inside, a rack of rigged sails, hanging upside down from the ceiling, rattle against each other, like skeletons of self-doubt at a Halloween ball.

That half-remembered soul wind wraps around my heart...

Centerport, NY
July 24, 1994

You do not wait for fulfillment, but brace yourself for failure.
—Eugen Herrigel[11]

Exhilaration, last night, to drive alongside pounding walls of surf, spraying foam over the dunes, onto the ocean road, as panicky forks of lightning and overwhelming thunder shatter the sky. It's easy to be happy in the full fury of a summer storm, while, secretly, you brace yourself for failure.

Not that I think of it that way. It's more of a maintenance-level disappointment strategy:

1. Do your best.

2. Brace for the possibility that no matter how hard you work, or how well you plan, it might not work out the way you want it to.

3. Find a way to learn something from every disappointment. There's a reason for everything but you may not understand it for a long time.

4. Remember: It's not always your call. There are higher forces at work.

5. Stop expecting everything to go your way. Then you won't be as disappointed when you don't get what you want.

6. Don't feel so much. When you throw your heart into living, you can get really, really hurt.

It works well, most of the time. But, as Herrigel's archery teacher might well have observed, a chronic state of expecting just a little disappointment is like running a low-grade fever. With a low temperature, you can function okay, and you can manage, but you'll never feel terrific. Similarly, a maintenance-level disappointment strategy lets you function on a fairly stable level. No great highs. No great lows.

No great anything, for that matter.

If you've graduated from the "Other People Have It Worse" School, you get into the habit of numbing out your own reactions. You forget how to feel, which, all things considered, isn't such a great loss. With 20–20 hindsight, even the most painful events—like labor—can be refiled under "That Wasn't So Bad." Even better is the "Maybe You Made It Up" technique. After a few choruses of "Maybe You Made It Up," it's hard to remember the facts. And, as long as you remember to forget to expect to forget to remember anything other than the possibility of disaster, who needs facts, anyway? All that counts is protecting yourself in case it happens again?[12] At least, that's the theory...

Packing a bottle of water, two apples, and a maintenance level six-pack, it's time to drive back to the Sound. After yesterday, with an entire night to second-guess, and what-if, maybe I should just stay home instead of daring to go back. *Who are you kidding?* I ask myself over and over again. *You can't possibly...* If the ghost of who I was before would just shut up, I could be sensible. Stay home. Watch TV, maybe. But something more compelling—soul memory, perhaps, or maybe some rich compulsion—is pulling me with unaccountable wanting toward another chance to step off this flat, unmoving plane, into that freeflowing, liquid universe that connects all continents and countries, mountains and cities, rivers and trees. Maybe those Druids were onto something when they described the water's edge as a sacred gateway into another world...

Simply being well enough to drive a car is like entering another world, one that I no longer take for granted. These days, any hour spent in motion calls up thankfulness, along with lost fragments of images and conversations I'd rather not remember. While reflecting on Socrates' ubiquitous tag line, "Know thyself," wasn't it Goethe who allegedly said, "Hey, man, if I knew myself, I'd run away?" Like a Vietnam veteran, returned to normal society after years in combat,

there's a part of me that never sleeps anymore, as if by staying vigilant, I can jump ahead to the next scene, thereby
preventing some incipient disaster. After years of numbing
out–yes, people die all the time–the idea of death becomes
a lot more personal, somehow, when it's your own.

More to the point: Critical, life-threatening flashes that
suddenly appear in the mind's eye, like dangerously jagged
rock formations, disturb the flow of that inner river of time
where each of us has our own running store of memories.[13]
There's never any telling when a few bars of music let loose
from a passing radio, or the sound of a child crying, or a
kitten's meow, or even the smell of medication, can trigger
the hypervigilance of a Vietnam veteran, crouching behind
a pile of Campbell's soup cans, machine–gun ready, just in
case the Cong barge through the cashier's counter. Welcome
to the land of Post-Traumatic Stress Disorder, domestic edition.[14]

Driving along the shore releases a chronology of sorts;
that is, if staccato bursts of dialogue and jump–cuts from
different years count as chronological order. There doesn't
seem to be much point in paying attention, although trying to stop the montage accelerates anxiety, which makes it
hard to drive. Better to let your peripheral vision absorb
the scenery–fluffy cumulus clouds and fishing boats–
anchored alongside the marsh's edge. (*Remind self,* "*This is
real.*" *Repeat,* "*Everything's going to be fine.*")

For a while it was.

Recuperation: one step forward, two steps backward.
After two years of collecting disability, my old job was long
gone. Like millions of baby boomer refugees from corporate America, scanning the field for possibilities, the likeli-
hood of my finding comparable employment seemed highly unlikely, given my age and medical history. *How about the
night shift at McDonald's?* I find myself thinking.

Then I think, *hey, other people have it worse, remember?* Like
Rocky, a double amputee who rolled, sang, and whistled his

way around the streets of an upstate New York town on a little wooden dolly. Rocky's story was the first one to land on my desk. Smiling into the camera, he described how his legs had been shot off in an argument during a poker game. Because he was always whistling and singing, people would stop him in the street to ask how he could be so happy. As it turned out, Rocky said, he didn't get that way overnight. When he woke up in the hospital the day after the shooting, he recalled, "Man, I cursed and yelled at God. 'Why me? Why me?' I kept goin' at God like that until one day I realized, 'Hey, I guess it had to happen to someone. And that someone happened to be me.'" Then and there, Rocky offered to volunteer at that same hospital. Ever since then, he could be seen every afternoon, wheeling his way up the ramp to the geriatric ward, where he taught little old ladies how to play poker.

In my private collection of Lemonade Makers, that little guy topped every list. I mean, what's a few years of chronic fatigue compared to what Rocky had to suffer? And if he could turn his catastrophe around, shouldn't there be a way for me to resuscitate some form of productive career?

Rocky's amazing attitude became a point of reference that led to a major turning point. Like Rocky, I would need to discover, within the framework of physical limitations, an opportunity that would become a blessing in disguise. By forcing me to develop a career path that would let me pace myself when I got tired, the aftermath of chronic fatigue would have to lead to work which would also allow me to spend more time at home as my daughter was growing up, which was what I really wanted. Although CBS News had asked if I would come back to work as a producer, I doubted that my health could stand up to the demands of unpredictable, erratic hours and jump-start travel assignments. Rather than look for another editorial job that would necessitate my commuting and hiring a full-time housekeeper, I felt it would be the right time to take a chance at writing books, at home.

Many people discouraged me because, as an unknown, there was incredible competition for publishers, and it would be impossible to predict one's income, especially in the beginning. There was one person who did think I could do it, by starting with smaller projects. My literary agent, Madeleine Morel, was a tremendous source of strength. With her help getting assignments, it was a natural transition from news and obituary producing to writing political biographies for young adults. I also began writing magazine features on subjects like the psychology of thrill seeking, the dynamics of "flow," or peak performance, and its opposite, performance anxiety. Subjects which touched on the mysteries of human behavior were becoming more intriguing than political bios and news stories.

Pursuing more indepth assignments led me to Judy Haims and Robert Stempson at Programs for Human Development in Greenwich, Connecticut. Judy and Robert taught people how to tap into their intuition using exercises that grew out of the work of neuroscientist Dr. Paul MacLean, who was the Chief of Brain Evolution at the National Institutes of Health. Dr. MacLean discovered that human beings have a triune brain, consisting of four separate brain systems which correspond to the four functions which Carl Jung had mapped out thirty years earlier. The left brain, which we think of as "the brain," is the brain we take to school. The right brain thinks in images and comes up with spontaneous, sudden flashes of knowing that are defined as intuition. The limbic system is the seat of emotional intelligence and the R–system is the center of organizational, structured patterns and routines. If you think of a computer screen divided into four windows, each one running a different software application, then developing a particular type of thinking would mean you placed the cursor, your attention, in that particular brain system to access its "software" of intelligence.

Our book, *Sixth Sense* reported on research and applications of intuitive intelligence, including secret government research into remote viewing of Communist military sites. I interviewed more than 110 people, from all walks of life, on how they used their intuition to make better decisions, and reported on the values and attitudes in education which punish children from using their natural intuitive abilities.[15] I also reported on children, like the girl who dreamed that her mother was locked away somewhere and told police about her dream. The girl's mother, who had disappeared two years ago, was discovered, murdered, in a locked freezer in the basement. Her father confessed to the murder.

To develop a system of intuition–building exercises, I entered a two–year program in neurolinguistic programming (NLP), a system for training the mind that combines hypnosis, linguistics, and visualization. NLP is probably familiar to people because of infomercials starring Tony Robbins, author of *Unlimited Power*. Although Robbins uses the term "neuro–associative conditioning system," it is NLP. I used NLP to develop exercises to help readers become more comfortable with their intuition, but it wasn't until *Sixth Sense* was published, in 1990, that I learned how powerful NLP could be.

Never having worked in front of a camera, or an audience, I discovered that just the thought of promoting the book could bring on a panic attack. One afternoon, I locked myself in the bathroom and cried at the thought of having to appear on "Oprah," like my friend Vicky Secunda, author of *When You and Your Mother Can't Be Friends*. Vicky was so phenomenal on the set that, while I was thrilled for her success, I also knew I was doomed, in comparison. If I was too phobic to promote a book, no one would know about *Sixth Sense* and the book would die on the shelves, along with my future career. Friends tried to reassure me, saying that more people are afraid of public speaking than they are of death. Makes perfect sense, if you ask me. If you're dead, you don't have to face any audiences.

How could I reverse a lifelong fear in just a few months, I asked my teachers, Steve Leeds and Rachel Hott, directors of the NLP Center of New York. What they showed me, over the next few months was a miracle. My NLP classmates, Ray Quezada and Ron Haugen also worked overtime to reinforce the NLP coaching sessions and classes. Ron even flew to Los Angeles for a last-minute coaching session the night before my first speech at the Beverly Hills Hotel. Surprisingly, it went well enough for me to work my way down the west coast, giving talks and workshops. I was scared, but somehow made it through each talk without hyperventilating and, after awhile, it started getting easier. Back east, I started picking up work as a seminar leader and lecturer. This was something I had never expected to be able to do! With help from my friend Mary Huff, a publicist in Atlanta, we promoted *Sixth Sense* from our living rooms. The first printing sold out in six months, and it went into a second printing. I was getting back on my feet.

Pete was doing well, also. He had hooked up with an entrepreneur who hired him as an operations manager for a financial services company. Since he was spending four hours a day driving to and from work, we put our apartment on the market, thinking that we would sell it and move within a few months. Two years later, we were still on the market. And the market was crashing. The value of our home had dropped more than 30-thousand dollars. It's not that we didn't have buyers. The co-op board, made up of one person from each of the four units, had voted to reject every potential buyer. Each time the other three families who made up the co-op board rejected yet another set of buyers, the value of our home dropped another ten-thousand dollars. Co-op boards function like fiefdoms, with absolute power to approve or reject anyone who wants to buy into the co-op association.

After two years, our equity was wiped out. So were our savings. Brokers in our neighborhood stopped listing our apartment because, they explained, "Your board is wacko." Wacko and increasingly hostile: spying on our visitors, listening in to our conversations with neighbors, and writing sarcastic memos designed to humiliate us. If Franz Kafka had written a version of *No Exit*, this would be it. If they hated us so much, why wouldn't they let us out? Things got worse when four real estate attorneys refused to take on our case, claiming that we would still need the co-op board's approval to move. It was too much trouble to deal with that kind of lunacy when they could close on an apartment house and make more money with less aggravation. (It must be pretty bad if a lawyer turns you down!) Then there was the joke making the rounds...

Q: "What's the difference between a co-op apartment in Park Slope and gonorrhea?"

A: "You can get rid of gonorrhea."

In the final months of 1990, Pete's boss sold the company to a Fortune 500 corporation that immediately went bankrupt. Pete lost his job. My new writing career stalled. The publisher's advance from *Sixth Sense* ran out. My book proposals were rejected. I had signed up for an independent study Ph.D. program, which had chewed into our funds, as well. The day Mindy qualified for the free school lunch program was one of the most humiliating experiences of my middle-class life. *It's only money,* I kept telling myself.

A little, dry cough, like the one William Hurt has at the beginning of *The Doctors* went from intermittent to persistent. *Remember: Other People Have It Worse. It's only money. Only money.* But it wasn't "only money," it was years of hard work: obituaries, space shots, elections, chemical spills, blizzards, earthquakes, and you name it. I tried a different approach: *Every misfortune is a blessing in disguise.*

The cough got worse. We had less than $1500 – not enough to make the next month's mortgage and maintenance payments–and were getting ready to inform the bank when my head started to pound as I was climbing up the stairs to the front door. I couldn't breathe. Pulling myself up the final four steps onto the landing, I leaned against the apartment doorbell.

"What's wrong?" Pete asked.

I could barely choke out words. "Can't breathe."

He sat me at the kitchen counter while he boiled water and mixed it with Vick's Vapo-Rub. Then he placed my head over a steaming bowl, sealing off the rim with a damp towel. After a few minutes, the steam started to work. I sat up, pushed the bowl away, thanked him, and walked to the bedroom, a little lightheaded. Pete, who had been complaining that my dry cough kept him awake, was now sleeping in the living room.

I lay down. A heavy weight pressed into my chest. It was cutting me in half. When I tried to sit up, everything went black. With that weight crushing down, each attempt to breathe felt like a razor slitting through my back. This was worse than labor, if that was possible. I tried calling out, but couldn't grab enough air to carry the sound of my own voice. Terrifying, to be silenced by such pain. Around me, the air felt thick, like gray soup. Another spasm. Someone was shouting inside my head, but there was no sound.

I guess I blacked out because I was now floating a foot or so above my head. From here, I could see a woman in a nightgown wracked by creepy-looking spasms and I could hear panicked coughing. Every few breaths, I got a jolt of searing pain. Then, I was floating. Across the room, on the far wall, a large, black door appeared. *The door to the other side. If I can just get over there, into that tunnel, to the white light that everyone talks about. Can't live with the pain...*

"You are not meant to live with the pain. You are meant to recover."

Who's that? Gotta get the white light.

"You are not meant to live with the pain. You are meant to recover." A man's voice.

But nobody's here. I must be gone...

This feels like swimming in your dreams. A few flutter kicks through the gray liquid and you can make it to the door. But something invisible pushes me back. No matter how hard I try, I can't force my way through it. It's making me angry.

"No." That voice again, as if he knows me. How come other people get the white light? And angels in white robes with halos? I know it's Brooklyn but why do I get some guy who sounds like he's wearing an eyeshade and smoking a cigar?

Over there...*Black door. White shape. I am definitely gone.* A very old man. Paperwhite. Translucent skin. Chinese? Tibetan? Floating in the air, across the room. Fading a few inches from my head. There's nothing to do but close my eyes. My left lung is getting warm. Again, I see the black door and white shape. Floating. Dissolving into the air. The warmth is now spreading to both lungs.

Black door.

White shape.

Arriving.

Dissolving.

Warmth.

Easier to breathe.

Saving my life.

The cigar-smoking angel says, "After tonight, your life will never be the same. You will use this experience to help other people."

I can breathe.

Sleep.

Wake up. Can make sounds. Sit up. Call doctor.[16]

"Status asthmaticus. Miracle you're still alive," grunts the doctor, injecting me with epinephrine. The shot makes me barf up something that looks revoltingly like placenta.

Frankly, I could have lived without seeing this. My heart has never sounded this loud, and my legs shake so badly that my knees crumple when I try to stand. "Rest," smiles the doctor. *Do I look like I'm running the marathon?* Might as well be. Breathing takes up every ounce of energy. In a few minutes, the gray gelatinous liquid that has been coating everything begins to clear away. I can feel my hands and my face. Funny, I didn't know they were gone.

"Good," he says. "Very good. Welcome back." I'm not sure where "back" is.

"No question. You could have died. Why didn't you call 911?"

"Couldn't speak. Black vise or something in my chest. Too weak. Couldn't move."

"What about your husband?"

"Living room." I can see one eyebrow going up behind his glasses, but I don't say anything else. What's the point? He's not a shrink, or a marriage counselor.

"You have asthma. Severe asthma."

"That's impossible. I'm almost forty-three. I've never had asthma."

"Well, kid, you've got it now. Adult-onset asthma."

"How do I get rid of it?"

He gives me a strange look. "You don't. You have permanent, irreversible lung damage."

Rapid onset cognitive dissonance. Ears ringing. He's lying.

I can't believe what he's telling me. "You have one of the worst sudden-onset cases I've ever seen. When you're well enough, you'll need to apply for Social Security."

"Social Security?" *This can't be true. He's lying.*

"Chances are, you'll never work again."

"But...."

"We have medications for you. Theophylline. Proventil or Ventolin inhalers. And I'll prescribe Marax, for emergencies, when the inhalers don't work. If the Marax doesn't work, call 911. You'll have to keep a diary, so we can figure out what triggers your attacks. And, of course, we'll do allergy tests and you'll come twice a week for shots. In a few years, you should find some improvement."

Fast forward twenty years. Same time, same place. Future episodes of "The Laurie Nadel Show" are not looking like fun. He's sharp, this doctor. He must know what's going through my head. "You'll get used to it. Seventeen million Americans have it. It seems to hit women your age. Hormonal changes, maybe. Perimenopause."

"Will I ever ride a bike again? What about windsurfing?"

"What's that?" Well, he *is* over seventy.

"Surfboard with a sail."

"Windsurf?" His smile reminds me of a teacher with retarded child. "You'll be lucky if you can walk up stairs."

No light at the end of any tunnel was ever brighter than this morning's. Who would have believed it would be me, here, smiling into an early sun glinting off an aluminum shed on this beach? Even if I wipe out, today is a triumph. Like being alive.

Without saying a word, the kid nods, walking me over to the long-forgotten simulator, a midsection of an old windsurfer, set onto a rusty spring. The rituals of my first lesson, in Port Washington, how long ago? Walking through the basics. He looks sad, watching me fall off his simulator a few times.

Seeing him shake his head, no, makes me defensive: "The sport isn't called 'simulating,' is it? This thing doesn't count."

Shrugging, he motions for me to follow him back to the shed, where he rigs up a stretched out, faded orange, 4.5 meter cloth sail. I help him carry the rig to the water line, where it looks as if the very first Windsurfer that was ever manufactured is banked on the tan-colored sand. Then, everything goes into a long, slow-motion, internal tracking shot: his hands' pushing the mast foot into a locked position, in the center of the board. With each of his movements, the muscles in my hands remember every push and turn. He takes the back of the Windsurfer; as if by rote, I carry the nose into the water until it's deep enough for me to stand next to the board, back to the breeze. One hand on each side of the mast foot. Push down hard. Body slides up, until I am kneeling with one knee on either side of the mast foot. Now comes the tricky part. A little shaky, but I'm up. Pulling the uphaul, hand-over-hand. The 4.5 meter sail feels like a sluggish fish on the end of a fishing line. Grabbing the boom, stepping back just a bit. Sheeting in. *Yes!* Breeze flicks the pocket of the sail and we're moving, again. Gently.

I don't want to think about the summers in-between, away from this reality. Peripheral images: sailboats flying delicious sherbet-lime and tangerine spinnakers, deep green hills with stone terraces and steps leading down to wooden docks, the roof of a mansion, red tile among deep green pines. Delighted with my day, until the clew line pops out of the cleat and the sail flutters into nothingness. I forgot about that part, where the equipment comes apart in the water, until you fix it yourself or yank the rig out of the slot, untie the clew and boom cleats, roll the sail around the mast, push the rig onto the board, lengthwise, climb onto the board quickly so the rig doesn't fall back into the water, lie, lengthwise, on top of the rig, and use your arms to paddle back to shore.

Arriving by kayak, the rescue kid reties my clew line. "Are you sure it's been seven years since you windsurfed? I didn't think you'd be able to stand, much less get this far."

"Can I have a bigger sail, please?"

"Sure." Paddling quickly to keep up with me, he calls out, "You know, most people who tell me they learned how to windsurf on vacation can't even stand up."

A 5.7 meter Bic sail has more energy. Intrigued, I let it take me, on a reach, two miles across the bay, to a stone breakwater separating us from the open Sound. Stopping on a sand bar, I make a slow, three hundred sixty-degree turn. I'm so far away from my worst nightmare: Choking on my own phlegm. Revolted by the death rattle sound coming from somewhere in my chest when I try to sleep. My reflection, gray, with dark bruises under each eye. "Permanent, irreversible lung damage."

Trying to come up with a list of the Top Ten Positive Things About Sudden-Onset Asthma:

Number one: You won't have to worry about getting cancer in your old age...

Number two: What old age?

My husband walks into the bedroom. Looks at me with loathing. "You're old and sick and I don't love you any more."

Merry Christmas.

Cutaways on the return leg: a two-masted wooden schooner, trailed by a couple of poignant sounding gulls, a seaplane over my head, halyards tinkling against an aluminum mast, heartache and gentleness balancing between shades of blue and a wide-angle view of new hills, new life.

Brooklyn, NY
July 25, 1994

It's not always easy to start again at zero.

—Albert Camus[17]

It's not that I wanted to die. But if anyone had cared to ask, right about then, life didn't seem like such a great deal.

Although life improved when the co-op board approved the people who wanted to buy our apartment which meant we could stop hemorrhaging money, we weren't happy with ourselves. Never mind that other families were going through worse times and that we were part of a downturn. We heard that other owners, locked into similar stalemates, who lost all their equity and walked away from their mortgage commitments. Coming from a middle class, professional family, I felt our slide into subsistence living was shameful. Never mind that, despite our best efforts to stay solvent, financial problems can happen to anybody at any time. In America, where there is an "implicit assumption that hard work will be rewarded,"[18] where success equals earning a good living, I had failed. Therefore, I was not a good person. Perhaps "they" were right and God was punishing me. That's what "they" used to tell me that God did if you screwed up. I had been warned about this a lot when I was young. If only I had been aware of anthropologist Margaret Mead's observation that "Americans have the underlying feeling that if they are sick, they are being bad."[19]

The possibility that Pete and I had been naive, and had not been given competent legal advice when we signed our contract to buy our apartment did not occur to us. No one had warned us that our financial survival would be in other people's control when it came time to sell. If the members of the co-op board didn't like a prospective buyer's religion or his pony tail (!), the board could vote to reject them with no explanation. If there was anything practical to learn from this, it was a) it's better to live in a tent or a camper than a co–op apartment and b) never buy into a multiple dwelling unless you buy the whole building! Not that we could think of owning anything. With Pete on unemployment, and my application for disability,[20] pending, the few thousand dollars we salvaged after closing on the apartment sale made up our emergency fund. As if constant respiratory pain wasn't enough of an emergency.

"Isn't there something I should be learning from all this?" If a question can develop a rhythm, this one was thumping along in rhythm with my heartbeat. Doesn't each life event contain a universe all its own, if only we can look through everything else to find the heart of it?

The first tier of learning was that severe pain can bring you across a threshold where the mind goes into a cold, gray empty place. It's described in *The Tibetan Book of the Dead* as the bardo, the place between worlds. If chronic fatigue had brought me through three tunnels of loss, asthma was forcing me through a twisted labyrinth towards social and psychological death. Researchers who have studied the physical process of dying say that social death sets in after a long period of absence from the physical world of healthy people...that world of conversation and laughter, phone calls and dinner parties that used to be "normal." Trapped in a diseased physical shell, the onset of social death occurs when illness or injury pushes you, again and again, into the cold empty void, alone. With no other options, and no companion to hold your hand, a patient struggling with severe illness experiences a form of culture shock. If you do not get well, social withdrawal leads to something called "psychological death," a narcoleptic netherworld of continual, dark sleep broken by incidents of sharp pain that are about as welcome as bricks and sharp fragments of glass coming through your bedroom window in the middle of the night. Not only are you dark and cold and alone, you no longer know if you are really here, or someplace else, and you don't care as long as the pain stops. If you don't come back from here, you will pass into the realm of biological death, where sleep becomes coma, or consciousness turns into some form of vegetative state. Not that you'd know, anymore. In the final stage, physiological death, when your organs no longer function, you are declared legally dead.[21]

Good days, for me, were like being stuck in a black, windowless room, listening to a cold angry voice: "You're old and sick and I don't love you any more. And P.S. This is all there is." The inner world, in which I had taken refuge during that two-year bout with chronic fatigue, was now easily as depressing as the physical world. My former identity—as a woman, as a writer, and a human being—was lying around, somewhere, fragmented and buried, like shards from an earlier civilization. It would have taken an archeologist years to locate the pieces, never mind fitting them together again. Anyway, that was too much to expect.

None of my usual techniques for psyching out a bad mood were working. Even holding up poor Rocky as a mood mirror didn't cut it—*I mean, how can you feel sorry for yourself when you think about what he had to go through?* In stories I had written about stress, I liked to quote George Bernard Shaw: "It's not the situation that happens to you, it's what you do with the situation that happens to you." Sure. That was easy for him to say. George Bernard Shaw had mobility. Now, the only quote worthy of respect was the first noble truth: "Human life is suffering."

Enduring the illness was hard, but worse was being hated for being sick. Whenever my husband walked into the room, I turned my head away, so he couldn't see what I was feeling. Not that he would have noticed. And who cared, anyway? It was over. Which was harder to bear?

Knowing what had to be done and not being well enough to take action? Or coming to terms with the icy stalagmites of contempt that driplocked around us, freezing out any warmth that might have helped us both? In silence, I blamed my husband for his lack of compassion. Only now can I see that I had none for him, either.

Pete had lost a job that he cared about, for reasons that had everything to do with the economy and corporate finance, and nothing to do with his skill or track record. He was helpless to protect his position, which disappeared, out from under him, while his life savings and his home were going under, as well. Now, his wife was not able to function and help out when he needed her the most. Was anyone at fault for feeling angry and betrayed? Weren't these inevitable human responses, given these disappointments and expectations? Seen through a geopolitical filter, weren't those expectations themselves at least partially at fault? If we had married during the Depression, or during wartime, or if we lived in a Third World country, wouldn't we have learned to expect that a good part of life and partnership in marriage would involve coping with survival issues, together? If we had been conditioned to expect a certain degree of economic struggle like most of the rest of the world, would we have been better equipped to pull together when times got tough, rather than each of us coming apart? Were we just a couple of disappointed yuppies?

Seen through any number of filters, the factors that led up to that series of losses and crises are complex. Were these events set in motion because there were courses I had signed up for before this lifetime? Were talents and flaws perhaps selected before, or perhaps even between lives, so that my soul could work off longstanding karmic debts? Was this debilitating illness a gift that would open a door to something greater?

Unraveling life lessons from just the past few years would take many more years. Lessons unlearned would pass with me, when I went through that door, to be completed in some future lifetime.

If I never got well enough to leave the bed, where would I find that teaching? My mind kept returning to the black door on the wall, the white spirit, and the guide who told me, in no uncertain terms, that I was meant to recover. Sometimes, in the middle of the night, freaked out and depleted by bronchial spasms, I doubted I would make it. *Use this experience to help other people? What does he know? And why did that force keep me from going through that door?* The big picture made no sense. My doctor, whom I saw three times a week, was pushing Social Security. It was a toss up whether the disease or the side–effects of the medication, theophylline, were more destabilizing: palpitations, nausea, dizziness, dry mouth, and muscle weakness punctuated by outbursts of anger and tears.[22] This was not me. At least, it was not the me I remembered. And it was definitely not the "me" I wanted to be. "You'll get used to it," my doctor chanted on a regular basis. "You can live a long time like this."

"Why would I want to?"

"There, there." His pity added another layer of embarrassment to the mushy batter that was my sense of self, now that it was starting to occur to me that this, essentially, was it.

"Killer disease. I'm impressed. You should write about it," chuckled the second opinion doctor. "You could be dead. Like that!" he snapped his fingers. "Sudden–onset asthma can progress to fatal, within minutes. People don't know that this is not just a children's disease. Of the seventeen-million Americans with asthma,[23] fewer than five million of those are kids. Of the five thousand or so who die from it every year, more than eighty percent of the fatalities are over forty–five. A lot of them are like you: They didn't know they could get it as an adult, so they weren't diagnosed and treated in time."[24] As Rocky would say, "Hell, it had to happen to someone." *Yeah, but why me?*

"Adult-onset asthma attacks women in their late thirties and early forties. Just as children with asthma often out-grow it when they reach puberty, there seems to be a con-nection between hormonal changes in perimenopausal women and asthma.[25] Genetics play a role, too. Does any-one in your family have asthma?"

"My grandmother on my mother's side. She developed it when she got older."[26]

"Hmm." He opened a drawer in his desk, pulled out a sheet of paper, and started reading it as if I wasn't there. Without looking up, he continued speaking, so softly that I wondered if he might be talking to himself. "...complex disease...triggered by allergic reactions to things like dust, mold, pollen, cat and dog hair."

"My daughter got a kitten for Christmas. Do we have to get rid of it?"

He laughed. "It's healthier for her, and for you, too, to keep a pet if you love it. You'd be amazed. Some of my patients say they'd rather get rid of their children than their cats!"

"I'd rather keep them both and get rid of the asthma. Maybe I can get a body transplant?"[27]

As though he hadn't noticed my attempt at humor, he went on, "You'll have to keep an Asthma Log. Write down every time you can't breathe. That way, we'll be able to fig-ure out your asthma profile. Everyone's triggers are differ-ent. Watch out for colds, bacterial infections, sudden changes in temperature, allergens, and..." Pushing that sheet of paper across the desk, he asked, "By the way, have you been under any stress lately?"

"No, sir. Before I got sick, I was thinking about getting a lower stress job as an air traffic controller."

This time, he smiled. I swear he did. Even though it was more like a subliminal smile, the affect made its way across the desk.

The sheet of paper he had given me contained a list of forty-three common life changes, called the Holmes and Rahe Social Readjustment Scale (see Appendix I, p. 306).

"Check off the events that you have lived through during the past two years. Then score those events according to the numerical rankings, or Life Changing Units (LCU's) provided," he explained.

In the next ten minutes, I checked off:

Marital problems

Death of a close family member (my father)

Illness

Fired from work (laid off while on disability)

Change in family member's health

Sexual difficulties

Business readjustments

Change in financial status

Change to a different line of work

Mortgage and loan over $15,000

Change in work responsibilities

Outstanding personal achievement

Spouse begins or stops work

Starting school

Change in work hours/conditions

Change in recreational habits

Change in social activities

Change in sleeping habits

Cumulative score: 722 LCU's.

Since a score of 300 or more means your chances of having an accident or developing a serious illness is around eighty percent, I had been a walking time bomb. "No," I smiled, pushing the checked list back, across the desk. "Not under any stress."

The doctor's eyebrows wriggled behind his glasses as he read off the items I had marked off. "Yes, I can see that. Not much stress. By the way, how many children do you have?"

"Two."

"Ages?"

"There's the one I married and the one I gave birth to..."

"Young lady." He removed his glasses. *Uh-oh. Whenever they call you "young lady," you're in trouble.* "I don't know anything about your world and it's not my place to tell you how to live your life. You are severely ill. There is no cure for asthma. You will probably never work again, as an air traffic controller, or anything else you used to do. Emotional stress and depression can exacerbate your condition. That means if you get too stressed out, your next asthma attack could be fatal."

"You are even more fun than the other guy."

He looked surprised in the way that serious people look when you haven't taken them seriously. Maybe surprised isn't the right word. Ambushed is more like it. And, like most of the serious ones I've met, he tried to squirm out by switching into a staring contest. Think: Clint Eastwood squinting at a cactus. As the resident cactus, it was all I could do to stare back.[28]

He came pretty close to winning, although I'd never let him know what. Maybe the phone ringing made him blink, or maybe he was getting bored, or maybe he wanted to let me win so I could feel good about something, even if it was only a stupid staring contest. Passing that Holmes and Rahe Social Readjustment checklist back to me, he said, quietly, "You are responsible for the child you made and not the child you found." Then he stood up, extended his hand, and gave me the strangest medical advice I had ever received. "Pay attention."

I had no idea what he meant, but at least he had helped me put a few pieces of the puzzle together. And he was more "fun" than the other guy.

A few weeks later, while I was lying in bed, my attention was drawn to a band of yellow sunlight slanting from

the top right corner of one window to the worn green carpet on the bedroom floor. Outside the window, a familiar
bunch of sparrows and pigeons were sounding more
enthusiastic about life than they had during the past few
months, a sign that the hours of light and warmth were
expanding out there. I couldn't remember how long I had
been stuck inside. My lungs still hurt when I tried to move
and each time I fell asleep, I woke up, choking. Reaching for
the inhaler was a reflex. When Proventil failed to stop the
spasms, there I swallowed a Marax tablet with water.
Seconds later, palpitations. Strange warm flushes, as though
someone was wiping the inside of my lungs with a warm,
damp washcloth. The rest of my body didn't agree that it
was so soothing but it was better than choking.

Magnetized by the sun coming through the window, I
would have given anything to be able to stretch out in that
shaft of sun, like a cat. That something so simple should be
out of reach floated me back in time, to a spring afternoon,
in 1973 when my friend Mindy, for whom my daughter is
named, had come home from the hospital. She had a rare
heart condition, which meant her life was spent in the hospital and in her own bed. On this particular day, she was
thrilled that we could walk to the end of the block, where
the Atlantic Avenue bus ended its route at a wide concrete
pier facing the skyline of Manhattan, across the river.

"Isn't it wonderful to watch the bus turn around?" she
asked with a poignant sincerity that made her seem almost
simple. "On the days when I can make it all the way to here,
I always wonder about who those people are, on that bus.
What are their stories? Did you ever think about that?"

No, I hadn't.

"Someone should write a story about that bus turning
around, and what happens to the people who ride on it,"
Mindy continued with her gentle, sad smile, taking my arm
for the walk back to her house. I didn't get it. As a twenty-
five year old action junkie, I was getting ready to leave for

South America. Watching a bus was, oh, too slow. Now, years later, lying in bed, too weak to move, it clicked. Atlantic Avenue was as improbable a destination for me, now, as the Andes had been for Mindy, who died a week before I came home.

For me to touch that sunlight across the room would be as great an accomplishment for me, today, as walking to the end of the street had been for my friend. I thought of all the ways in which I had brushed off people who were sick during my life and recognized how that attitude might have affected friends or family members at the time. There grew in me an awareness of countless other women, men and children who were lying sick in bed, like me, forgotten by the world at large. In a culture that values good looks and achievement, getting sick instantly makes you an outcast. If you can't produce, you are you? If you aren't attractive, who cares? Your ideas and feelings don't count to the world. You have nothing to offer. It's as if you no longer exist. You might as well be dead. Now my own lack of concern for this suffering struck me as self-centered and callous. All I knew was that if I could ever walk, talk, and breathe well enough to have a normal day, I would never forget to be thankful.

A few days later, three two-foot tall green parrots showed up in the apple tree outside our window, at six in the morning. Pete opened our curtains carefully, so as not to scare the huge green birds away. Even the kitten, who had jumped onto the windowsill, looked respectful and surprised. Fog from the bay, three miles down the road, curled around the early buds and tiny leaves, making the three birds look even more like apparitions from another world. Which, of course, they were. A world that had been mine, years before. (Flashback: One Sunday afternoon, flying above the green Amazonian ocean in a DC-3 cargo plane, with the copilot sitting on an oil drum practicing an aria from Rigoletto, while I read off the gauges, in Spanish, to the pilot.)

The Amazonian parrots were bringing me a message. "If we can make it, so can you." I sat up, quickly. It didn't hurt.

My wake-up call came a few nights later. "I hear you're going to my doctor," said my uncle Norman. "I've had asthma for ages. You're in good hands. He's been my doctor for thirty years."

"Thirty years? Have you been my uncle's doctor for thirty years?"

"That's right." Innocuous question, innocuous smile.

"With all due respect, sir, thirty years is not exactly a success story in my book."

"What?" Maybe not so innocuous...

"I have no intention of being anybody's patient for thirty years. Within two years, I am going to get off this medication and go back to work."

"You are?" I've seen that look: *You? You're going to windsurf?*

"My body never "did" asthma before. I could sleep through the night just fine. I never needed medicine so that I could walk as far as my kitchen. If my body never had asthmatic reactions before this, there must be some memory pattern of normal breathing within me."

"I've never heard it explained that way before, but it makes sense." The way he leaned back in his chair to observe me made me wonder if I had now been reclassified as some kind of interesting specimen. This must be how a microbe feels under a microscope.

When he spoke again, it was his turn to surprise me. "You have quite an attitude, young lady. That's good. Most of my patients don't fight their diagnoses."

"I need my life back. I need to feel the sea and the wind taking me across the bay." It was hard to keep tears out. "There has to be a way..."

"There is. Very few of my patients want to do the inner work that can make the critical difference. Fortunately, you got angry. Now, we can start."

Brooklyn, NY
July 26, 1994

[When] enough soul-wind has been raised to cause the psychic vessel to sail far and away...the atoms leap.

—Clarissa Pinkola Estes[29]

"Would it be all right if I told you I loved you more than yesterday?"

It's impossible not to smile. "How could I say no?"

"I do. I feel better just hearing your voice." We tend to stop talking at this point. It's fairly impossible to speak when your heart feels like it's going to cry. At least, mine does. I can't speak for him.

"Me, too." For someone who doesn't have a hard time with words, I'm having a hard time.

"I missed you yesterday. I thought maybe you had run off with a surfer."

"He was too young."

"Hmm."

"You're in no danger..."

"I don't know what I'd do without you in my life."

"Hmm."

"I mean it."

"You're doing that again..."

"What?"

"Like you don't know. Reading my thoughts."

Weird. Like that dream where I could feel him behind me, with his arms wrapped around my shoulders, so real that it scared me awake. In the morning, Neil said, "You didn't have to wake up. I wasn't going to let you go. I never will."

"How was it?" he asks, breaking the pause.

"Like being sprayed into fine mist so that you blend

with the sun."

His breath catches. That's something I can't get used to–the feeling that anyone cares about the tiny moments of my day. When I try to tell him how unnerved I am by his desire for closeness, he interrupts, "You'll have the rest of the journey to get used to me."

I relax.

His voice is silvery and soothing. Like a quiet afternoon on an autumn lake.

Neil and I have come together like two drops of water, or the flames of two candles, touched together. Coming out of a marriage where I discovered what it was like to be needed but not loved, I have a hard time believing this is real.

"I know what it is to be loved but this is the first time I know what it means to love," says Neil.

Coup de foudre. Lighting bolt love. The kind that strikes unexpectedly, in the middle of nowhere, after years of numbing out. It's like seeing the color blue for the first time and realizing that you've never seen it before.

Solar eyes. Looking into an eclipse must be like this, when everything else in the world stops moving and you can't tell if that's the earth or the moon or the sun ringed with fire. "I've been waiting for you," Neil with the solar eyes said, a year and a half ago. "I had a dream that I would meet you here." Cornering me in the hallway during a conference on behavioral medicine, he touched the sleeve of my navy blazer as I was walking out of the conference room with my friend, Joe.

Dr. Joe Schippa and I were in North Carolina, presenting a workshop to doctors, psychologists, and nurses on mental strategies for overcoming asthma. Neil, who had used meditation to heal from prostate cancer, was sitting in the first row.

That cigar-smoking, eyeshade-wearing spirit guide had been right, as it turned out. I was not meant to live with that pain. With the help of my doctor, keeping a dream journal, three friends who had studied NLP with me, and my teacher Steve Leeds, I was able to wean off theophylline and begin rebuilding my life. Mark Newman, Ray Quezada, and Ron Haugen each took their time to visit me while I was too sick to function, talking patiently to my unconscious mind while I slept. If my eyes were open and I was alert, they would "walk" me through as many different mental exercises as they had in their collective quiver. Together, they marshaled an eclectic approach to communicate with the part of my Unconscious[30] that felt like it was "trying to kill me." Together, we coached the healing intelligence back to work. I was particularly impressed at Steve's use of indirect trance, a form of hypnosis that was like an interview with the Unconscious mind. Steve would ask questions of the submerged part of the mind that controlled my breathing. Although I was too deeply "under" to recall the conversation, in just two sessions, the nocturnal wheezing attacks were gone and my inhaler consumption was soon down, from one a week, to one every two months.

Getting strong enough to get to Steve's office in Manhattan had been a journey and a half in its own right. Meditation had helped me to recover from chronic fatigue syndrome but since I was too sick to sit up, I experimented with NLP exercises. In my own version of Time Line Therapy[31] I imagined myself floating over a river of time, representing my past, present, and future. Down below, I looked for bright shiny places along the river that were experiences of flow–effortless concentration, vibrant health and energy. Scenes from the Zone: windsurfing across Lake Montauk with Pam, and those splendid solo crossings of the Great South Bay. I also found two healing events–times when I knew for certain that I would recover form measles and from a broken arm. These experiences, which Dr. Herbert Benson of Harvard Medical School calls "remembered wellness" events, were retrieved and replayed, as if I was living through them again as lifesize, colored, moving, three-dimensional movies. I could see, hear, and feel each event as though it was happening right at that moment, so that muscles I had forgotten about began to tingle. Like a blindfolded Zen archer hitting the bullseye, an intuitive montage of sights, sounds, smells, tastes, and sensations of peak performance I had found while windsurfing flowed from some deep archive of the emotional brain.

Part of my psyche was still in shock at the doctor's prognosis: that the intimate merging with the soul of the sea would be off limits for the rest of my life. For me, to have windsurfed was to have lived life to the fullest. In the neurophysiology of remembering, perhaps new circuits of optimism were running, like electrical pulses, recharging shut-down sections of the brain, rebooting the cognitive processes needed for healing. If so, then these "remembered wellness" events of windsurfing and recovery would turn out to be the best gifts I could ever give to myself.

As mysterious as the magic of new skin forming over a cut or bruise, something was happening during each "remembered wellness" session. In quiet celebration, I could feel those bronchial passages opening up.

Seven months after that Near-Death Experience, I began weaning off theophylline. I went back to work on my dissertation, earning a Ph.D. in psychology. Once a month, I would attend a weekend workshop on some aspect of mind/body healing. During Steve Leeds' course in Ericksonian hypnosis,[32] the guide's prophecy began coming true. Joe Schippa was a fellow classmate at the time, and he told me how he, too, had almost died from a sudden attack of adult-onset asthma. In his search for alternatives to steroids, he had come upon the healing modalities of NLP and indirect hypnosis.

With Joe's encouragement, I enrolled in a second doctoral program through the American Institute of

Hypnotherapy of Irvine, California.[33] The directed independent study program included mandatory coursework in medical hypnosis for psychogenic, or stress–related conditions and the history of medical hypnosis and hypnotic anesthesiology.[34]

Believing that our paths had crossed for a reason, Joe and I launched a series of workshops for people struggling with adult–onset asthma. That North Carolina conference on behavioral medicine put us in front of the medical community for the first time. Talk about stagefright! I could hardly believe that I was presenting to an audience of physicians, psychologists, chiropractors, and nurses. And Neil. A high school physics teacher, Neil had studied meditation and NLP after being diagnosed with prostate cancer five years earlier. With his cancer in remission, Neil now taught meditation and NLP to cancer patients in hospitals around the country and in Europe.

"You were magnificent! You are living proof that our beliefs can make us sick or well," he said, smiling and linking arms with me as we found our way to the next workshop.

It's true, I think, up to a point. Beliefs don't create bacteria or viruses, although our attitudes, values, and responses to stressors can damage the immune system, making us more vulnerable to infection. Nor is there any cognitive blueprint for human immortality, no matter what we believe or how "advanced" we are in the application of psychoneuroimmunology to our own health. As I like to remind anyone who expresses skepticism, "Nothing works all the time for everyone. Not even aspirin."

What it comes down to is: I'm hesitant about taking a lot of credit for being alive. Clearly, I would have been dead without spiritual help. I didn't visualize or "make" that black door or that Tibetan spirit appear. They did not show up because of my beliefs, one way or the other, any more than believing in electricity makes the lights go on and off.

"If it was simply a question of what we believed, then

happy people would never get cancer and only depressed people would get sick," I remember telling Neil as we embarked on our ongoing, goodnatured dialogue about mind/body healing that he calls "The Laurie and Neil Show."

We both agree that illness can blow your world apart, taking you on a journey inside yourself. That cancer or life-threatening asthma could have been the catalyst for our career paths to shift, transit, and merge was simply another indicator of how pain can work, paradoxically, as a springboard to new understanding.

"Just think, if I had not had cancer, I would never have met you," he said the day after we met. We were standing under a gazebo, having walked around the conference center grounds. Neil was spinning projects for our future. "We'll give workshops together all over the world. We'll become co-conspirators and write books. We'll commit acts of great heart!"

"I'm flattered. But I'm a housewife from Brooklyn. I don't get out much."

He looked as if he didn't believe me. "That's true," I smiled. "This is the first conference I've been to since I got sick. It's hard to believe this is real..." I was starting to say when he covered my mouth, gently, with his hand.

"Soulmates." First kiss. His eyes. The color of wild clouds blown across the sky after a summer storm, kicking away foundations of everyday reality and common sense. A sensation of stepping off the platform of time, as all those years from before collapsed within seconds and all that mattered was the two of us, here, in the center of "o," in the middle of now.

It happened so quickly. Neil hired a castle–gray stone, with turrets–on a windy hill overlooking the sea, flying me to Europe for a media tour and again, for a series of motivational workshops, where we shared the platform in front of hundreds of people. We're working a book with mind/body exercises for healing. "This book will honor our soul connection," Neil says.

Those times that we spend together, Neil has a way of looking at me that breaks through barriers that have been in place a long time, maybe even my entire life. He calls it "unconditional acceptance." I call it "that unbearable gentleness." It finds its way through the cracks of my maintenance level disappointment. When we walk through our respective northern cities, hand-in-hand, Neil has a habit of walking up to strangers to announce spontaneously, "I'm here because I'm in love with her. We're going to live together in the fall."

When of course people stare, as would any self-respecting New Yorker in the presence of such boundless enthusiasm, he swings his arm around my shoulder protectively, or pulls me against his chest. "Don't be such a New Yorker," he'll whisper if I haven't smiled yet. "We'll be together for the rest of our lives."

"Are you sure?" Maintenance level disappointment requires that I ask. Just in case. "If any part of you has any concerns or doubts, any unfinished business... Or if there's even a small percentage of a chance that you might change your mind, for any reason, please tell me so that I can prepare for that possibility. That's only fair, don't you think?"

"Of course it is. If there was a problem, we would work it through together. When are you going to start trusting again?"

"In my next life?"

"How about right now? The only thing I believe in is you and me. If anything happened, and we couldn't be together, I would be committing emotional suicide."

"Life doesn't always work out the way we want it to."

He is quiet for a while. Then he says, "I want you to write each and every belief that's holding you back from trusting me on a piece of paper. Then I want you to tear that paper into dozens of little pieces and put it in the blender."

So far, I haven't done this, even though Neil has been known to check on me ten or fifteen minutes later to see if I have.

Today, I wait to hear the phone go dead before I hang up. A few minutes later, when it rings again, Neil says, "I forgot to ask you something. The next time you go out windsurfing, please take a cell phone in a ziplock bag. I couldn't stand it if anything happened to you."

Lazy Point, Napeague, NY
July 28, 1994

So, if women must, they will paint blue sky on jail walls....Women
will draw doors where there are none, and open them and pass
through into new ways and new lives. Because the wild nature
persists and prevails, women persist and prevail.

–Clarissa Pinkola Estes[35]

As squirrelly as the road got back there, when it felt like I was
"exiled, paralyzed, deprived of all pleasures...reduced to the
existence of a jellyfish...(and) horrible to behold,"[36] there
were friends who called, who offered prayers, and who let me
know that I was in their thoughts. My women friends, going
as far back as kindergarten, checked in from points as close
as across the street and as far away as the other side of the
world. Like blowing gently on a dying fire, their caring
helped bring me back from the embers of the bardo. True
friendship helps us find beauty in the darkness.

The best part about being alive again is girl time.
There's a freewheeling lightness to driving underneath
overhanging trees, past marsh ponds and windmills and
potato fields with Catherine, a blonde attorney whom I met
while working on a human rights project for writers and
journalists sixteen years ago.

"Do you remember that afternoon in Port Washington,
when I hung on to the back of your sailboard while you
were windsurfing?" she laughs. "I still have those pictures."

Yes, I remember.

"Do you think you'll get into windsurfing again?"

"Only if I rent equipment. The thought of hauling all
that heavy gear around is overwhelming." The mere
thought that I might be capable of hauling all that heavy

gear around is just plain absurd. I'm wondering if the idea of my windsurfing isn't equally absurd. That is, until I spot the sign: WINDSURFING SWAP.

Before I promised God that I wouldn't complain ever again, as long as I could walk and talk and breathe, I used to complain about people who liked to stop the car to browse for antiques. Certainly, I would understand if Catherine complained about this.

"Would you mind if we stopped in at that windsurfing swap?" I'm half-hoping that Catherine will give me one of those irritated looks that I used to give friends who wanted to stop for antiques, but her face lights up. "Are you thinking about getting a board?"

"Of course not!" But I am already out of the car, moving around the brightly colored sails and used windsurfers, trying to gauge whether or not I could lift any one of these onto the roof of this 1992 Honda Accord in the unlikely event I got a roofrack. *How much would it cost to get back in the sport?* I think, and calculate a quick estimate: *board, mast, universal, mast foot, boom, sails, wetsuit, harness, and roofrack? About two thousand dollars. Out of my league.* "I've made up my mind to rent equipment. It will be easier."

I seem to be talking to no one in particular when, like Alice in the Red Queen's rose garden, I come face-to-face with a ten-foot-ten purple windsurfer, standing on its tail. A sign in front of it proclaims, "NEW FROM GERMANY–XANTOS 310–WEIGHS 16 POUNDS!" Lighter than a bicycle. My mind's eye sees a slim, silvery wake fanning out behind my heels with three hundred sixty degrees of prussian blue water radiating sunlight capped by a bowl of sky. Right there, in the store, I catch a scent of afternoon wind off the ocean. The back of my ears tingle. Breeze. *I had forgotten about that…* Intuitively, my knees go into flex mode as I lean back a little. This feels oddly like meeting someone you used to be in love with but you broke up and you thought it was over but then you saw him again. Damn.

"It's a brand new design, called a no-nose." I delivered this comment to Catherine while shooting left across the westbound lane of Montauk Highway in order to grab a carlength of space in the eastbound lane, aware that it may turn out to be one of those non sequiturs that gets remembered forever, due to astrological conjunctions of that particular day, hour, angle of the sun, and the manic speed you were driving. Years later, Catherine will say, "Remember when we were trying to make that turn into all that traffic on Montauk Highway and you started talking about someone's nose?" At the same time, there's a growing, but dim awareness that the succulent tidbit of information have just passed on is of no interest whatsoever to the person sitting next to you.

"It's one of the first Xantos boards to arrive in this country from Germany." *Am I talking to her or to myself?* We have slipped off the main road, dodging south, behind Easthampton's Guild Hall, under an arch of old trees, swinging east past an astonishingly wide curve of the road, through the middle of the Maidstone golf course near the ocean. When our trajectory intersects Montauk Highway at the eastern end of Amaganssett (settled 1680), instead of hanging a right, toward Catherine's mom's place in Montauk, I gun the accelerator for a lunge across the highway, onto a rough, pitted macadam road that curves around the edges of pine forests and salt ponds. "You don't mind?" I ask with the kind of slightly nervous laugh that people must have when they know they have done something socially gauche, like hijacking. Fortunately, Catherine has one of those musical laughs that makes you think of arpeggios, even if you're not sure what arpeggios are, music education not having been a mandatory subject in the Brooklyn public school system. Reassured by her laughter that it's okay, we continue north until sand from the forest spills onto the road where it forks sharply. Turning right, we pass a couple of vans stacked with windsurfing gear.

"Getting close," I say.

"You're not...are you?"

"Well..."

Lazy Point Road ends at Napeague Bay, a flat stretch of water that picks up steady ocean winds throughout the summer. Years ago, when windsurfing was a way of life, I had heard that the combination of steady thermals, flat conditions, and waist high water gave Napeague a reputation as the Bonaire of the northeast, one of the most popular windsurfing sites on this coast. I had wanted to sail here years ago but this will be the first time I'm attempting Napeague and I probably should have my head examined. The wind is coming from the southwest, around twelve knots, and it looks like anyone planing out there must be half my age. *What am I thinking? That Xantos doesn't even have a daggerboard. I'll keep falling off! Everyone will laugh at me.*

Introducing myself to Bill and Jeremy, the two young men renting gear out of the "Main Beach" van parked at the water's edge, we chat about my windsurfing experience so they can choose a sail that's right for my skill level and the wind conditions. I'm having one of those disorienting mind moments where you seem to be having a normal conversation and inside, anxiety is making your teeth chatter but fortunately, no one can see them. Watching them rig up a new, 5.7 meter clear Mylar Neil Pryde sail, it occurs to me that in the eight years since I was last on the water, there has been a great technical leap between my old, clunky HiFly and these new F2s. This generation in sail design looks like an F-16 compared to those old Wright Brothers' planes. Considering that I'm the kind of person who gets intimidated in a hardware store (what are all those gadgets for, anyway?) it looks like I'd need a masters in nautical engineering just to put that rig together.

"Why did I say I would do this?" I mutter, as Catherine pats me on the shoulder for encouragement.

Back to the wind, with the board at a perpendicular

angle, I jump onto the Xantos, kneel, then quickly stand. This is the point where I usually fall backwards on a short-board. The board is rocking back and forth, yet it feels strangely stable. Hand over hand, the uphaul lifts the sail through the water, until the mast is nearly upright. Hands find their way home, gripping the boom and sheeting in, intuitively.

Liquid fire. Sun hits the brain. A moment of surrender, like seconds before an orgasm, when molecules in your body fuse and all around blazing, white, hotsilver light flashes through a star-sapphire afternoon. *I forgot, I forgot.*

"You're good," Bill and Jeremy nod as I head back in. "Go take another run."

A gust of wind yanks the sail, but instead of losing grip, my legs crouch. My weight now holds the sail. I lean back, against the wind.

Onshore, Catherine is clapping for me. *Weren't we supposed to be at her mom's place in Montauk?*

"Want a bigger sail? A harness?" *Harness? I would end up face-first in the sail.* Still, their enthusiasm is tempting.

"No thanks. We're on our way to Montauk."

"You were really good out there," they smile.

Such unexpected, outright praise is embarrassing. I remember one of my last times on the water: *"Why aren't you as good as that woman?"* I never thought I was any good at windsurfing.

Brooklyn, NY
August 10, 1994

It is better to judge someone, not by what she owns,
but by how much she gives.

−Samoan proverb

Barely able to look at each other, Pete and I threw out the remains of the Shark a few days ago. How did I ever know how to connect the stainless steel rods with those metric nuts and bolts? We were both sweating in the hundred degree heat and covered with soot as we combed through the cartons and old inner tubes: A much loved pink bear baby bottle frequently filled with apple juice and water. The ubiquitous wedding gift, a wok. A teak daggerboard. One hundred pounds of beeswax that Pete ordered, thinking he would start a candlemaking business. Wetsuits with rusty zippers. A torn yellow lifejacket. Blue canvas duffelbags packed with neatly coiled lines of different thicknesses. A set of dinnerware. Affection, good times, and dreams rotting in the soot and heat. Debris of a long marriage.

He and I lurched back and forth through a number of attempts to separate, followed by apologies, tears, reconciliations, counseling sessions and long nights without speaking, encamped in our own disappointments. "You two can't afford to divorce," our accountant reminded us, leading to another edgy round of counseling. One time, having agreed to move out, Pete broke his leg while chasing two robbers who were running through our next-door neighbor's back garden. Limping around on one leg and crutches, well, couldn't we try again? Years of my fearing conflict, or his temper, meant it was easier for me to give in to what was keeping us locked, for years, in a limbo of erosion which one divorce attorney said could last for more than a decade. Finally, when we started navigating the locks of the divorce canal, I was required to stand firm, to not change back by giving in. It was a reversal of roles, one which I probably could not have handled without Neil.

It would be great if life was like a book and you finished one chapter before moving into the next. But this time, life was messy, with endings and beginnings soaking into each other like warm, sticky liquids on a kitchen counter. Now, one year after our divorce, Pete and I are beginning to look at each other with a sad respect. I admire his truthfulness, as harsh as it has been, and his loyalty. He is committed to his daughter. What I get from him is that he values my work ethic, my concern for him and love for Mindy. Even though she has her own philosophy about her Mom and Dad's breakup, which she confided to me last Thursday when we made our weekly afterschool stop to feed the swans in Prospect Park, the breakup of our family is something that the three of us will always carry in our hearts with a certain regret. "You aren't sad and Daddy's not angry any more," is Mindy's take on it. "I get to spend time with each of you, now, and it's easier."

Putting the pieces back together, as a single mom, has meant, first and foremost, taking a look at reality, which has never been one of my favorite activities. Financial reality tends to be an especially distressing place to visit. Like many women who were "creative," I was never trained to understand the dynamics of money. Somehow it would work out. If you worked and saved. Yeah, right. Another fantasy bites the dust.

Along with starting life over, from scratch, breath by breath, step by step, I have had to learn about that fragile, invisible line that weaves between positive thinking, wishful thinking, and denial. As I was telling Neil this morning, my worst fears have come true, bringing me to this midlife transit point as a newly self-employed, divorced single mother. Remembering to say thanks for every day that I am strong enough to care for both of us.

> *"May I be safe from harm.*
> *May I be happy and peaceful.*
> *May I be strong and healthy.*
> *May I take care of myself with joy."*
> —Metta (Lovingkindness) Meditation[37]

Sitting up. Speaking. Walking. Driving my daughter to school. Continuing on to Manhattan where I share an office with another psychotherapist two days a week. In one-on-one private sessions, providing each person who comes to see me with his or her unique set of tools to overcome any number of stress related factors that can damage our health. Receiving help and referrals from the medical community. Being invited to develop seminars based on *Sixth Sense* for the business community. Helping with homework. The way back sometimes has been like windsurfing alone in choppy seas, on the edge of a storm at nightfall, not knowing if I'll make it back. Little by little I'm starting to believe that I can start over, rebuild. Little by little, I'm beginning to trust that I am truly cared for.

My biggest problem now is money. More precisely, it's my relationship with money, which has been the most problematic relationship of my life. In the hour or so before 6:15 AM, when the alarm goes off and I hit the ground in that running assault maneuver designed to wake, feed, and dress a child in time for the half-hour drive to school, I wonder how things got so complicated. That must have been someone else, back there, who was content with three hundred dollars in her pocket and plane ticket to her next underpaid assignment where she would interview a few people, take a couple of rolls of film, fly home, and sell that story for rent and another ticket. (The Number One Rule: Never own more than you can move by yourself, in your own car.)

The fact is, money scares me. Writing a check with more

than two zero's can bring on a migraine. During the fifteen years that Pete and I were together, I never so much as wrote out a check for any of the monthly bills, nor did I balance a checkbook. Seriously. The nerve-fraying prospect of having to maintain my own accounts was one of the main reasons I froze up whenever we started talking seriously about splitting up. I stayed frozen, in a dead marriage for so long because I just couldn't deal with money issues. Yet when it came down to the critical choice of whether to replace a carburetor or operate on the kitten, each of which cost $1,000, and neither of which we could afford, Pete tossed the decision to me. "I would let the cat go," he said. "Because you can always get another animal. But I know you don't think of it that way."

All I could think of was the scene at the window, three days after her fifth Christmas, when Mindy held up her new kitten up and pointed outside. "Look! You haven't seen any snow since you left the North Pole." What kind of burden would it place on her in the future, if she grew up thinking she was poor because her parents didn't have $1,000 to save her kitten's life? Well, we could always get another carburetor. What really bothered me was being handed all the responsibility for the decision, from which would follow the responsibility for finding a way to bring in that thousand dollars. Me. The creative impractical dreamer. Didn't Pete realize that if I have to be the grown up in this relationship, we are in big trouble?

"Tell them to go ahead with the surgery," I said, after one of those nights when you lie awake next to someone who's a thousand miles away.

At the heart of my troubled relationship with money is an even more distressed relationship with numbers. Second grade. Long division. Miss Dalton berating me in front of the class. "You're so stupid," she hissed. My mom, an accountant, tried her best to fill in the educational gaps, but was frustrated at times because numbers are "so logical."

(Subtext: What's wrong with you?) Adding to my overall ambivalence about the subjects of money and numbers is an overriding willingness to give anything to anyone who seems to need it more than I do. If you gave me five dollars or five thousand dollars, and you airlifted me into the middle of the rainforest where there were no stores and nothing to buy, I would go for a walk and, an hour later, come back to the airstrip with one or two children, a tropical bird, some stones, a few gourds and strands of beads, a wonderful old lady with wizened eyes and magical stories, a monkey or a cat, no money, and a big grin.

Wanting to buy that Xantos 310 is giving me major angst. First of all, I can hardly take in that I am actually considering dropping about two thousand hard-earned dollars on myself. Never mind that this is the first time in eight years that I have had two thousand dollars available. My stomach gets knotty even thinking about it. Living lean, working hard, I'm stashing as much as I can in the hopes of buying a small house in a safe school district by the time Mindy enters junior high school in two years. Looking at the big picture, I realize that two thousand dollars is not going to affect my ability to buy a house. The fear is if I buy this board, then hit hard times again, I will have wasted that money on a frivolous purchase. *Think practical.* I tell myself. *No beads, old women, or monkeys. OK, kid?* But I can't stop thinking about that shot of liquid fire and that exquisite knowing, again, of what is to dance...

"A couple of thousand dollars is a small price for anything that brings you so much happiness," Neil reassures me. "If I could buy it for you I would, but I wouldn't even begin to know where to shop."

"It seems so selfish."

"Then please do it for me."

"For you?"

"Next time we're together, you can teach me how to windsurf."

Brooklyn, NY
August 20, 1994

Dream: Clear yellow light filters through the clouds.
   I am both participant and observer.
   I am windsurfing in a river with the Dalai Lama.
   Whitney Houston is singing, "I Will Always Love You."
   The guide who sounds like he's wearing an eyeshade and smoking
a cigar is giving me a message.
   He says, "Don't look for the road. The road will come to you."

Napeague, NY
September 9, 1994

'The Shuar stick to the jungles – except when they psychonavigate.'
'Psychonavigate?'
'Happens when a shaman enters a trance. They say he flies to
far off lands.'

–John Perkins[38]

I'm driving to Napeague. Brand-new Xantos, Bic boom, and
two sails (Bic 5.7 and UP 4.5) are tied down, atop the
roofrack. A fiberglass mast mounted in mast hooks points
straight ahead.

I'm crying.

Today was going to be our day of celebration.

"Take lots of notes," Neil said. "I want to feel as if I was
there with you." That was four days ago. Then, for no
apparent reason, Neil disappeared. Or at least, he stopped
trying to reach me. In the past year and a half, we had
never been out of contact for more than a day, and this
sudden break in communication felt scary. At least, he
could have left a message if something was wrong.

Around four AM, a fax came through, shattering the
night:

Laurie:
I am not able to pursue a relationship with you. I am moving
back home with my wife and children.
Please do not communicate with me again.

Neil.

This can't be real. Can't be real. Something must have
happened. Reach for the phone. He's there.

"What happened?"

There are many kinds of silence: nursing a baby in the middle of the night, standing becalmed in a marsh, watching an egret, or listening for that space between breaths after making love. Then there's that malevolent silence, seconds before life as you know it gets ripped away.

"Oh, it's you. You got my fax." A serrated edge of contempt cuts through me. Like falling into icy water too early in the season, when your solar plexus seizes up as you try to breathe.

"Neil?" The voice. This isn't Neil. It's someone I've never met before, someone who hates me.

More silence. Is it possible to feel someone else's teeth clench in hostility from a distance? I must be making this up.

"What's wrong? Can I help?"

"You?" That's an unmistakable sneer. "What could *you* possibly do to help?"

"What happened?" *I want Neil back. What did you do with him?*

"You got my fax. What else do you need?"

"That's not enough." *Like I should need to say this?* "Neil, whatever it is, please. We can work it out together. That's what you said, remember? I am part of you and you are part of me?"

A split-second catch in the back of his throat. Like a first breath of wind moving across a lake...the real Neil. Or is it?

"Because of you, I alienated all the people who really care about me."

Cognitive dissonance. This does not make sense. How can someone care about you one day and, overnight, with no provocation, delete you as a human being?

"What was I, 'Entertainment Tonight'?" Freefall. Why didn't intuition protect me? "What about our book? Remember? Soul connection? Work together?"

"Ha. I wasn't aware that my choice of work or where I choose to live would impinge on you."

He rents a castle for me, then breaks up by fax? What's

wrong with this picture? And what's wrong with me, that I feel like throwing up everything I ever digested?

"I can't believe you had a change of heart like this, overnight."

"I'm not going to kill myself for love. I'm nearly bank-rupt. Thousands and thousands of dollars in the hole, thanks to you."

"Me?"

"Ever since I met you, every project I've started has turned to shit. I thought you were famous. You were on *Oprah*."

"Neil. I told you that fifteen minutes as a talking head doesn't qualify as fame. And even if it did, why would that matter? You said you didn't care if we had to sleep on a mattress on the floor, as long as we were together."

"Stress is bad for my health, you know. My cancer could come back."

"What happened to maintaining strong, positive beliefs for optimal results?" I hate it when my voice gets high and squeaky. No control. "What about us?"

"There is no us."

"What?"

"We had nothing in writing."

The end.

Nice work, Doctor. What kind of therapist is he, any-way? "Nothing in writing." Driving east, on Sunrise Highway, the two Neils ricochet in my head. "Write your doubts on little pieces of paper and tear them up and put them in a blender." And now this: "Nothing in writing."

How could I have missed the signals? There were no signals. As Bill Murray says in that movie where his fiancée is murdered, "I thought she was my reward for trying to lead a good life. But there is no reward." Life is a series of deals that fall through.

Question: How long does a skydiver have on the way down if her emergency parachute doesn't open?

Answer: The rest of her life.

The rest of my life. Not like this. Please not like this. A wall of fire across the river of time. Solar eyes. "We'll go dancing on an evening cruise around the harbor." Wall of fire. Napalm. The future is napalmed. Can't see the road ahead. Can't stop crying...

Uh-oh.

That is not supposed to be there. A head. Man's head. In front of the windshield. Floating. *Can't be real. Must be a mirage or something. Must be making it up.* Look down at the steering wheel, dashboard. Check your hands. Feet. Look to the left. Traffic moving in a normal pattern.

Man's head still floating in front of the windshield. Check dashboard clock: 12:20 PM. Just passed the Pine Barrens. Three dimensional. Color. Coconut brown skin. Black hair. Jet-black eyes. Kind, very kind. Feels like he's telling me not to worry. Sending wave-thoughts. Speaking without words: "I know you're hurt and I want to help.. You're not alone. I know you're hurt." Infinite kindness flowing from his eyes to my head. Red and yellow head-band around his forehead. Check your hands. Speedometer. Doing 60 in the right lane. Head still floating in front of my windshield. *Heads don't materialize over Sunrise Highway in broad daylight,* I remind myself. *You're gone, kid. Over the edge. Out to lunch. Has two brains — one is lost and the other is out looking for it. Wackadoo, to use a technical term. DSM IV to the max. Bellevue time.*

Westhampton. Thank God, he's gone. Must have made it up.

Shinnecock Canal. Sacred Native American land. He's back but fading. What the hell was that? Old, wizened face. Exceptional eyes. A man of infinite compassion.

I must be in really, really bad shape.

Can't stop crying.

Damn Neil, anyway.

Napeague, NY
September 10, 1994

It is an odd time, a paradoxical time, for we are aboveground, and yet below ground. In Jungian terms, this state is called "the tension of the opposites.." Among storytellers from my culture, this state is called nacio dos veces, being "twice-born." It is the time where a second birth occurs through a magical source, and whereafter the soul lays claim to two bloodlines, one from the physical world, and one from the world unseen.

—Clarissa Pinkola Estes[39]

It looked a lot easier in the store but when I laid all the windsurfing gear out on the road, it kind of jumbled together and I couldn't remember what to do first. My head felt fuzzy from crying, but the wind soon blew it clear.

Make a list: universal, mast foot, mast, boom, and sail. Common sense would put the universal into the foot of the mast first. Then the sail gets threaded onto the mast. Okay.

An hour later, there I am, wrestling with the damn downhaul, this crisp four hundred–dollar 4.5 meter sail that the salesman let me have for $125 is in agony, making harsh sounds as it flips around on the tarmac. The camber, which locked easily onto the mast when he showed me how to rig it in the store, last week, keeps jamming. No matter how hard I pull on the line, the sail won't straighten out.

A German sailor takes pity on me, sitting down on the ground and pushing his heel hard against the mast foot. "Sail is steef," he says. "Thees is pain in the ass sport, for sure." Fifteen minutes later, he is satisfied enough with his work to let me carry the rig to the water, fastening it to the base in the metal mast track in the center of the board.

Foaming silver wake mixes with a Grateful Dead track

blasting over the water from a van parked on a mound of sand half a mile away. Intoxicated. Synesthesia: the music of sea air on the tongue, each breath pulling in indigo from the edge of the horizon somewhere, finding its way to those muscles stretching past the aching until something expands into the openness and there is no disappointment. No longing. No heartache.

That is, until the final reach across the bay, when orange sunset explodes behind my eyes, and tears come, without my permission.

He is gone.

Brooklyn, NY
September 28, 1994

Spiritual emergencies: ...dramatic experiences and unusual states of mind that traditional psychiatry diagnoses and treats as mental diseases...actually crises of personal transformation....an opportunity of rising to a new level of awareness, or 'spiritual emergence.'
    —Stanislav Grof, M.D. and Christina Grof [40]

I once knew someone who had a breakdown, once. The real kind, where they take you to a stone building on a hill with no phones so you can "rest" and people in lab coats bring you meds that work like novocaine, temporarily numbing the surface of your pain so you can't feel where you're slit and bleeding inside. The person who had a breakdown was the Africa desk editor at a television news agency in north London where I was working as a secretary hoping to become a newswriter. As one of those meticulous worriers who overplan for every contingency, then obsess about each thing that could go wrong, the Africa man was found sitting at his desk at two AM one Sunday morning, wrapped in an afghan crocheted by one of the staff translators, reciting the weekly flight schedule from Abidjan to Paris out loud, while rocking back and forth. "Air France 308 leaves Abidjan 8:45 8:45..." the night editor heard the Africa man chattering as he was escorted down the hall, into a waiting car that whisked him off to one of those stone buildings on an English hill. The following morning, when I reported to work, I found that flight schedule, in his precise handwriting, minute enough to fill a two-inch square. I also found that I had been promoted to newswriter, a serendipitous exchange of bad and good fortune that impressed me, even then. Crisis equals danger plus opportunity, no? Every painful experience contains something we need to learn, although it may take years before we figure out what it is. Or, as the magnet on my fridge says, "This life is a test. It is only a test. Had it been a real life, you would have received instructions on where to go and what to do."

I should be over him. But inside, my soul feels charred and burned like a dead worm. The worm is that part of me that trusted life. Past tense. Poor dead worm. When I close my eyes, I can see myself wrapping it in sterile gauze soaked in cool seawater. Seawater, like tears. *Tough it out, kid, I tell myself. You've been through worse.* But nothing helps. When I sleep, a clammy nausea seeps through my skin, through my dreams. I feel like vomiting all the time, and this is what scares me, I can only eat white food. Last night, when I opened a can of "Spaghetti-Ohs" for Mindy, those little red pasta circles made me throw up. Today, I can't decide which is worse: having this abnormal reaction to colored food or serving "Spaghetti-Ohs" in the first place. Sinking this low in the nutrition department makes me feel guilty, and is there anyone more prone to guilt than an overwrought single mother? Later, in bed, trying to warm up the dark, empty place where the dead worm lives, I found myself on the other side of the room, observing myself curled into a foetal position. *If this is madness, it's more scenic than a migraine but damn, this is not supposed to happen.*

Wake up. Retching. It feels like there's ground glass in my intestines. I sleep through the alarm clock. At ten to eight, the aftershock of getting kicked in the stomach forces me out of twilight sleep into twilight day. I had a ticket to visit Neil today. I force myself to get up. Get ready for the drive to school. Hot tears are running down both sides of my face, sticking in my hair. Apple tree outside the window. *Where are the parrots? The signs from nature that things will get better? No messengers from far away. Far away. Not coming home. Not coming home.*

If it was just about me in this nightmare, it would be hard enough. But when your profession is helping other people to hold it together, and you yourself are, well, dysfunctional, you can't pretend to yourself that something isn't seriously wrong.

Which is how I find myself, today, sitting in a booth in a coffee shop named after the Greek goddess of wisdom, asking the psychiatrist across the table if I'm having a nervous breakdown.

"Breakdown or breakthrough," Sherman says, studying me through his wire-rimmed glasses while he pretends to read the menu. "Do you think that lady sitting at the counter is a transvestite?" His eyes are twinkling over the menu. Dr. Sherman Schachter, director of the New Hope Guild mental health clinics, always gets me to laugh. Right now, that's a good sign.

"A transvestite? Next door to a Russian delicatessen on Kings Highway? You must be kidding."

"She's here every day, as am I," Sherman smiles. "I always wonder about her."

When the waitress comes, I order oatmeal. "I have this thing about white food. I sound like a mental patient, don't I?" Sherman has been briefed on the basics, so why screw around? I'm counting on him to tell me if I'm out to lunch.

"White is the color of grief, according to the Chinese. You're not Chinese but everything you are describing sounds normal for someone in a state of extreme grief."

"This isn't like me. I can hardly function."

"You just had the ground ripped out from under you. What do you expect?"

"I expect to get back up in twenty-four to forty-eight hours, like a cork that floats up to the surface of the water."

"This isn't a twenty-four to forty-eight hour thing."

"I don't get it. Neil always said he was so grateful for our relationship. He would walk up to people on the street to tell them he was in love with me. I can't understand how anyone who feels that way can turn on the person he loves. Just like that. No explanation."

Thoughtful, Sherman chews an English muffin. "I'm sure that what he feels for you is real. It sounds like when he's with you, here, he has a powerful fantasy about the strong man he wants to be. And when he goes home, with all of the old associations and memories and expectations from other people, that fantasy collapses. Please eat your oatmeal." He waits for me to work through four spoonfuls before he continues. "It sounds like that soul connection was profound for both of you. Having had that once, you will probably never be satisfied with anything less. But the term "soulmate" is loaded. It's often used when someone idealizes his or her partner and projects special or magical qualities onto them. In fact, a so-called soulmate or marriage of two souls may bring up areas where each of you needs to grow, to express a deeper potential which seems to have been awakened by your coming together at this time."

"You mean in real life, nobody lives happily ever after."

"Whatever gave you the idea that they did?" he laughs. "As for your concerns about your ability to take care of your daughter, let me ask you a few questions. How many times have you not been able to take her to school because you were too upset?"

"Just today."

"Are you able to go to work and concentrate?"

"Most of the time. If anything, I feel more empathic to what someone else is feeling."

"Yes," he smiles, pleased. "That is so."

In spite of myself, I smile back.

"The human psyche is a self-correcting mechanism," he adds. "You'll be fine."

I'm glad to hear that but I'm not convinced. "You mean I'm normal?

Sherman can't stop laughing. "What do you think?"

"I asked you."

"I'd say that most of us are guilty of pseudosanity.

What's normal?"

"You're asking me?"

"'To be normal is a splendid ideal for the unsuccessful,' Carl Jung wrote. 'But for people who have more ability than the average...for them restriction to the normal signi-fies...unbearable boredom, infernal sterility, and hopeless-ness. As a consequence, there are as many people who become neurotic because they are only normal, as there are people who are neurotic because they cannot become normal.'"

"Wasn't it Freud who said that neurotics are the creative torchbearers of civilization? I could probably light up a city!"

Confession time. "I saw a man's head floating in front of my windshield, on Sunrise Highway, in broad daylight. I was on my way east, to windsurf the day Neil broke it off. I couldn't believe what I was seeing and kept checking my hands and feet, paying attention to the steering wheel and the speedometer. Everything else was normal. I have my menu of neurotic behaviors, just like anyone else but hal-lucinating three–dimensional heads in broad daylight has never been on the menu."

Sherman, I notice, is not looking at me as if he thinks I have lost it completely. *Good sign.* After a few minutes with-out speaking, he looks directly into my eyes. "You are describing a spiritual emergency."

"As in...?"

"A crisis that opens up spiritual perception, like the vision of that man's head."

"How do you know that's spiritual rather than psychotic?"

"I don't. Run your experience through a conventional psychiatric filter, and it sounds like brief reactive psychosis. Except for a few key points. One: You describe what hap-pened in an organized way. You're not incoherent or hys-terical.

"Two: You were aware, at the time, and now, that you were observing something that was out of the ordinary. Simultaneously, while observing, you were able to concentrate and perform a physical task, like driving, without interruption."

"It was as if my attention was in two places at once."

"For thousands of years, people all over the world have had similar experiences. It's not uncommon after trauma, such as experiencing someone's death or going through a Near-Death Experience. People who have had NDE's may even be more susceptible to these types of transpersonal experiences."

"It feels like a death."

"It is. Not only have you lost a great love, you've lost your dreams for the future. In other societies, they say that a piece of your soul splits off when you lose a dream."

"Why would I have a vision like that? It's foreign to everything I know."

"One of the characteristics of a spiritual emergency is that it serves as a gateway for transpersonal experiences. In other words, instead of a classical breakdown, you are receiving information that comes from a source beyond your own ego, or your own individual history. You may eventually discover the reason."

"This is going to sound weird, but I am working on getting a magazine assignment to write about an expedition into the Amazon. Last April, in Boston, I met an author, John Perkins, who takes Americans into the rainforest to meet with healers and shamans. I asked if he would take me along if I would write about his work for a major magazine."

"So there may be a connection."

"I haven't landed any work yet. Thirty-six rejections, and counting. So it looks like I won't be going."

"Hmm."

Giving me a bear hug outside the coffee shop, Sherman says, "Grief takes time to work itself through. Everyone's journey is different. Get lots of rest and take a day off when you feel you need it. It may not feel like it today, but this will pass." Through the window, I can make out the possible transvestite drinking another cup of coffee. Across the street, on the post office roof, a southwest wind is teasing an American flag.

At home, the answering machine is blinking. "John Perkins here. I think it's important that you join us on the Amazon expedition."

3 PM.
With Mindy in the passenger seat, we follow the breeze to the south shore. It's low tide when we arrive and Manny, a retired fireman who hangs out at Plumb Beach every day, is stretched out in a green canvas deck chair.

"You were here the other day," he says, shading his eyes with his hands. "You wanna sell me that Xantos?"

"I just got it." Manny's old Ultra Cat is perched on a muddy sandbar.

"You wanna use my board today?"

His generous offer takes me by surprise but hey, why not? Barefoot, wearing our shorts and shirts, Mindy takes the nose and I carry the heavier tail of the sailboard through the mud flats until the water is deep enough to float the Ultra Cat with its daggerboard extended. Even though the wind is gentle, I'm so depleted that I can't raise the old, cloth 6.3 meter sail out of the water until my daughter gently lifts the mast tip so the wind can help us.

There is something elegant and life-affirming in the grace of sailing in and around New York harbor on a warm day in the middle of the week. Gently, steadily, we skim through a small ripple of waves where the tide is filling in a sandbar, at home in the water, like dolphins, laughing into the hazy orange heart of this late September afternoon. I point out the World Trade Center and the Empire State Building. No King Kong today. She giggles as we chase a seagull back to shore, "Mommy, this is the best day of my life!"

Centerport, New York
November 5, 1994

A shaman is a man or woman of excitable temperament who gets called by the Spirit, after an illness that cannot be treated through conventional means, to take up a path of healing.

—Marina Nelson[41]

"Anyone can go to a mountaintop and meditate," one of the Beatles was quoted as saying. "The trick is to be able to do it on Broadway." It's similarly easy to experience something miraculous in a faraway place. The trick is holding onto the magic when the xerox machine breaks. Or when, after an hour of bungling, a 5.7 meter sail takes on a renegade shape, with bulging battens and a bunchy mast sleeve. Oh well, nobody's perfect.

The air temperature is seventy degrees, yet the water is almost too cold, even with a 3.2mm wetsuit. An offshore breeze, about eight knots, nudges the board toward the burnt sienna hills where three sets of stone steps connect private docks to the homes hidden from view by the pines. I spent a wretched afternoon sitting on a mossy step, observing a fog bank filling in the spaces between where I was and where I needed to be. Like my mental state at the time...

Was it just one month ago, when Pete came to stay with Mindy for a week so I could go on assignment for *Elle* and *Maxim*?

Before my brother called me "Princess X-Files?"

Just a month ago in Miazal, Ecuador...

It was just after dawn when I noticed the scorpion crawling out of my sleeping bag. Fortunately, I wasn't inside, having just come back from what is euphemistically called "the john." Not that anything even remotely resembles plumbing in the Ecuadorian Amazon. A call of nature means squatting in a pool of steaming mud behind a giant banana plant, hoping you finish before you get too close to any of those friendly, primeval insects that look as if they were genetically engineered in Jurassic Park.

The scorpion was taking its time, crawling across the dirt floor of the hut that served as the gathering place and shaman's lodge for the Shuar Federation of Indians, an isolated tribe that still hunts with blowguns and poisoned darts. Described for many years by neighboring tribes as "hostile and aggressive," the Shuar were known among travelers to these parts for their quaint custom of decapitating their enemies and shrinking their heads. But that all changed when the missionaries and Christianity arrived. At least, that's what they told me before I signed on to this expedition. When we arrived, we were told that a few days earlier, three headless bodies had been found close to the mission where we were spending the night. Like biting your nails or smoking cigarettes, shrinking heads must be a hard habit to break.

On this particular morning, as my eyes tracked to the scorpion, I noticed Kitiar, the Shuar's senior medicine man, chanting strange syllables as part of a healing ceremony for one of the women in our twelve-member expedition. As he leaned toward her, Kitiar collapsed. The shaman lay unconscious on the floor. His face was grey. But that was nothing to the angry faces of the Shuar who seemed to think that their senior medicine man's collapse had something to do with us. A dozen Shuar now blocked the exits. We were trapped. Even if we could escape, it would take twenty-five days of trekking through 105-degree heat to reach the nearest road—if we could ever find the road.

Expedition leader John Perkins huddled with the tense Shuar leaders for a few minutes. John has known the Shuar since his Peace Corps days in the 1970s. John and I met at the Interface Center in Boston, where we had been giving workshops in our respective areas of expertise. John's range of platform skills includes the shamanic practice of breathing fire, definitely a show-stopper. Immensely charming, especially to the women who flock to his classes, John has published three memoirs about his adventures with various shamans. The founder of Dream Change Coalition, a not-for-profit corporation in Palm Beach Gardens, Florida that is helping to fund my trip in exchange for coverage, John is passionate about saving the rainforest. "Every individual in the U.S. produces approximately four tons of deadly carbon dioxide a year. It takes about three acres of pristine forest to offset this effect," he says. For $29 dollars a year, anyone can lease three acres of rainforest through Dream Change Coalition's P.O.L.E. (Pollution Offset Lease for Earth) Program.[42] Catching a glimpse of his face as the Shuar huddle progresses, he does resemble Harrison Ford, an obvious comparison given the setting and the feeling that we've been dropped into an Indiana Jones movie. Beth Beloff, a member of our predominantly female group, calls us "The Indiana Joans."

Standing in a circle around Kitiar's body, the Joans look pretty shaken when John explains that the Shuar think Gino, a fellow expedition member, caused Kitiar to fall on the ground, unconscious. Gino had objected to his wife participating in a jungle healing ceremony with Kitiar. Ergo, Gino had done something to make the shaman sick. "They won't let us out of here until Gino heals the shaman," John shrugged.

With his pink Ralph Lauren sports shirt and gold wire-rimmed glasses, Gino, a banker from Milan, knew as much about healing a sick Amazonian medicine man as you or I. Probably less. As I wondered how I'd look in a glass case in the Smithsonian, years of newswriting now kicked in: "Reporter's Head Shrunk in Tribal Ritual." Hopefully the Shuar would grant my last request: *"Cuando tu cierres las labias de mi boca, favor que pongas el hilo azul. Va igualar mejor con mis ojos."* ("When you sew up my lips, please use the blue thread. It will match my eyes.")

Whatever possessed me to sign up for this? Just yesterday, I found myself standing on the edge of a rocky gorge, facing a swinging wooden bridge with no handrails and missing slats, about two-hundred feet in the air. "No way," I said. "I happen to have a phobia of heights. I avoid visiting friends who live on high floors, refuse to ride glass elevators, and can't even stand on a chair." But the newspaper and magazine assignments I had persistently sought, and which had materialized a week or so before the trip, were reports on how pharmaceutical companies were working with rainforest shamans to develop tropical plant-based drugs. Unfortunately, the pictures I needed to shoot–of an innocuous bamboo hut with a garden of healing plants– lay on the other side of the gorge.

Three steps onto the bridge and my field of vision blacked out. I staggered back to the cliff, shaking my head as if that would get rid of the darkness. Only when John's partner Raul walked in front of me, my eyes focused on his shoulders and the back of his head, clinging for dear life to hands kindly extended behind his back, could I inch my way across.

The relief was short-lived. After shooting two rolls of film, I joined up with the others on a "hike" to the sacred waterfalls. Three hours later, in oven-like heat, and under a constant barrage from stinging ants and mosquitoes, we had fought our way across a sheer rock face, six rushing rivers, and hung onto twisted vines to avoid slipping off treacherous ledges. The waterfalls were worth it: a set of silvery, twin cascades twisting over a cliff studded with wispy clouds, one aqua waterfall warm from underground thermal energy; the other, clear and icy cold.

After swimming in the pools at the foot of the twin falls, we started back. On the far bank of the first river, as I was climbing over a tree trunk wedged between two boulders, it was necessary to find a foothold in the sheer rock face that needed to be crossed. Wearing knee-high, heavy rubber gumboots added to the challenge, I discovered, as I wedged my left foot into a small crevasse while my right leg scraped against the rock face, feeling for a toe-hold. To steady myself, I grabbed at a vine but it broke off in my hand. *Uh-oh. I signed a release!*

The next three seconds were very, very slow as I studied the straight drop down to the jagged boulders hundreds of feet below, aware that half of my body was dangling in mid-air while the other half was losing traction on the rock ledge. It is said that in such moments your life passes in front of your eyes but I was serenely aware that every fraction of a second, I was slipping... The next thing I knew, someone slammed me back onto the rock ledge, saving my life. After inching across the rock face to a pit of stinking mud, it took a few hours for my legs to stop shaking.

Slogging through boiling mud the next day, Waiti, a plant shaman, did his best to teach me how to identify medicinal herbs and plants. Still tired from the day before, I was struggling to lift my feet, a prerequisite for making it through the hot, sticky mudfields that acted like quicksand. Within minutes, boiling gunge was sucking at my legs like a scene from a Japanese horror movie. Waiti and another Shuar guide grabbed me under the arms, yanking me to safety, leaving my gumboots slurping in the steamy muck. Later, someone retrieved them so that I could rejoin the other Indiana Joans, who laughed and called me "Mudwoman."

Zen in the art of windsurfing was one of the farthest things from my mind at that moment, but years of falling in the water made it easy for me to laugh at my new nickname, even as Waiti was instructing me in the Zen of staying alive in the jungle. "Watch your feet and hands. You must think and move in the now," he chanted over and over, a forest monk instructing an apprentice. Mindfulness here was essential. A one-second mistake could be fatal. Sure enough, as I grabbed a tree stump to balance, Waiti knocked it away, pointing at a crawling, seething mass of large, red insects. *"Veintiquatros,"* he said. "Killer ants. Very dangerous. One sting and you're dead in twenty-four *(veintiquatro)* hours." After yesterday's close call on the cliff, death was, once again, inches away and my life had been saved by a man who could just as easily have decapitated and shrunk my poor head which was starting to reel from this crash course in impermanence.

Mild shock, intense heat, mud, and stinging insects were also taking their toll as I began to hallucinate: Ice cubes in large glasses of Coca-Cola. Grinning Eskimos. Air conditioners. Refrigerators.

After wading through whitewater rapids at the end of the day, we arrived at the lodge where we would spend the night. Sore, insect-bitten, and covered with mud, I headed for the river to wash my dirt-encrusted self and clothes in the river. Suzan Lang, who joined the expedition in search of a shaman to heal her chronic asthma, was standing behind me washing my hair with a thin square of lumpy Ecuadoran soap when a long, black caiman cruised by. We held our breath as he swam away without tasting so much as a toe.

Just when I thought the surprises must be over for the day, I walked up the riverbank, through a clearing, carrying Mindy's green and yellow "Crayola" sleeping bag into the open frame, thatched longhouse. Seated on a tree stump was the same old man whose face had appeared over the road as I was on my way to windsurf six weeks earlier. I'd like to be able to think that he gave me some sign of instant recognition, but no, he just smiled gently at all of us. In Spanish, I asked Waiti to explain to Kitiar in the Shuar dialect that he had already presented himself to me. What, in fact, had really happened? Was he aware that he had seen me six weeks earlier, in another country? How could he explain it? Do people in states of spiritual emergency emit some kind of electromagnetic signal that can be downlinked by a medicine man on the other side of the world? To both men, my questions seemed more extraordinary than the event. The hardest thing for them to understand was the description of "driving." Neither of them had ever seen a road, let alone a car! As for his psychonavigation skills, Kitiar grinned, "Sometimes my spirit goes out travelling to help many friends in North America." It made as much sense as any other explanation but I'm not sure which is less weird, imagining a floating head that looks real or seeing one that is.

At nightfall, when the rainforest sounds like a Tarzan soundtrack, Kitiar began calling in the spirits. He and Waiti poured a concoction that looked and smelled like tar in a tin cup. Kitiar and I would each drink from the cup. This would give him the power to see into my soul and heal any places that were broken. Thoughts of Neil had surfaced on this trip but the breakup seemed small and faraway from here, so I didn't think I needed help with that. Like the Wizard of Oz, Kitiar wanted to know what I requested from the ceremony. No cowardly lion, I knew I had courage. Any scarecrow would agree that my brain was already fried. And even Dorothy and Toto would feel that going home right now was out of the question. Kitiar's deep charcoal eyes looked into mine for what seemed like a long time before he passed me the cup.

"Can you open my spiritual vision?" I asked in Spanish. Waiti translated for Kitiar, who nodded and laughed.

"He says that one's easy for him," Waiti grinned. The two shamans then gave me a shot of trago, strong Ecuadorian liquor, to wash down the tarlike drink and told me to lie down until it was time to vomit. Lying on a carpet of man-sized banana leaves, sounds grew feathers and rainbow-colored fireflies streaked across the room like falling stars.

When the aurora boreolis came down from Canada to dance across the thatched roof, I felt my stomach start to go and I crashed outside, stumbling over seven other Joanses wrapped in sleeping bags. Just outside the doorway, it felt like someone was watching me. Turning to find out who it was brought me face-to-face with a dead tree–and it was laughing at me. The tree made faces, winked, and stuck out its tongue.

"Señora, are you all right?" asked one of the Shuar guards.

"Look, Manuelo. The tree is a person."

"Of course it is." He looked pleased that a *gringa* had fig-ured this out for herself, even though it should have been obvious. What was becoming obvious was that the Shuar were on to something. If you spend enough time in the rain forest, the trees start talking to you. Coming from New York, I knew nothing about laughing or talking trees. There were only three categories of trees: Christmas trees, regular trees, and palm trees. Now a grove of musical trees, with faces like the roses in Walt Disney's *Alice in Wonderland*, started singing purple and pink into the night.

A grand chorus of Ecuadoran roosters turned night into morning. John tapped me on the shoulder and walked me back inside, where his eighteen-inch stainless steel hunting knife had been placed on a bamboo shelf the night before. A quarter-inch thick in the middle, the knife had snapped in two at the thickest point. No one had touched the knife, nor did the Shuar have metalworking capabilities, John was saying when Kitiar collapsed.

No trees were singing now as a sweaty Gino, shaking a gourd rattle, kneeled frantically over the unconscious med-icine man. A half-hour later, Kitiar was still out cold. John was trying to stay calm but his face was paperwhite and his pupils dilated. We were in real danger. Perhaps if we all lay hands on the shaman...?

Nothing of a healing nature occurred to bring him back,

but Carol Feinhage, a physiotherapist from Maine, diagnosed him as having suffered a stroke. He needed medical attention urgently. After some negotiation, John persuaded the Shuar to let us fly him to the nearest military hospital for treatment. The men unblocked the exits and we were free. Sort of.

"Run to the airstrip!" John and Raul shouted. We plunged through mud, leaping into dugout canoes that were standing by to take us downriver to the airstrip. Somehow, the Shuar from the lodge managed to beat us to the landing area, even though they had started out on foot after we left. Twenty minutes later, a four-seater Cessna skidded to a stop. Gino was shoved onto the plane first. Six men carried Kitiar aboard and laid him carefully on the floor behind the seats. Waiti, John, and Gino's wife took that flight into the Andes while the rest of us looked at the airstrip with the fear and longing that comes from sleep deprivation, hunger, thirst, and the feeling that your insect-bitten skin is going to crawl away in protest.

Centerport, NY
November 6, 1994

So Princess X-Files, how do you put all of this together?

—Eric Nadel

I wish I knew.

Neil called yesterday. "I haven't stopped loving you," he said. "And I never apologized for loving you. I'm sorry we lost our way. Don't give up on us. Keep the faith." I should have hung up but I froze like a deer in the headlights.

This afternoon, releasing the outhaul, unclamping the boom, and pulling the mast down, through the sleeve of the sail, my questions lead to more questions: Why me? Why Kitiar? How did that happen? What does it all mean?

If I had answers, I could retire. In the meantime, I'm as confused as ever.

But I believe that now I'm confused on a higher level and about more important things.

1 There are two variations of this quote, in print. Albert
Camus' essay, "Return to Typeset," appears in *The Myth of
Sisyphus and Other Essays* (Alfred A. Knopf, 1995), page 144.
Nagakawa soen–roshi's haiku appears in *Nine-Headed Dragon
River: Zen Journals* by Peter Matthiessen (Shambala, 1998), p.
62. By the author's account, Soen–roshi read "his own new
haiku" in 1977. The metaphor of discovering an invincible
summer within oneself transcends distinctions between
existentialism and Zen. The question of whether or not
Soen–roshi might have read some version of Camus'
quote, in passing, and absorbed it, subconsciously, or
whether this is a synchronistic literary event, cannot be
determined, as both authors have passed away. Camus'
version of this quote was printed on a popular 1970s wall
poster.

2 The three essentials of Zen practice are discussed at length
in *Zen Philosophy, Zen Practice* by Thich Thien–An (Dharma
Publishing, 1975), pp. 42–46.

3 Isn't this quote too good to pass up? Thanks to Albert
Camus' *American Journals* (Paragon House, 1987), p. 137.

4 Camus, ibid., page 107.

5 Statistics on chronic fatigue are imprecise because the
symptoms are similar to mononucleosis, depression, and
bereavement. Symptoms of chronic fatigue can be due to
the Epstein–Barr virus or, in my own case,
cytomagelovirus (CMV). The statistics quoted in this section come from several phone conversations I had, in 1987,
with public information officers at the Centers for Disease
Control and the National Institute of Health.

6 Christian's study of Sika deer and its implications for
understanding the effects of stress on the adrenal system
are well described in *The Hidden Dimension* by Edward T.
Hall (New York: Anchor Books, 1990), pp. 19–21.

7 Research on chronic fatigue syndrome by the Centers for

Disease Control, published in various sources, 1987.

[8] Judy Mahle Lutter's article, "The strength-sapping sickness: chronic fatigue syndrome," appeared in *Women's Sports and Fitness*, volume 13, number, October 1991, p. 22-23.

[9] Dr. Herbert Benson of Harvard Medical School began a series of controlled studies on what he called "the relaxation response" and other forms of meditation in the late 1970s. At first, his research was highly controversial in the medical community, because it questioned the assumption that health problems are 100 percent physical in nature. In 1999, before this book went to press, I started studying with Dr. Benson at Harvard Medical School's Continuing Education Program. In June 2000, I completed Harvard's postgraduate course in Clinical Training in Mind-Body Medicine.

[10] Starting from the base of the spine, or root chakra, representing grounding and stability, the other six chakras are: creative/sexual, solar plexus/identity, fear, and anger, heart/love, throat/communication, third eye/inner vision, crown/higher consciousness.

[11] The author quotes his teacher, the Zen master archer. Eugen Herrigel, *Zen in the Art of Archery* (Pantheon Books, Inc., 1953), p. 30.

[12] Although I'm jumping ahead of the reader, here, it is relevant to note that not all Near-Death Experiences give you that "saved by the light" glow. Ongoing research on NDE experiences reported by as many as eight million Americans indicates that "NDEers may feel a sense of distance or separation from people who have not had similar experiences; and they may fear being ridiculed or rejected by others—sometimes, of course, with good reason…People who have had unpleasant or frightening NDEs…may be troubled by terrifying flashbacks of the experience itself." Quoted from "Counseling the Near-Death Experiencer" by Bruce Greyson and Barbara Harris in *Spiritual Emergency: When Personal Transformation Becomes a*

Crisis, edited by Stanislav Grof, M.D. and Christina Grof (New York: Jeremy Tarcher/Putnam, 1989), pp. 202–203.

[13] The "river of time" metaphor for memory appears, first, in Canadian Richard Bucke, M.D.'s classic 1901 text, *Cosmic Consciousness* (Arkana Books, 1991 edition), p. 20. Later in the 19th century, American psychologist William James developed a metaphor of memory looking like beads on a necklace, in which the connecting string or filament represented neutral memories, and the "beads" represented emotionally charged memories.

[14] The American Psychiatric Association Diagnostic Manual, or DSM IV, defines Post-Traumatic Stress Disorder (309.81) as being present when a person has "experienced, witnessed, or was confronted with an event…that involved actual or threatened death or serious injury, or a threat to the physical integrity of self or others" and his or her response "involved intense fear, helplessness, or horror." The traumatic event is re-experienced through "recurrent, intrusive distressing recollections of the event, including images, thoughts perceptions…dreams" and "acting or feeling as if the traumatic event were recurring." These feelings may come through flashbacks, resulting in symptoms that can include sleep difficulties, irritability, difficulty concentrating, hypervigilance, and exaggerated startle response, and "a sense of a foreshortened future, e.g., does not expect to have…a normal life span." Diagnostic Criteria from DSM–IV (American Psychiatric Association, 1994) pp. 209–210. At a postgraduate course at Harvard Medical School's Institute for Mind/Body Medicine in June 2000, I learned that PTSD affects the anterior pituitary region of the brain which produces arousal hormones. In addition to flashbacks, PTSD sufferers experience a 'deer frozen in the headlights' type of panic where they are unable to protect themselves from approaching harm. Medical experts believe that PTSD never completely heals or goes away.

[15] Yes, this theme was later exploited in the 1999 movie *The Sixth Sense.*

[16] It's not the classic, "white light" Near-Death Experience (NDE), but, according to Sogyal Rinpoche, it falls within the paramaters of a "standard" NDE. As many as eight million people, or one out of every twenty Americans, has had at least one Near-Death Experience, according to a 1982 Gallup poll. In *The Tibetan Book of Living and Dying,* Sogyal Rinpoche lists the main features of a Near-Death Experience: "an altered state of feeling, without pain or bodily sensation"; finding (yourself) "separated from (your) body"; becoming "aware of another reality...entering a darkness...a tunnel." He adds, "They may reach a bound- ary beyond which they cannot go...return with a sense of mission and service...to fulfill the purpose of their life, which has not been accomplished." (p. 321)

[17] When revising the third draft, in 1999, I came upon this poignant reference to tuberculosis comes from Camus' journal, as quoted in Olivier Todd's biography, *Albert Camus: A Life,* Alfred A. Knopf, New York: 1997.

[18] Hall, op. cit., p. 63

[19] Hall, ibid., p. 53.

[20] The insurance company disqualified me and refunded two years of premiums.

[21] These definitions of death have been summarized coher- ently in a manual developed for a seminar called *Working with Seriously Ill and Dying Patients* by Judith A. Skretny, M.A. (The American Academy of Bereavement, Tucson, AZ: 1999.)

[22] In updating this journal, I have found two medical abstracts that address these symptoms. "Asthma Medication Can Have Psychiatric Side Effects," an article in the *Annual Journal of Allergy, Asthma, and Immunology* (January 1999; 3: pp. 95–504) and a 1996 report in the *New England Journal of Medicine* on "Drug Therapy: Theophylline in Asthma,"in which pediatricians Miles Weinberger and

Leslie Hendeles of the University of Iowa Hospital, Department of Pediatrics express concern about the toxicity of theophylline, which has been prescribed for asthma for more than 50 years. (*New England Journal of Medicine* 1996; 334; pp. 1380–1388).

23 According to Forecasted State-Specific Estimates of Self-Reported Asthma Prevalence–United States, December 4, 1998/47 (47), pp. 1022–1025, "approximately 17-million persons in the United States have asthma." The state with the largest estimated number of asthmatics was California (2,268,300); New York came in second, with 1,236,200 asthmatics.

24 Data collected from interviews and reports produced by the Centers for Disease Control in 1990, updated when I was editing the third draft in 1999. In Table 58, "Number of selected reported chronic conditions per 1,000 persons, by sex and age: United States, 1995–Con., 73.6 women aged 45–64 are asthmatic, as compared to 31.4 males of the same age. *CDC Series 10, No. 199, p. 80.* A Harvard Medical School study in 1995 confirmed my doctor's hypothesis that "estrogen plays a role in the pathophysiology of asthma." (*American Journal of Respiratory Critical Care Medicine, October 1995, 152 (4 Pt 1): 1183-8.*) A 1994 Wisconsin Research Network (Wren) Study determined that "56.7 percent of patients with undiagnosed asthma reported that their symptoms began in adulthood." ["Diagnosed and possible undiagnosed asthma: A Wisconsin Research Network (Wren) Study" by D.L.Hahn and J.W. Beasley. *Journal of Family Practice, National Library of Medicine, MDX Health Digest, Volume 38, Issue 4, pp. 373.9.*] Hypothyroidism and hormonal changes during perimenopause have also been shown to be factors exacerbating airway inflammation in asthma. (*Journal of Allergy and Clinical Immunology, 1999; 104: pp. 595-600. The Annual of Allergy, Asthma, and Immunology, 1999; 83: pp. 222-228*).

25 "Cykotine Shifts and Perimenopausal Asthma," *The Annual*

of Allergy, Asthma, and Immunology, ibid.

26 Dora Eisman, my maternal grandmother, died in the emergency room of Coney Island Hospital, after being accidentally overdosed with theophylline, according to medical records. She was 96.

27 The doctor didn't crack a smile. My friend Jane commented later that if I was well enough to joke, it must be a sign that I was getting better.

28 You can never outstare a Sarah Lawrence girl.

29 Clarissa Pinkola Estes is talking about what happens when the soul comes out of a long period of incubation. *Women Who Run with the Wolves* (New York: Random House, 1992.) p. 435.

30 Unconscious is the term Carl Jung coined. It encompasses the repressed desires of Freud's "subconscious," while including such intelligences as creativity, healing, and spirituality. Jung believed that the Unconscious was a doorway connecting us to a collective or greater Unconscious which contains a reservoir of universal symbols (archetypes) that appeal, across-the-board, to the human psyche, regardless of culture or upbringing. By tapping into the power of the Unconscious, we can connect to our deeper Self to tap resources that go beyond our individual ego identities and personal histories. Other methodologies refer to the Nonconscious.

31 Time Line Therapy was developed by Tad James, Ph.D., and Wyatt Woodsmall, Ph.D. in the 1980s. It is a working model of a metaphor for memory storage and activation attributed to psychologist William James, who said that memory was like beads on a necklace, with the emotionally charged memories as the "beads" and the neutral memories as the "string" that holds the beads together. I like the imagery of a river.

32 Based on the work of the late Milton Erickson, M.D., this method employs storytelling, metaphors, and a gentle interviewing technique which opens up new lines of com-

munication between the conscious and Unconscious minds. There are the usual jokes about "watch waving," and "turning people into chickens and ducks" but indirect, therapeutic hypnosis bears no resemblance to stage hypnosis or the parodies of hypnotists seen on TV.

33 In 1991, the American Institute of Hypnotherapy was located in Santa Ana, California. For more information: 1.800.USA.9996.

34 I earned my Ph.D. in psychology from Greenwich University, Hilo, Hawaii, in 1991. My faculty advisor, Ronna Kabatznick, Ph.D., was a prominent psychologist who had been the psychological advisor to Weight Watchers, International for many years. She was an advisor to Mark Cutler, M.D., coauthor of the Dalai Lama's 1998 bestselling book, *The Art of Happiness*. In 1994, I completed my doctorate in clinical hypnotherapy at the American Institute of Hypnotherapy, Irvine, California. Although neither degree is from an accredited institution, both Greenwich and A.I.H. are licensed by their states' Departments of Education. Contrary to what many people think, "non-accredited" does not mean that the school operates illegally.

35 Pinkola Estes, C., op cit., p. 203.

36 Why reinvent the wheel when Jean-Dominique Bauby has done it so eloquently, already? What could me more haunting than this masterful description of life after a stroke, which he communicated, to a transcriber, by blinking out Morse Code. *The Diving Bell and the Butterfly* (Alfred A. Knopf, Paris, 1997), p. 25.

37 Over the years, I have come upon any number of versions of this Buddhist meditation. This one, which crossed my desk as I was completing the third revision, is simple and strong. It comes from *Reflections: Peaceful Dwelling Project Newsletter, Autumn 1999, vol. II, No. 4*, edited by Rev. Madeline Ko-i Bastis, BCC.

38 *Psychonavigation: Techniques for Travel Beyond Time*, John Perkins.

(Rochester, VT: Destiny Books, 1994.) p. 4.

[39] Pinkola Estes, op cit., pp. 460–461.

[40] According to Grof, a Czech psychiatrist who has conducted extensive research in the field of transpersonal psychology, "spiritual emergencies have a positive potential and should not be confused with diseases that have biological cause and necessitate medical treatment." *Spiritual Emergency: When Personal Transformation Becomes a Crisis* (Jeremy P. Tarcher/Putnam: New York, 1989), p. x.

[41] Marina Nelson is a shaman in Fairfield, Connecticut who trains with her teachers in Ecuador.

[42] For information on Dream Change Coalition and/or the POLE program, go to *www.dreamchange.org* or call DCC at 561.622.6064. (Dream Change Coalition, PO Box 31357, Palm Beach Gardens, FL 33420.)

Part Three
1995–1997

As the body lives
so does the spirit,
and both must be born, and broken
in order to reach the light.
−BERYL BAINBRIDGE [1]

Atlantic Point, NY
June 13, 1995

The sea is high again today, with a thrilling flush of wind. I have escaped to this island with a few books and the child. The villagers say that only a sick (person) would choose such a remote place to rebuild. Well, then, I have come here to heal myself, if you like to put it that way.

—Lawrence Durrell [2]

Sunrise.

Through an octagonal stained glass window, first light splashes over cream stucco walls. On the ceramic tile floor, in a green water glass, one pink cabbage rose acquires translucence as dawn passes through the room.

Like Darby, Durrell's narrator who begins *The Alexandria Quartet*, I have come here in search of a safe place for Mindy to complete her schooling. "Here" is a seven-mile long barrier island with a year-round population of 35,000 people, clean, private beaches, a community of year-round surfers, and a small fleet of charter fishing boats. "Here" also satisfies the clause in my divorce agreement that stipulates she and I must live within a fifty-mile radius of the Empire State Building so her father can continue to see her on a regular basis.

"I want to make myself an empty room:
Quiet whitewashed walls with slant sunshine
And a fresh breeze through open windows." [3]

Drawn to the island's canals and eccentric cottages, Neil and I had wandered these back streets looking for a future home. This house has the bayside location and fireplace that were high on our wish list, yet I would not have moved here now, had it been simply a question of satisfying myself. Too much blood on the tracks, I guess. It's hard not to think about those dreams when there are so many reminders of our happiness around.

A year from then, life feels raw around the edges, at times. Still, who's to say, maybe it's better for us both like this, rather than moving to a new home with a new partner. Talk about adding points on the social readjustment scale! There's no point to replaying "coulda-shoulda-woulda" scenes late at night, either. Better to put one foot in front of the other and say, like an old farmer in a Chinese legend whose farm burns down, "Good news, bad news, who can say?"

When his scorched land grows back into a field and the king sends his horses there to board, the farmer becomes wealthy again. His neighbors come to congratulate him on his good fortune but the old man shrugs, "Good news, bad news, who can say?"

When the king sends his favorite wild stallion for the farmer's son to train, the horse throws the young man to the ground, breaking both his legs, so the boy needs two canes for getting around. His neighbors wring their hands and say, "What bad fortune."

But the old man merely shrugs, "Good news, bad news, who can say?"

Years later, when the kingdom goes to war and every healthy young man in the land is drafted, the farmer's son is spared because of his disability. "What good fortune!" his neighbors say. Shaking his head from side to side, the old man repeats, "Good news, bad news, who can say?"

Had anyone told me, when I left the newsroom for a week of bed rest in 1987 that it would be nearly a decade until I could get back on my feet, I would have argued, "No way! I can't live through all that." Maybe that's why no one told me, then. Nor would I have believed that six months of "transition" would stretch into four and a half years. How my mom put up with our chaos, upstairs from her impeccable apartment where no speck of dust would dare to settle, I'll never know. I would have said, "No way," had anyone suggested that I would ever buy a house, on my own. For fifteen years, I never looked at a checkbook or paid any bills. The husband is supposed to be doing this. Everyone knows I have the math skills from hell. Good news, bad news, who can say?

Waking up in this house for the first time makes me wonder if I have been in a state of suspended animation. There is something surreal about traveling simultaneously backward into a quieter time, and forward into a new beginning. Perhaps this is an "archway which one prepares to pass through, to a new manner of knowing and being."[4]

"Barn burnt down —

> *now*

I can see the moon." [5]

What a privilege to be able to start life over.

The house is practically empty, apart from this Posturepedic mattress and a suitcase with sheets and towels in the corner bedroom. A Bic aluminum boom, a two-piece, gray fiberglass mast, and an orange 5.7 meter Bic sail lean against a wall. The Xantos 310 is stashed on a grass strip next to the concrete driveway. A 3/2 millimeter Body Glove wetsuit hangs from a pole, in an open closet alcove, in a small room that smells like a poultry market in Chinatown in mid-July. The previous owner disliked closet doors, bred finches and canaries in the back room, and apparently performed no significant repairs on the interior of this house for twenty years, which is how I have managed to afford it. The living room floor is covered in linoleum the color of congealed blood which even Dracula must have rejected. Stucco walls in every room have been painted different colors. The peeling pink and motley blue rooms are calling out for neon ring ceiling lights and plaster madonnas to give it that Mexican bordello look. Even though Charlene says I could give Martha Stewart a heart attack, I promise to resist.

On Monday, walls and ceilings will start coming down. Soon, we will have real plumbing and closets. Then the books, computers, and my three pieces of left-over furniture will start to arrive, inevitably followed by brand-new clutter.

What would it take to simplify my life, so that all I need comes down to this: a windsurfer and a wetsuit?

This emptiness holds promise.

Atlantic Point, NY
August 8, 1995

*A house constitutes a body of images that give mankind proofs
or illusions of stability. We are constantly re-imagining its reality:
to distinguish all these images would be to describe the soul of
the house; it would mean developing a veritable psychology
of the house.*

—Gaston Bachelard[6]

Disgust and fatigue roll in, one after another, like sets of
waves. If only I had known...

Standing in the street, watching fishing boats pass at
the end of the block, Gary Mangus, my redheaded windsurfing architect friend from the holy city of Brooklyn,
unrolls my orange sail on the sidewalk in front of my little
blue house. A deep pit, the size of a midget's coffin, has
reinvented the space of the garden. Gary and my godfather
have had to rip out the front deck to make this pit, the
cedar planks leaning at a forty-five degree angle against a
four-foot sand hill next to an unfortunate magnolia tree
that used to be a garden centerpiece. The Gerry Adams
I.R.A. Memorial Bunker, as I call it, looks like something you
would crouch behind after throwing Molotov cocktails at
the enemy, which might not be a bad idea, if I knew just
who the enemy was. The Bunker does not exactly endear
me to several of the neighbors. Most people here have been
friendly, but one woman, in particular, has been heard to
snarl, "Who asked you people to move here, anyway?"

So much for that cliché about the sweetness of life in a
small town. "God, I miss Brooklyn," I sigh while Gary sizes
up the boom in relation to the sail. "There, at least, people
stab you in the front!"

So far, five local plumbers have inspected the two

month–old pit and promised to return the following day to move the house trap from its present place in a doorless closet to the pit. The town plumbing inspector has ruled that this is the only way we can legally install a modern bathroom. The Catch–22 which, with 20–20 hindsight should have kept me from buying this place had I known about it, is a local law that makes it illegal for homeowners to use any plumbers, electricians, or contractors who are not licensed by this town. Even more draconian are the informants, who reportedly call the building inspector if they see an out–of–town contractor's truck parked in front of anyone's home. Or, they call the police if they feel you're a few inches too close to their driveway. I've already learned about that one the hard way after my car got towed to the pound, two towns away, the day after I moved in. It cost me $330 in cash to retrieve the vehicle, which is even more expensive than retrieving a towed car from the pier in midtown Manhattan! And no, I wasn't blocking their stupid driveway. Neighbors down the block say that when they moved here, two years ago, someone informed on them when they called in a fencing company from another town. They were fined $800 for installing a $2,000 fence!

Finding a locally licensed plumber who will actually show up to move the house trap to the pit is becoming critical, if this house is to be livable by the first week in September, when Mindy comes back from her summer vacation to start school. So far, none of the "legal" plumbers have come back after promising us that they will. Whenever I call to inquire, they mutter something mysterious about pre–existing violations and being afraid of the plumbing inspector. Where is Franz Kafka now that I need him? Or is this a Graham Greene novel–in–waiting? Opening scene: Frustrated new homeowner finds a dead plumber in the pit, only to learn that a neighbor has called the police to accuse her of the murder.

And what's this about a housewarming?

Q: "What would you like for a housewarming gift?"

A: "How about camouflage khaki curtains with bullet-holes? We're going for the Sarajevo look."

Purgatory must look, sound, and feel like this. It was probably developed by a contractor and a building inspector. Inside the house, black marcusite planks covered with soot have at least partially covered up the Type A negative linoleum in the living room. The planks go all the way through the cottage to the kitchen, where the burners on the stove have, apparently, been home to nine generations of the Spaghetti Factory. Sure, I checked the inside of the oven. It was clean. Who removes the burners from the stove during a walk-through? I also checked the dishwasher before making an offer on the property. It was filled with books. After more than two years of showing our apartment, who could forget those mad dashes to clear off all counters before prospective buyers arrived? Not wanting to embarrass the owner, I didn't say anything when I discovered his books stacked sideways, in the racks, like dishes.

The realtor told me that all appliances would be hooked up when I moved in, but, along with disliking closet doors, the previous owner apparently did use his dishwasher for book storage. After eight years of standing, unused, its rubber gaskets and hosing have rotted out. So have the hoses under the kitchen and bathroom sinks. The faucet handle on the bathtub fell off on the first day, right after the shower head dropped on my foot. At least half of the electrical outlets are nonfunctional, but, hey, doesn't the I-Ching say that obstruction is the flip side of success? None of this is going to kill me. After all, it's only plumbing. If I was watching this in a movie starring Carol Burnett and Walter Matthau, I'd be laughing. But it's not a movie. This morning, when the washing machine started spraying water everywhere, I burst into tears.

Maybe if I could go windsurfing. There's nothing like walking on water for reawakening a sense of wonder but even that's not working. It takes an hour to rig the damn thing. By the time I get it together, the sail is half-wrinkled and I'm too fed up to enjoy it. It's impossible to steer or navigate unless the sail is properly rigged. Those old cloth sails were so much easier. These new babies require a degree in nautical engineering. The main problem seems to be getting enough downhaul so the foot of the sail is fully stretched to the mast foot. No matter how hard I pull on the crescent, cleated, aluminum rigging tool, the bottom of the sail gets stuck six inches from the mast base. That's if the sail-eating plastic boom clamp hasn't chomped on a finger or two, here and there. My finger or two, to be specific. I can't seem to hold the mast against my leg and grab the boom clamp without sucking in a section of the sleeve. It would be easy to blame the gear but I know the problem is me. I'm just a klutz.

"No you're not," says Gary. "You just need rigging lessons."

I'm not sure if he feels sorry for me or if he really believes it's simply a question of one-on-one demo and practice.

"It is stiff," he concedes, making me feel somehow vindicated as he tries to thread the mast through the sail's luff sleeve. The main problem seems to be getting enough downhaul to the mast foot so the sail is properly trimmed, or stretched. Sitting on the pavement, he shows me how to brace the bottom of one foot against the base of the mast while pulling on the downhaul line. The trick, apparently, is to pull down on the line while you push against the mast base with your leg.

"From a standing position, pulling down on the line with your arms won't give you enough strength," he explains. Curious about the drill, a couple of surfers walk over. "What's that?" asks one.

"A windsurfer. Also called a sailboard."

"Like on TV?"

"There are more surf shops than schools in this island and you've never seen one of these?"

"Not in person."

It is already dark and time to cook dinner when we roll the sail up and push it into its black Da Kine sail bag. Carrying it, inside, horizontally, we duck under the contractors' ladders and scrape past Jimmy's lathe standing next to the fireplace. Jimmy Judge and his crew are meticulous in reconfiguring the shape of the house to match Gary's blueprints.

In the room where I was sleeping on the floor, a Brazilian white pine table with brass candlesticks has been set up along one wall. The rolled-up mattress stands against the opposite wall. My godfather, who taught me how to swim when I was eight years old, and whose family took care of Mindy when I went back to work, has been sleeping here for the past six weeks. If he hadn't been here to replace broken pipes, fix appliances, negotiate with different work crews, and help me scrape the remains of the Spaghetti Family into a final resting place, I would have lost it, totally, by now.

Ron, a Vietnam veteran who once worked for infomercial king Tony Robbins, has been powerwashing grease, tobacco, and bird dropping stains from the walls to prepare them for primer and paint. Grumbling about the amount of work involved, he throws a question into the general mayhem: "Don't you think Home Depot should have a hot list of people who are never allowed to buy home improvement supplies and paint? Like, whoever did this to your house should be number one on that list."

The guys are busy placing bets on whether the Gerry Adams I.R.A. Memorial Bunker on the front lawn will be history by Rosh Hashana, Halloween, or Thanksgiving when Jane arrives with a bottle of holy water from Lourdes. Were it not for my having visited Jane every summer for the past twenty years, I would never have known about this island. A single mother who has raised her two sons in this town, Jane signed on as one of the first seven women in the New York Police Department after working the night shift at ABC News while putting herself through journalism school. There's something about being the only two women awake in New York City at two in the morning, on a Tuesday in December that can forge a lifelong friendship.

That particular Tuesday had been a wild night in the control room where we were waiting for an Apollo space shot launch that was going to be delayed for at least three hours. Three Japanese television executives, who were buying very expensive satellite time for the launch shot, were getting antsy. The executive producer, whose general resting state could best be described as somewhere to the right of panic, sent Jane into my cubicle with a black and white, two-inch videotape of Harry Truman's obituary. Truman was dying, and the producer thought it would save the Japanese money if we used their satellite time to transmit the Truman obit; otherwise, they would be paying for what would, essentially, become dead air time. It wasn't a bad idea, but when I screened the tape I asked Jane to warn the producer not to use it. Soon, the phone rang. For a few seconds, all I could hear were sounds of someone hyperventilating. "What's wrong with the Truman obituary?" he managed to wheeze. "Does it have scratches?"

"No scratches, sir."

"Then send it, goddamn it."

"I don't think that's wise, sir."

"Wise? What are you, some kind of a wise ass?"

"No, sir."

"I'll send the goddamn thing myself."

A few minutes later, red-faced from rushing down the hall, the producer shuffled into the room, ordering the tape editor to cue up the Truman obituary.

"We are sending this," he said through clenched teeth.

I was just telling him, "I think you should check it out,

first, sir," when the local weatherman, Tex Antoine, stuck his face into our booth, muttering, "What are those fuckin' Nips doin' in our control room? Don't they know it's Pearl Harbor day?"

"Get him out of here!" the producer yelled. "Cue up the tape!"

"Check it first, sir. Please."

"Okay, okay. This better not be a joke, or you're history."

The reel started with file footage of Truman shaking hands, smiling with Bess, walking around the White House. Then the "Victory at Sea" music came up, followed by an ominous drumroll, under a wide shot of a mushroom cloud. "Hi–ro–shi–ma," the announcer chanted, in time to the drumbeats. "Na–ga–sa–ki....Possibly the most momentous decision of Truman's career...the bombing of Hiroshima and Nagasaki...saving countless thousands of American lives."

Were those tears or sweat running down his face?

"Thank you, thank you, thank you." Tears.

"No scratches, sir."

"No scratches."

In the middle of the night, Jane and I were still laughing. "No scratches, Laur."

"No scratches, Jane."

The barman at the White Horse Tavern probably thought we were nuts that night, until Jane introduced me as "that woman who lived across the street, the one whose toilet had broken on Thanksgiving Day."

"That was great for us," the barman grinned. "We must have had thirty people in here buying drinks and using the restrooms. We made so much money the night your toilet broke. Let me refill those drinks. On the house."

"Her toilet broke because she got called into work that day, and her friend Paul, who was supposed to cook the turkey, also got called into work. He's a chauffeur and he had to pick up Joanne Woodward's mother at Kennedy

Airport and drive her to Westport, Connecticut."

"Joanne Woodward's mother broke the toilet?"

"No. Paul's friend, who was missing a few cards, if you know what I mean—he got sent to her place to watch the turkey. Only the turkey caught fire and the house filled with smoke, then he grabbed hold of the chain to flush the toilet, and the box fell off the wall, and the water sprayed everywhere."

"No scratches, though."

"No scratches," we chant, still laughing as Jane pours holy water from Lourdes into the pit, with a couple of Hail Mary's for the plumbers. Tomorrow will be better. I always tell myself that, even when reality means unremitting heat, filth, construction headaches, and the arrival of bills with so many zeros they look like the gross national product of some Third World country. *Why did I do this?*

"Someone tell me: How is renovation like falling in love?" I ask.

When no one answers, I smile at my friends sitting around the table, grateful for each one. "Each time I do it, I swear I'll never do it again!"

Acadia National Park, Maine
July 22, 1996

Dreams are, if not a door, a hatch into other worlds…a journey of unthinkable dimensions…that make us…perceive the inconceivable.
—Carlos Castaneda[7]

Jungians say that, if you listen, an introvert will tell you what she's thinking. Extraverts, on the other hand, have a pipeline from the brain to the mouth. Since introverts spend more time in the inner world of concepts and ideas, than in the external world of people, activities, and things, you need to *ask* an introvert about what she is thinking.

Since extraverts live in the present, where do introverts spend most of their time? The past? The future? An introverted scientist, like Einstein, would hang out in the future. An historian, on the other hand, might well prefer to reside in the past, like the antique book collector who told me that he had a map in his head of 19th century London. He could never bear to go there today, because, he said, " I know that twentieth century London would break my heart. It could never live up to my imagination. " So, where *do* introverts live? For starters, not in the here–and–now. Nor do we bubble with crosstalk, preferring to drift together, in silence, unless called upon to speak.

As one of the Indiana Joans, Carol and I had last seen each other in the Amazon, where her amazing, hands–on diagnosis of the shaman's stroke probably saved everyone's head. Literally. Smiling shyly as she drives this hilly, coastal backcountry of silver birch and pine where she grew up, Carol slows down from time to time to check on her ten-year old son and his friend, asleep, in the back seat. Every hour or so, she says, "Great to see you." Or, "remember that giant bug near the shower?" And we laugh.

"Isn't it funny that we became such good friends because of our phobias?"

"Remember that giant bug?"

"I remember you screaming, 'Laurie, Laurie!' at two in the morning."

Laughter. "It looked like a manta ray or something."

"Then you almost killed us walking across that swinging bridge, " I remind her. "Right after we got down from that rock wall where the branch came off in my hand."

We laugh and laugh, reliving how she grabbed my hand when we got to the next hazard: a field of twelve-foot high grasses, said to harbor poisonous snakes. *"Manuelo, cuantos viveres quedan por aqui?"* ("Manuelo, how many snakes do you have around here?") I had asked the cook, who was leading four of us back to our camp. He had thrown his head back, laughing at the sky. *Bastante!* (Meaning "just enough.")

"Remember what happened on the bridge?"

"I'm the one with the height phobia. You were supposed to walk in front, with your hands behind you, so I could hold on," I remind her.

In the middle of the swinging bridge, Carol froze. No matter how I pushed gently, urging her to move, she stayed glued to the spot. Manuelo decided to rescue us. As he clomped onto the bridge, my worst nightmare was coming true. The bridge began to sway, uncontrollably, back and forth. "Go!" I screamed, pushing her to move before we got knocked off the swinging bridge into the sacred river, below.

Like a lot of things that were terrifying at the time, now, it seems hilarious.

We become quiet again.

"When did you get back?" she asks.

"Last week." After enduring six months of adventures in plumbing last year, I felt I was overdue for a break. On this second trip to the Ecuadoran rainforest, I was working as a back-up interpreter for Marina Nelson and Suzan Lang, mutual friends who lead women's expeditions to Ecuador. Proceeds from these trips are donated to Earth Dream Alliance, a not-for-profit foundation that buys tracts of cloud forest for preservation.

"How was it?"

"Well, you know." We smile. Carol and Suzan spent a month there, after the 1994 expedition, living with the family of a shaman who allegedly cures people of various illnesses with bee stings. She knows that I thought the guy looked like Charles Manson, but hey, it must work for some people, since they travel to him from all over the world so he can sting them with bees.

Quiet worlds, quiet thoughts. Images: snowcapped volcanoes and purple clouds, like cotton candy tufts on tropical trees. *Arutam.* The great force of life. "May the great force of life take care of you," the Indians say.

About half an hour drifts by. "Surreal," I say, in response to her earlier question.

"What is it that Don Juan tells Carlos Castaneda, 'how difficult it is for the mind to allow mindless possibilities to become real?' And 'new worlds exist…wrapped one around the other, like skins of an onion.'"[8]

"Sounds like the vine of death talking."[9]

"Once was enough." Something in my tone of voice makes her turn her head, sharply. "What happened, then?"

"Six weeks before Marina and Suzan invited me to accompany them, I dreamt that I was in a bamboo frame hut with a sloping thatched roof, looking up at the stars and the moon. There was something strange about the roof, because I could see the sky clearly, and at the same time, feel the bamboo slats underneath my back. The moist, rotting jungle smell was real. Then the dream became lucid: I was in the dream and observing that I was dreaming. The content became transpersonal, taking me outside any personal experience I had lived. Castaneda describes them as dreams in which you journey into a different reality."

"Sounds like fun."

"I'm not sure I'd call it that. Interesting as hell, though. In that bamboo frame hut, a fierce, older Indian woman arrived and began blowing cigar smoke all around me. I could smell the smoke, an important element in Native and South American cleansing ceremonies. I could feel small rocks and pebbles under my feet when I stood up."

"Then...?"

"Last month, when the three of us arrived in the rainforest, it felt strangely like home. When someone told us about *la abuelita*, the little grandmother, I wanted to find her. We had to slide down a steep mud cliff, ford a river, then climb up the other side."

"Don't these people ever live on main roads?"

"Near a strip mall where you can get insect repellent? No. When I climbed up the far riverbank, there was the open-frame, bamboo structure from my dream. Only half of the sloping roof was thatched, which explains how I dreamt I could see the sky and that thatched roof simultaneously. *La abuelita* lives nearby in a similar bamboo hut with a steep, thatched roof."

"And...?"

"Same woman who blew smoke in the dream! 'I expected you sooner,' she told me. 'Six weeks ago, I dreamt you were coming with your two friends. I wondered where you were, until this morning, when you showed up in my dream again.' Then she performed a cleansing ceremony in which she dusted each of us off with something that looks like a brush made of giant leaves. And yes, she blew cigar smoke all around my head, just like in the dream."

For a few minutes, neither of us speak. "Castaneda calls dreaming 'a vast, open-ended world...where the impossible might even be feasible,'" Carol says softly. "Why do you think you dreamt about her, and she about you? Didn't you have that vision of Kitiar on the highway? What do you think is going on?"

"Beats me. My brother calls me Princess X-Files."

"'The implication (is) not only that you will live those possibilities, but that one day, (you) will comprehend them.' Castaneda. *The Art of Dreaming*," she half-whispers.

"Comprehension would be a nice change. My rational self thinks this is all too weird," I comment, looking out the window. "I'm constantly arguing with myself. Mr. Spock, the voice of reason, says, 'This is not logical. It does not compute.' But how can you deny synchronicities[10] like dreaming about a healer in the rainforest before you knew you were going there, then meeting that same person to discover that she was dreaming about you at the same time?"

"How do you explain it?"

"I can't. But there's a good quote that sums it up. 'There are two excesses: to exclude reason, and to admit only reason.' Blaise Pascal."[11]

"So, why do you think your dreams crossed?"

"If I knew that, I'd have a key to one of the mysteries of the universe."

Carol smiles. "Haven't you interviewed scientists who study intuition? You must have a theory."

"The popular theories are based on physics, but honestly, I don't understand them. I think a lot of it is due to how we're wired up, genetically. Some people have musical ability, others are mathematical geniuses, or athletes, or brilliant in emotional or intuitive intelligence. Molecular biologists have found that every cell in the human body has an electromagnetic receptor, or receiver, as well as a chemical receptor. My theory? Intuition functions like a satellite dish in the brain. Maybe some people have receptor cells for certain electromagnetic frequencies."

"In this case, the dish picked up the Rainforest Channel."

"Something like that. I did run the "satellite dish in the brain" concept past the Dr. Roger Sperry a few years before he died. He won the Nobel Prize for discovering the left and right brains. 'That's a great theory, young lady,' he laughed. 'No one can ever prove you're wrong.'"

"None of this explains why you picked up transmissions from Kitiar, and now from *la abuelita*, before you had ever met them!"

"Probably just a coincidence." We look at each other, then burst out laughing.

"Does it really matter how it works? When you get in an airplane, do you have to understand the laws of thermodynamics, or is it enough to trust that they're stronger than the law of gravity for the duration of your flight? When you turn on your TV, do you have to understand how the picture and sound gets there?"

"You mean, those little people don't live in the box?" Carol jokes.

"Niels Bohr, a Nobel Prize winning physicist, tells about the time he was hammering a horseshoe over his door when a neighbor said, 'Surely, Dr. Bohr, you don't believe that thing really brings good luck?' And he answered, 'I understand it works whether I believe it or not.'"

"You've got a point. Did *la abuelita* tell you anything else?"

"She offered to train me in the art of dreaming."

"No way! Are you going?"

"She wants me to stay for a month. I can't leave Mindy for that long."

"There's always summer camp."

"I have clients and bills. You know, real life."

"You're hedging," Carol smiles. "What's the real reason?"

"Sometime near the end of the month, the Indians take you to a cave, somewhere in the jungle, and leave you there for a few days without food or water. *La abuelita's* people believe that nine generations of shamans have reincarnated into the bodies of their local anacondas. When they leave you in this cave, you're supposed to wait for an anaconda to show up."

"And..?"

"What do you mean, *and*..? Isn't that enough?"

"It's called a vision quest. Native Americans do it, too," she smiles. "The anaconda would come to acknowledge your learning. It would give you a message. Are you afraid of snakes, too?"

"Not as long as they're visiting other people."

"So, are you going to train with her?"

"Maybe I'll try a singles weekend at the Concord."

"What's that?"

"A joke."

The crisp blues of a late summer sky give way to a furry mist around Acadia's beige rock cliffs. The boys in the back seat wake up from their nap. We give them some water and ask if they're hungry.

Carol's son hits me with a stream of questions: "Are you the only lady with a purple windsurfer? Do you know any other old people who have one? When are you going to put it together? Can we try it?"

"There is no wind."

The boys look at each other, impressed. "How can you tell there's no wind?"

"We'll look for flagpoles as we drive around. If the flag moves, there's wind. Also, if the tree branches are moving."

"Cool." Meaning, it's a cool trick but, hey, no flags or trees have shown any sign of life for the past few hours.

Carol has just turned around to drive home, when her son taps me on the shoulder.

"Look at the trees over there!"

"You're right." Smiling to herself, Carol takes a sharp turn onto a one-lane road that ends at the southern tip of Acadia Lake. Parking on the righthand shoulder, she and the boys get out of the car, studying the tops of the trees.

About eight to twelve knots out of the southeast.

"Well?" she says. I think she means "I've been driving you around all afternoon looking for the damn wind, so put up or shut up."

The boys are jumping up and down, offering to carry the sailbag, mast, and boom to a clearing. For the first time since I bought this thing, I manage to put it all together. It takes about an hour and I'm still not sure it's going to hold together on the water, but, nonetheless, this is progress. Pulling on my wetsuit and neoprene boots, I step onto the water, positioning the sail, so that the wind whistles over my right shoulder. Entering that fine mist, the wind and I streak toward blue-green hills across the lake that looks so much like Loch Lomand that I half expect to see a mammoth bearded Scot in a tartan kilt appear between the trees on the far shore.

"What ever possessed you to do that?" Carol wonders, when I make it back. "I couldn't imagine going through all that work."

"Neither could I."

Having held onto the back of the board for a few rides, the boys are exuberant. "When can you come back and teach us?"

My friend is studying me and I can almost hear her thinking, "Yes, when?"

As we take the mast apart and the boys to carry both pieces to the car, something about this afternoon reminds me of the last chapter of *Zen and the Art of Motorcycle Maintenance*, a story about a man and his son, on the road.

"'Can I have a motorcycle when I get old enough?'

'If you take care of it.'

'Is it hard?'

'Not if you have the right attitudes. It's having the right attitudes that's hard.'

'Oh.'

After a while I see he is sitting down again. Then he says, 'Dad?'

'What?'

'Will I have the right attitudes?'

'I think so,' I say. 'I don't think that will be any problem at all.'

'And so we ride on and on and on....'" [12]

Southampton, NY
June 15, 1997

In the beginner's mind there are many possibilities, but in the expert's, there are few.
> −Shunryu Suzuki, *Zen Mind, Beginner's Mind* [13]

I'm going to get divorced from this "sport," if that's what it's called. Last week, the boom came apart, half a mile from shore. Swimming is good exercise, but the whole point of windsurfing is to be on the water, not in it. Having owned this gear for three years, I feel as dumb as if I bought myself a Porsche and never learned how to work the gears.

Giving up makes sense, in a way. Carol was right. It's all so much trouble, and I have no natural ability for it, whatsoever. *Sell the gear. You'll never be able to windsurf again. Give it up. Why make yourself miserable?* Then I remind myself that miserable is when you give up on something or someone you love. Imagining the unimaginable has gotten me this far. Replaying lost images of windsurfing during the years when I was so sick was a powerful source of motivation. A symbol of what doctors told me would be impossible became a personal metaphor for overcoming obstacles. Without those dreams, who knows, maybe I would be living a half-life, collecting Social Security. In the words of don Juan, "Freedom to fly off into that infinity out there...to dissolve; to lift off...is an adventure with no end, in which we risk our lives and much more for a few moments of something beyond words, beyond thoughts or feelings...To seek freedom is the only driving force I know." [14] To give up windsurfing would be to give up.

Knowing what I don't know is the next logical step. In Zen, it's called beginner's mind, "don't know" mind. To get there, I have to give up the idea that I know how to windsurf. Which shouldn't be hard. Since the formula for success is to have "great faith, great doubt, and great determination," theoretically, all things are possible. But I will need help.

Enter Jace. A six foot five, nineteen year-old Southampton boy, Jace moves with the liquid confidence of a young Mick Jagger. He has deepset blue eyes and a wicked smile but more than that, he reminds me of Tenzing. Tenzing Norgay Sherpa and Sir Edmund Hillary became the first men to reach the summit of Mount Everest on May 29, 1953.

"The only things that are important when climbing are determination and interest. That is all that counts," Tenzing told me when we met in 1978. Focused determination and interest are reflected in Jace's piercing blue eyes. His mouth smirks a little while he listens to a frenetic two-minute version of what is and isn't working. When I mention these journals, which I would like to use as the basis for a "Zen in the art of windsurfing" book, Jace's eyes narrow and he taps the side of his head. "Where's your book? In there?"

"No," I laugh. "It's handwritten, in a blue silk-covered notebook I've been carting around."

Nodding slowly, he takes in this information, then turns to observe Peconic Bay with a stillness that mirrors the calm water. Although I have not yet seen him move on the water, the efficiency of those few, minute movements contains an encyclopedia of knowledge I could spend the rest of my life trying to understand. It comes down to this: Jace Panebianco's DNA is way different from mine. He has mercury for spinal fluid. Ball bearings in the hip sockets. There is more than flexibility and poise at work here. He gives off quiet intelligence within the soul of an adventurer. In a flash of knowing, that comes from who knows where, I sense this young man from Southampton will accomplish something extraordinary.

"Not much wind," he says, to my relief and disappointment. No wind may mean no lesson, but it also means I can't embarrass myself. "Let's get a system," he continues.

"Why don't you lay your equipment over here and let me take a look at it?"

"No wonder." Watching Jace make a face at the boom makes me laugh. "For starters, it needs to be shorter. You're losing too much air at the clew."

As he walks through how each piece fits together, my mind begins to slows down. "Lately, all I've been doing is yanking my way to nowhere. And cursing."

"Rigging is the part that girls hate the most about wind-surfing," he observes, matter of factly. At least I'm not alone.

Like Gary did, two years ago, Jace demonstrates how to sit on the ground and push the mast foot with one leg while gripping the rigging tool, cleated on the downhaul line with one hand. It took Herrigel a year and a half before he learned how to hold the archery bow; even if I'm as slow a learner as I seem to be, *Zen in the Art of Archery* would recommend that I be patient, especially when starting over:

"'What must I do, then?' I asked thoughtfully.

'You must learn to wait properly.'

'And how does one learn that?'

'By letting go of yourself, leaving yourself and everything yours behind so decisively that nothing more is left of you but a purposeless tension.'

'So I must become purposeless—on purpose?' I heard myself asking.

'No pupil has ever asked me that, so I don't know the right answer.'

'And when do we begin these new exercises?'

'Wait until it is time.'* [15]

"There are good ships and bad ships and the difference between them has nothing to do with them being seaworthy. If I was fanciful I might say some had souls," writes Beryl Bainbridge in *The Birthday Boys*, her novel about Sir Robert Scott's failed expedition to the South Pole.[16] The

Xantos has a soul; that first sail, at Napeague, the connection was unmistakable.

Now, whatever it takes, I'm going to get *it* back.

Southampton, NY
June 29, 1997

The purpose of life, after all, is to live it, to taste experience to the utmost, to reach out eagerly and without fear for newer and richer experience.

–Eleanor Roosevelt

These words, from a former First Lady, reach to my spirit like a hand extended after a fall. Had I chosen to relearn how to play the piano, there would be scales and chords to practice, over and over again. But this instrument, a hand-held boom, hooked to a fifteen-foot fiberglass mast, plays different riffs—breeze, catching in the pocket of the sail; battens flipping into place, after a tack; seawater, whooshing, off each side of the bow. Baby step by baby step, forgotten movements and positions for hands and feet. In Zen, "to shift the attention to the soles of the feet...(may) seem to do little to penetrate stress and confusion...but such efforts are like pouring water into sand: although the water seems to disappear, over time the sand becomes more moist and workable."

"The way of the soul...leads to the water," Carl Jung has observed. There is something inherently healing in the ritual of driving thirty miles east on a straight two-lane road, a few yards from the edge of the Atlantic. At the highest point on a causeway bridge, a sweeping, wide-angle view of white mainsails reaching across the Great South Bay to Fire Island, opens a place within me, that, apparently, has been shut for years. In these seconds on top of the bridge, I "knock on the sky and listen to the sound."[17] Is it possible that everything up until now has opened this ability to wonder, in appreciation of light and majesty?

At the marker for the Long Island Pine Barrens, I slow

down, looking for signs of Kitiar. I'm glad he's safely home in the jungle with his red and yellow feather headband and his blowgun instead of floating around in search of souls in distress. Even with my insatiable love of adventure, one spiritual emergency is quite enough, thank you.

Adventure can take many forms. Falling in love is one, although it can also feel like falling off a cliff. Giving birth is yet another. If, in the course of a soul's journey through one lifetime, each of us gives birth to our selves, over and over, then what better way to celebrate renewal than through creating adventure? And what could be even more adventurous than excitement fed by streams of possibility? Juice. Buzz. Charge. Stoke. And, as Louis Armstrong alleged- ly once remarked about jazz, "If you have to ask what that is, you'll never get it."

John Ford, Jace's boss, and the owner of Windsurfing Hamptons, must be mainlining stoke. After years of wind-fed adrenaline, who wouldn't be, but John's happiness is dangerously contagious. Nobody leaves the store parking lot, with its orange, Sailworks sail, feeling less than high, I'm sure. Windsurfing Hamptons on route 27 is a relatively unknown landmark, although millions of people pass it every year on their way in and out of the Hamptons without recognizing the sloping, white shed on top of a small rise that is the nerve center for the best windsurfing resources in the New York metropolitan area: state of the art gear, wetsuits, drysuits, videos, and instruction.

"Great wind! Are you ready?" John asks every Sunday. Frankly, I'm terrified. Fear of humiliating myself, looking spastic, and not being able to get out of my own way make me wonder if I'm out of my mind. But one look at that knockout smile and I'm almost convinced this is worth it.

"Jace is already down at the beach," he says, every week, as part of the ritual, usually when I'm placing the receipt for today's lesson into my wallet.

It's then, when I look up, that I'm sunk. In that second

or two of eye contact, one thing is unmistakable: John Ford believes I can do it. He looks so sure, that my doubts feel ridiculous, even to me.

"Yup. Ready." I think I'm smiling.

"You can do it! Go out there and have fun!"

Across Montauk Highway, the back road winds past a saltwater pond, a children's camp, hiking paths, and acres of protected woodland, ending in a shiny crescent of white sand fronting the bay. After unloading the roofrack and trunk, I wave to Jace, who is generally kayaking alongside some other windsurfing student. Preparing to go through the steps of assembling the rig has become a less frantic exercise, although there's still anxiety about making a mistake. *"Anxiety,* the next gumption trap, is sort of the opposite of ego. You're so sure you'll do everything wrong, you're afraid to do anything at all...You jump to wild conclusions and build all kinds of errors...because of your own nervousness. These errors, when made, tend to confirm your original underestimation of yourself," observes Robert Pirsig in *Zen and the Art of Motorcycle Maintenance.*[18] I couldn't have said it any better myself.

Although I did not set out, consciously, to design a mental focusing technique for rigging, arranging gear on the ground and stepping around it, slowly, clockwise, starting from the bottom of the mast, helps me to pay attention to each piece, instead of worrying. Carefully, step by step, I unroll the sail, insert the mast foot, and begin to thread the tip of the mast through the luff sleeve. When I remember to angle the sail, downwind, there's less wrestling required.

Checking the places where the rig is most likely to come apart–downhaul, boom clamp, and outhaul–Jace nods approval. After fitting the mast foot onto the circular mount in the middle of the centerboard, the second phase of training gets underway. Carefully modeling what must be an ancient technique, I extend my arms, shoulder height so that my elbows are bent with palms facing forward. As unlikely as it seems, I am about to become a human wind-mill, turning carefully, 360 degrees, in the sand, so that my open palms catch the wind. Kneeling down, I then draw a line, in the sand, pointing to the wind. A second line, per-pendicular to the first one, points to the angle of sail.

At first, the windmill exercise reminds me of those odd-ball activities—egg candling, bed making, pet grooming,—that led to Girl Scout badges.[19] Then it became kind of cute, in a Sancho Panza sort of way. Now, I can see how this exer-cise works on several levels. First, it slows down the mind. Second, it focuses the mind on the wind. Third, it uses the whole body, so there is no cheating. You cannot "try" to do this, nor can you do it in a half-hearted way. Something about standing with your arms bent, palms forward, quiets you down right away. And quieting down is the most important part of mental preparation. As Tenzing put it, "Some people are excited when they get to the mountain, but it is better to be calm. Don't race. The mountain is not going anywhere."

Since the sea is not going anywhere, either, Tenzing's words hold equal relevance here. After last year's ill-fated Everest expedition in which eighteen climbers were killed, Tenzing's son, Jamling, said, "My father often saying that the mountain gave him great strength."[20] Jace and I must get our strength from the sea. I can't help thinking that Tenzing would find a certain similarity with this young man who, at the age of twelve, was taught windsurfing by his father, Richard, much the same way that Tenzing passed on his love of the mountains to Jamling.

Like climbers who acclimate at different altitudes, Jace and I are starting to get to know each other out here, in the middle of the water. His twin sister, Nova, is a biologist in Nepal, his mom is an accomplished artist, and his father, a local doctor. Our most important talks are about our dreams. Jace wants to compete on the pro circuit and pit his skill against Hawaiian waves the size of buildings. For my part, I joke about being a single mother who dreams of chasing across the water again in higher winds. This probably doesn't seem like a dream-quality ambition to anyone who moves as naturally on water as he does on land. But it would be a huge accomplishment for me. As we talk, there's no question that I've been handicapped, not simply by asthma and chronic fatigue but also by lower physical resilience due to aging and a challenging self-image as a klutzy girl nicknamed "Dumbo." The klutziness is easy to joke about, now, but it's my secret sore point. I would never say so out loud but in my darker moments, my most disappointing relationship is with myself.

"I fall, I stand still...I trudge on, I gain a little...I get more eager...every struggle is a victory," wrote Hellen Keller, compared to whom, my challenges are purely metaphorical. But isn't this ongoing journey to a place between light and water a respectful metaphor for breathing life into a dream and making it real?

It must be difficult for someone who is naturally athletic to understand someone like me, especially when I get emotional over mistakes that are, well, technical. Wasn't it Thomas Edison who said that he hadn't *failed* to develop a working filament for a light bulb 3,999 times; rather, he had *discovered* 3,999 ways not to make a working filament? And isn't that what I tell my students? A mistake in windsurfing hardly makes me an idiot nor does it bear any reflection on what matters most–integrity and kindness, in general; being a great mom and a great friend. In the end, whether I windsurf or not affects nobody's life, one way or another. To keep it in perspective: a ten-second slip, and you fall in the water. A ten-second slip in brain surgery, and you've killed someone.

"What's that look on your face?" Jace is as quick to perceive lightning changes in emotion as he is to notice a

214

minute hand misplacement on the boom.

"How did I get so far in life with so little confidence?"

For a second, he looks surprised. Then he smiles, "You're doing great. Move into the boom, flex your hips, then step back. And pay attention to the uphaul," he reminds me. The uphaul is the braided rope I am still using to hoist the sail instead of crouching in the water and positioning the sail across the board so that it hoists me.

"That's easy for you to say." When you're twenty, you believe anything is possible. Still, something about Jace's optimism makes me wonder: Is anything possible because you believe it, or is it really true that anything *is* possible? Before giving it another shot, I take a good, long look, scanning his expression for signs of doubt. But his eyes lock onto mine and that expression of confidence becomes my emotional uphaul.

Southampton, NY
July 1, 1997

Zen and raising a child may seem like unrelated activities.
      −John Daido Loori[21]

Q: How is life as a self-employed single mom like wind-surfing?
A: It's a balancing act and an ongoing, simultaneous effort to stay afloat.

Juggling three careers−as a therapist, consultant, and occasional author−so that I can work at home, three days a week, most of the time, is an art unto itself.

My original fantasy about working at home was born in the middle of the newsroom during a blizzard. Instead of standing in a control room with a phone in each ear, coordinating multiple satellite feeds of snowstorms, I'd be home baking brownies, watching children build a snow-man in the yard. We've had quite a few blizzards since then and several dozen trays of brownies but like many fan-tasies, the "mommy in the kitchen" scenario hasn't quite panned out as expected.

"Why can't you be a regular mommy?" I hear this a lot.

Just because the refrigerator holds half a package of hot dog rolls, an empty carton of Tropicana Original orange juice, seventeen clear plastic packets of Chinese duck sauce, and five rolls of ASA 100 Sensia film, there's no need to complain. We have not retreated to the Spaghetti-Oh option and there's always a choice between take-out and delivery. One of Neil's running jokes had something to do with my not being able to cook, although after fifteen years of mar-riage, cooking is one of two domestic skills I learned well.

In real time, working at home with a child running in

and out of your workroom, has its own brand of hazards.

"Sarah broke the fishtank!" Mindy's S.O.S during a radio interview went out live across five Western states. The talk show host had introduced me: "Here, in our studio, in Salt Lake City." His horrified reaction went out all over Utah, Nevada, Wyoming, Colorado, and a corner of Idaho! Two weeks later, when we tagged around the west on a mommy-daughter book tour, a lady remembered. "Whatever happened to your fish tank, dear?" she asked my five-year old.

On the phone with a magazine editor, in a crunch deadline for a story on recovering from sports injuries, a scream from downstairs made me drop everything. It was only a twisted ankle but deadlines go out the window when your child needs emergency x-rays. Not only deadlines fly out the window. My so-called professional image has disappeared from view more times than Houdini. Like this morning, when bloodcurdling screams and explosions of tears interrupted a telephone planning session with a client from the Federal Reserve Bank. "How do I get the bananas out of my hair, Mommy?"

After reading, or rather, ingesting a story in *Seventeen*, about using fresh fruits and vegetables as cosmetics, Mindy had mashed bananas into her long hair with a fork!

"My face once turned green from an avocado face wash I read about in *Seventeen*!" On the other end of the phone, my client, who is also a mom, confessed, making us all laugh.

"Honey, I think you're supposed to puree the bananas in a blender before you shampoo them in." Patiently, after I've located and retrieved every visible chunk of banana, she is shampooed and getting psyched about this afternoon, when she'll take her first windsurfing lesson. Well, I'm psyched.

"You were out windsurfing before, only I didn't know I was pregnant."

"So what?" At a certain point in parenting, no matter what you say or do, you're screwed. Like now. If only there was some kind of weekend orphanage program, where you could check-in your kid from Friday night through Sunday so she would appreciate you on Monday morning.

From the top of the Captree bridge, I point out a sail-boat, heeled on a reach.

"Big deal."

"This is going to be fun." No comment. "Looks like the wind's out of the south, about eight knots."

Suddenly curious, she turns to look at me. "How do you know?" Actually, what she says is, "How would *you* know?" Still, it makes me smile to show my daughter how to read a flag for wind direction and general speed. Taking this in, she nods, as if I have finally said something worthwhile.

When we arrive at the store, it seems that I'm not the only one psyched about her first lesson. "All you have to do is have fun!" John's smile says it all.

Involved in the rhythm of rigging the Xantos, out of the corner of my eye, I see her standing on the simulator, hold-ing the boom as if she was born with it in her hands. When I pick up my head, a few minutes later, she is about five yards offshore, with Seth Korbin, Jace's partner, paddling alongside in a kayak. Of course. Her father had it, too. Rugby, surfing, and ocean swimming came naturally to him. New research shows that people with athletic ability, called "kinesthetic intelligence," may be wired up different-ly in the basal ganglia and cerebellum, those sections of the brain that regulate timing, movement, and balance. I'm simply glad she has her father's coordination instead of mine and I'm proud that she's taking to the water, but for a second or two, a hint of jealousy flares up, like seaweed washed in by the tide.

When it's my turn, it's deja vu all over again, as Yogi Berra would say. It's impossible to stand and the harness lines are too high, so that every attempt to hook onto the boom lines launches me into the water. Without a wetsuit, my shins and knees are scraped and bleeding after an hour. My arms are black and blue.

"The drunk falls from the cart but is not hurt.
You throw hesitation aside but look stupid.
To be truly uninhibited is a rare grace." [22]

"It's just a surfboard and a sail," she points out, later, with all the philosophical correctness of a twelve year old. "Why are you so angry?"

"Because my body won't do what I tell it to. More important, how did you like it?"

She smiles with her eyes, and her happiness, as always, makes my day.

Southampton, NY
August 3, 1997

When you meet a master swordsman, show him your sword. When you meet a man who is not a poet, do not show him your poem.

–Lin-Chi [23]

This morning, a struggle with depression. Or is it malaise? Maybe I should stay home and do the paperwork I have been avoiding. After two days of presenting workshops at a conference in Sarasota, there was the madness of changing planes in Atlanta. We landed at La Guardia at midnight, then it was an hour's drive home. I couldn't stop thinking about the young woman who came up to me, during a break to thank me for my presentation. "I want to be like you when I grow up," she said. "But I have a feeling I don't want to go through whatever you had to go through to be you." Tomorrow, it's back to the platform, again; this time, at the Federal Reserve Bank. After seven years of giving workshops and seminars and being graded by the people who attend them, standing in front of an audience is a continual source of amazement, perhaps because that old public speaking phobia always feels as if it's simmering below the surface, rather like volcanic lava. Every night before, during, and after a lecture or seminar brings on rampant insomnia. My head reels with endless questions that could potentially trip me up. Performance work demands a lot of energy, nonstop. Which is why, for relaxation, I decide to take up an equally unforgiving activity. Why can't I just walk down the block and read a book on the beach?

Now this computer is acting weird. Why can't these things work like refrigerators? All you have to do with a refrigerator is plug it in. It doesn't need special programming for milk or beer or lettuce. It knows just what to do. When you open the door, it never beeps, "Access denied. Cannot read Shelf C." A refrigerator never refuses to let you retrieve the cottage cheese because you forgot to save Ben and Jerry before you shut the door.

As a nineteenth century mind in the twentieth century, I resent being so dependent on machines. Which probably explains the nontechnical appeal of winging it to the horizon, hanging on to a pole attached to a floating plank.

"Why don't you practice using your harness?" Robert calls out across the water from the Mistral Equipe which he and his wife Peggy are using as a float to keep cool. The organizers of the Peconic Bay Marine Conservation Society, Robert and Peggy Gans have been cheering me on all summer. Despite their enthusiasm today, there's hardly any wind. After the ritual 360-degree impersonation of a human windmill, the only thing moving is sweat. Mine, to be precise. Which is a great excuse for walking into the water, to float upside down in a yoga posture called "the bow." In fact, this is exactly what I was doing a few days ago, in the hotel swimming pool, before the conference...

"You should really oil that wheel on your suitcase."

Flipping over, to tread water, I look around to see who's speaking. A sandy-haired, freckled man with a round face moves from his beach chair to the edge of the pool.

"Are you talking to me?"

"You're the one with that squeaky wheel, right?"

"Yes?"

"Why don't you oil it?"

"It doesn't bother me."

When he smiles, his upper incisors look peculiarly sharp.

"You were married for a long time. Your husband didn't understand you," he continues. "He wasn't a bad guy, really, but after awhile there was nothing between you. Even so, both of you were very responsible, caring parents and it was very difficult to separate. Now, you work very, very hard. What is it that you do, exactly?"

"I go to the country club, get my nails done, and yell at my servants."

There's something odd–or is it vaguely menacing–about this conversation. Who is this person? If he knows so much about the intimate details of my marriage, wouldn't he know what I do for a living? He looks quickly at my hands without looking as if he's looking. Which means that, at least for a second, he believed I had servants.

"Why do you work so hard?"

"The money fairy doesn't know where I live yet. Who are you, anyway?"

His eyes are hidden behind the sunglasses, and his mouth curls when he smirks, "And you haven't had great luck with men."

Uh-oh. Who the hell is this guy? And why do they always find me? I suddenly remember being on the picket line, outside CBS headquarters, during the Writers' Guild Strike. That funny old man in the mustard–stained brown coat started walking in step with me, chanting, "I saw Morley Safer in an elevator once. I saw Morley Safer in an elevator once."

Right behind me, the sports producer started hissing, "You made eye contact. You made eye contact."

"I did not. I did not."

The old guy in the brown coat continued, "I saw Morely Safer in an elevator once." For four hours!

Then there was the bow–legged Mexican, with his cardboard suitcase tied with string, and his mesh bag of onions, who accosted me in Indianapolis airport. "Here." He shoved a blue, airmail envelope at me, pointed to a scrawled phone number, and said, "Please?" When I dialed, of course, the number was out of service.

"*No funciona,*" I told him. His guardian angel must have pointed to me because I was probably the only person for a hundred miles who spoke his language. When I told him the phone number was out of order, the little fellow started to cry. He turned the envelope over, so I could see the address.

"*Mi amigo,*" he pointed. "*Mi amigo me espera.*" My friend is waiting for me. Sure. In Minneapolis, according to the return address.

"*Estamos en Indianapolis,*" I explained, pointing to the return address. "*Es otro apolis!*" Yes, this is a different Apolis altogether. How had he gotten to the wrong Apolis? A friend in California had bought his ticket. No, he didn't have enough money to get another flight. How long would it take him to drive to Minneapolis? Let's see: Indiana, Ohio, Illinois, Wisconsin, Minnesota—that's five states. Just like on Sesame Street, now, let's do it in Spanish. So, we traipsed, first to the Hertz desk, where, no, the little guy didn't have a license or a credit card; then, to the ground transportation center, a twenty minute walk, during which we must have looked like Mutt and Jeff to everyone we passed; me, standing almost six feet tall, in heels, in a short skirt, and blazer, trailed by Senor Crescencio Garcia and his mysterious bag of onions. They always find me. And, no, I never make eye contact.

Now, every alarm bell in every cell is going off and I know I should grab my towel and get gone. But I am relentlessly curious, especially when it comes to intuition. How does it work? Why do some people have more of it than others? I have my theories, and over the years, I get more skeptical about people who claim to be intuitive or psychic. I'm not sure whether this guy is some kind of clairvoyant show-off, or if he's a snoop who has, for some bizarre reason, investigated my marital history. Either way, it's pretty creepy, even for Princess X-Files.

"How do you know that?"

He smiles again. He really needs to see a dentist about filing those bizarro teeth.

"Tacit data."

"Tacit data? Cool." What are the chances of him talking to someone who knows anything at all about tacit data? "Isn't that the unconscious absorption of information? It's how we learn the rules of syntax when we learn our native language, so that instead of pointing, and grunting 'me-cookie,' we learn how to say, 'May I please have a cookie?' No one teaches babies how to do that. They learn through tacit data. Right?"

"You are good. But you never got over a man who disappointed you. He was the one you really loved."

I should have left right then. "Tell me. How do you do that?"

"Your face."

"Oh, right. Just like that."

"Just like that. Tacit data. Would you like me to tell you more? You get very lonely sometimes."

"I'm never as lonely as I used to be when I woke up next to my ex-husband and we were both a thousand miles away. That was real loneliness. Besides, who doesn't get lonely, at times?"

"But you never got over the other one, did you?"

"Who are you?"

"Ed Ridder. And you? What's your name?" As he holds out a freckled hand, with short, square fingers, I notice he's wearing a class ring with black onyx. I'm not about to take his hand or give him my name. Chances are, he already has it. Either he has bribed the desk clerk or he's following me. If he's bribed the desk clerk, then he's already had run my name through a computer.

"Are you having me followed? Am I under investigation for something?"

He laughed. "You're good. No, this is just a personal hobby of mine."

"What is?"

"Following my intuition."

"And what does it tell you?"

"You're one of us."

"Right." Do I have a light over my head, like a taxi, flashing "WEIRDO?"

"You know."

"No."

"Intelligence."

"Maybe you can answer a question for me. Why is it that whenever I give a lecture, one of you guys comes up to me after everyone has left, to half-whisper, 'I'm in intelligence.' D.I.A. Navy Seals. Vietnam operatives. Why me?"

Either he's strangely quiet or quietly strange. Or both.

"They must have thought you were one of us. I did."

"Me? Why?"

"It's the way you look us straight in the eye. We're trained to do that. It sets us apart from everyone else. Obviously, you've had some kind of advanced mental training."

"You're kidding, right?"

"Of course not." Watching him carefully, as he removes his sunglasses, I feel like Clarice Starling being chatted up by Hannibal Lecter. "You'd be very good in this line of work."

"What line is that, sir? Assassin?"

"We prefer the term 'contract players.'" *Where is Scully, now that I need her? And what's that strange sound in my chest?* "After two years in our training center, you would be able to go out and kill anyone, when you're told."

"Thanks for the job offer. I'm flattered." Although I can't see his eyes, we're locked in a staring contest. "I really don't think I'd be very good at this line of work, sir. You see, I have a very strong belief that killing people is not okay."

"What if we could have murdered Adolf Hitler in 1938?" Nice try, you psychopathic little creep. "What if you were sitting in the control room with God, watching a satellite feed of your men murdering Adolf Hitler? What would God say?"

He fidgets on the edge of the pool. I seem to be making him nervous. "Well, the Old Testament God would be angry. The Christian God would be merciful. The native Americans would see God in nature."

There is a point in any staring contest where it starts to feel like indian wrestling. "What do you think God would say?" he asks.

"How would I know? Maybe God sees us as little points on a map, like some cosmic general. If God sees past, present, and future, and all of our past and future lives, and individual and collective karma, then who knows? God wouldn't be thinking like a human being. When you start killing people, that's playing God."

Now, in the full Florida sun, his eyes change color, from light hazel to cornflower blue, shiny like a glass marble. It gives me the chills, like maybe I'm in the presence of something that's not entirely human. "You would say that," he mutters.

"This is a very strange conversation to have with someone I just met. It's very invasive. I should have left twenty minutes ago, but I'm too curious for my own good."
As I stand up, he grabs my arm.

"Don't leave. You have beautiful eyes. Let me walk you to the elevator."

"Leave me alone." Staring into his strange vacuum eyes, I wonder if evil is, like someone once said, essentially mundane, a chit of paper like a parking ticket scrawled with bureaucratic codes that mean nothing to anyone, really, except the person getting killed. Death by memo.

I've almost reached the door when he calls out, "Have you seen them in the airports?"

"Huh?"

"Take a look, next time. They're watching you."

"Sure. 'Oh, look, she's going to Cleveland! No, it's Chicago!' Don't you people have real work to do, like catching terrorists?" Slamming the door behind me, I run through the hall, to the elevator. Remember that old 60s joke? Just because you're paranoid doesn't mean they're not out to get you!

A whisp of wind. Swim back. Unload the board, sail, boom, mast, and rigging. Carry the board to the waterline. Lay out the sail. Assemble the mast. Where's the universal? I washed it last week. Usually I put it back in the antique, yellow mesh bag that says "URGENT CBS NEWSFILM" but it's not here. Not in the trunk. Nowhere inside the car. Damn. I must have left it on the dryer near the kitchen. The one piece that holds everything together!

Skydivers drop through light fog as I head west into the glare of a forgotten afternoon. My body feels achey and heavy. My head throbs in the heat. I feel isolated and hot, frustrated and exhausted. Just one of those days when nothing seems to hang together. Least of all, me.

Southampton, NY
August 15, 1997

It is the full involvement of flow, rather than happiness, that makes for excellence in life.

                                             –Mihal Csikszentmihalyi, Ph.D.[24]

Our ongoing dialogue concerns this question of flow, the "complete immersion in an experience...a sense of effortless action (you) feel in moments that stand out as the best in (your) life." What is it? How do you get and maintain it? What's different about flow and non-flow? Is the art of Zen about finding flow? If it is effortless, like love, then it can't be found.

I've had many more non-flow than flow sessions, whereas Jace's seamless transitions on water look like he's never out of flow. Csikstentmihalyi, the guru of flow: "...your full attention is focused on the movements of your body...There is no room in your awareness for conflicts or contradictions; you know that a distracting thought or emotion might get you buried face down...(This) is so perfect that you want it to last forever."[25]

Hitting a flow state after practicing an activity, sport, or movement, methodically, for years can become the kind of transforming event that forms a point of reference for the future. Take Herrigel: "Bow, arrow, goal and ego, all melt into one another, so that I can no longer separate them. And even the need to separate has gone. For as soon as I take the bow and shoot, everything becomes so clear and straightforward and so ridiculously simple..."[26]

Gusting 10 to 15 out of the southwest, this wind makes me nervous. Looking terrifically organized, Jace rigs a pink Simmer 4.5 meter sail and ties purple and yellow lines to a short aluminum boom. Observing his steel blue eyes locked on the wind patterns, like Captain Jean-Luc Picard studies the galaxy from the bridge of the Starship Enterprise, I wonder if he's thinking it's too strong for today's lesson.

"We'll practice using the harness and tacking. Be stubborn when you tack. Hold your hands together and pull the sail all the way back. Go suit up."

This little sail scoops wind as we shoot offshore towards the Shinnecock Hills. Jace windsurfs a few yards to starboard on a Bic Veloce, one of this summer's hot sellers.

"Put pressure on the rail. Use the balls of your feet. The balls, not the heel!" he hollers. *Balls. Heels. Who cares?* I think. *When in the world did I ever think about my feet?*

It's almost impossible to coordinate where to stand on moving water with hand positions and the flashy, pelvic thrust-squat that hooks you to the boom line, especially when the wind is pushing so fast from behind that everything around you is a blur. Adrenaline filters out hesitation. My brain becomes a zoom lens that magnifies each high-speed frame of life. Time encapsulates itself into microsecond units of performance: The harness hook grabs the line, I push off the rail, counterbalancing the sail and all the vertebrae align, relieving pressure in my shoulders and back. Contoured to the water, the edge of time expands to the horizon. And beyond. E-words, missing for nearly a decade, cascade over each other: ecstasy, excitement, energy, excellence, exhilaration.

For five minutes, that is. "It's Ascension Day," I call out from the water. "If you go into the ocean three times, you will be healed. Do you think it counts if you fall in?"

Wacko. I bet that's what he really thinks. If only you could press a button on a remote control and see a cartoon bubble over someone's head, so that you'd know, for sure. He's giving me that compressed intelligence look: simultaneously quizzical, amused, objective. Pushing back up, onto the board, I confront him. "You've got that Jace expression again."

"Do you know what you just did?"

"Hooked in!"

"That was great. No, it's not what I meant, though. What happened to your feet?"

After all that, he wants me to remember my feet? "Huh?"

"That's what I mean."

Sometimes it strikes me that an observer who overheard these terse exchanges bordering on the non-sequitur would wonder how Jace and I understand each other. But nuance and syntax come through via some mysterious Vulcan mind meld. In Zen, the mind-to-mind connection between master and student can become so seamless that "communication seem(s) like the internal dialogue of a single person." As a coach whose intellectual empathy skills easily match his athletic talent, Jace mentally puts himself in my position in order to explain how to correct a movement, hopefully in time to prevent a fall. This mental approach to windsurfing is teaching me, again, that it is okay to make mistakes. It is even okay to make mistakes in front of someone else. Falling is part of the flow of learning, moment by moment, with no right or wrong.

"My feet keep getting caught on each other. My hands find their way along the boom, just fine."

He laughs, "I remember when I was at that stage."

"You're just being nice."

Jace is getting at a missing step: linking the internal visual images of what needs to happen into a smooth, confident series of movements. In *Sacred Hoops: Spiritual Lessons of a Hardwood Warrior*, Phil Jackson, the L.A. Lakers coach who teaches his players Zen meditation, describes the process: "A lot of times players can visualize the necessary change, hear what is needed, but their bodily reactions can't adjust. Instincts (habits) are hard to break, players (must go) through the physical act of making the adjustment until the repetition replaces the instinct. It takes time."[27]

Part of me knows what to do and the other part can't seem to catch up. My feet must be learning disabled.

"Keep your butt in. Release that death grip on the boom. Wiggle your fingers!"

With each micro adjustment, it's easier to finesse the swell. The wind hits the sail's center of effort. We plane, picking up speed until sky and bay become a white blur and the molecules in my body must be vibrating at a higher speed, like in *Star Trek*, where they beam you up. This is it! Buzz. Charge. Juice. Stoke. Flow.

"That's a phenomenal grin," Jace has to shout for his voice to carry, in the screaming wind. "What are you thinking?"

Feathery rays of white light fan down from the back of a cumulus fan, backlighting the sky, teasing the outer reaches of Peconic Bay. Breath by breath. Step by step. Hand over hand. Mind over mind. Soundbites: Irreversible lung damage...Social Security...disabled for life. From the edge of survival to right here, right now. This "impossible" triumph.

"I'm thinking about that doctor who said I'd be lucky if I could walk up stairs!"

Southampton, NY
August 31, 1997

When you understand one thing through and through, you understand everything.

−Shunryu Suzuki[28]

Middle of the night sounds: cicada concertos, a fishing boat making its way along the Intracoastal, the harmony of soprano and tenor wind chimes.

"There's no news on TV, Mommy," Mindy said last week.

A metaphoric pinch of salt over one's shoulder: "Don't say that, honey. It tempts a news god."

Old superstitions die hard: a news god smoldering in the collective unconscious with a latent antipathy to an absence of disaster. A sudden death, like Princess Diana's, shatters illusions of predictability.

"The voices of ghosts are so familiar,
They whisper to me every day.
You, so young and rich,
Make assumptions with absolute assurance." [29]

Ghosts most personal: a young woman, married to a man who needs but does not love her, visibly pregnant, rushing some celebrity's obituary through a corridor filled with soap opera props, pushing through the door of the control room just in time to make air. Friends checking in, "Remember that time...?" And, "No, she wasn't in the 'ghoul pool.'" No obituary in the can, ready to air for someone so young. Ghosts most personal viewed through the lens of Tao: "In life, where so few things are stable enough to serve as true reference points, death is one of our few assurances...No one knows death definitively. The closest we may come is a supposed Near–Death Experience, which, by definition, cannot be death itself...There is only one universal goal, a gracious death with no regrets."[30]

A Chinese philosophy that dates back to the Zhou dynasty (around 300 BC), the Tao, or Way through adversity is not through confrontation or blaming forces outside or within ourselves. In the past few months, personal questions about preconceived limitations have morphed into generic themes: How do we, as human beings, develop and incubate fears and what we can do to overcome them? If fear is like a wall that blocks a view of ourselves so that we fail to see our positive options, then how can we get over that wall and become fearless? Is it possible to absorb traits like confidence, optimism, talent, and courage through empathic osmosis?

This time spent aligning with water and wind has given me more than I expected. Not only have I learned a few basic physical and technical windsurfing skills, I have also challenged my losses, redirected my ability to learn, and rediscovered confidence. For the first time in ten years, I am awake. Body, mind and soul present and accounted for. In giving me a range of qualities to model—focus, determination, patience, and being in the moment—Jace has done a lot to rewire my vulnerable belief system. In a few days, he leaves for Maui to do something few people ever attempt: live his dream. Maybe that's the answer to my own line of questioning: To become fearless, we need to live our dreams.

"Think big! Who ever heard of Alexander the Average?" I call across the water as he carves a freestyle jibe.

"Let's review your work. Your goals were to become self-sufficient in rigging, and to use the harness."

"Compared to 1986, when I came down with chronic fatigue syndrome and stopped windsurfing, I've met and gone beyond my goals. Especially when you consider that the Xantos is, technically, a shortboard."

"You've also gotten pretty good at hooking in and out."

"Thanks to you."

Taking that one with a smile, tilting his head slightly to one side, Jace says, "For the future, it helps to be aware of your purpose, or goal, even if you're just going out to have fun."

"Phil Jackson tells his players it's about waking up, becoming alert and awake for each moment."

"Sounds good."

We have arrived at a tricky patch of swells where I usually fall in, but this time, pushing down on the rig keeps it stable.

"Nice save. Now, hook in! Relax your grip! Watch the surface of the water. When it starts to ripple, there's wind coming in. Now tack!"

Tacking this no-nose board is problematic since it has no weight in the bow. Placing a foot in front of the mast, while raking the rig to stern will sink it fast. I'm not quick enough to jump around the front of the mast but my success ratio is up to 50 percent, so I'm not complaining.

"Wind coming up! Hook in, but don't count on it!"

"Sounds like my last boyfriend!" Within seconds, a lull, followed by another gust tips me into the water. Counting ten breaths, I pull myself back up, one knee on either side of the rig; from here, into a standing position, pulling the uphaul, hand over hand, then crossing over, so my right hand grabs the front end of the boom. A new edge: hooked in, hiked out. Breathing in seafoam kicked up from the froth of the board's cutting wake.

"Do you now understand," the Master asked...one day after a particularly good shot, "what I mean by 'It shoots,' 'It hits'?"[31]

It makes sense now. At least until I hit a slopy stretch of water, where I catapult, face first, into the boom.

"What were you thinking about?" the teacher asks, sweeping close by, to check that I'm all right. "I could see your thoughts change."

A flash frame of Neil, backlit by morning sun, his eyes bright with gentle affection, reaching across a table to hold my hand. His voice: "When we're together..."

Tears, saltier than the bay, run down, into my mouth. STUG: Sudden Temporary Upsurge of Grief. *Damn. I thought I was over all that.* Trying to choke back the sound of crying. This is so embarrassing. I don't let people see me cry, especially people I don't know. "I don't want to talk about it."

With sun in his face, Jace watches me like a sea hawk eyeing prey that's trying to get away. "Pow-wow?"

"No. Thanks." I shake my head, pull myself back up, ready to uphaul.

Jace is sitting on the Veloce, patting the space next to him. "No. Thanks."

Damn. I think he's going to outstare me. "Well..."

It's hard to get going, but like Forrest Gump at that bus stop, sitting here on the sailboard, with Jace's arm around my shoulder, the story spills into the sea. Yes, I've been to therapy. Of course, I've gone on dates. Well, only two. One, a Park Avenue architect, straight out of Woody Allen, had a phobia of leaving Manhattan. I diagnosed "Manhattanitis" when he had a panic attack on the Brooklyn Bridge. The next one...well, my heart's not in it, really. I'm still not over Neil, even though someone who can turn on you, on a dime, and walk out of the life you had together with no explanation, is...is...

"The thing is, I'm not good at relationships. I'm too naive, or something."

The Tao says to "create the poetry of your life with toughness and determination," but, having fallen in the water, again, with my mouth and eyes full of salt water, it feels like I can't punch my way out of a paper bag. Even so, I've come to feel that it's better to have broken and healed a few times than to believe that you will never get hurt. From right now, looking around my universe with the eyes of the sea, how can I possibly be sad when a late afternoon sun is silvercoating life with sparkles, everywhere, the essence of love itself?

Oak Beach, NY
October 14, 1997

The time to contemplate the ending is before the ending.

—Deng Ming-Dao[32]

"It's all in the knots," as K. loved to tell me, laughing. A successful comedienne, K. moonlights as a phone sex dominatrix. "You have to know your knots, or the callers know you aren't really Mistress Dominique."

Bizarre comparisons to S&M notwithstanding, on a bad day, rigging can be torture. Even on a good day, "it's all in the knots." Tying harness lines to the boom. Half hitches to secure the uphaul line to the mast foot. Sitting, pushing the heel of my right foot against the mast foot while pulling in, hard, on the downhaul with my right hand, cleating in the clew. Fingers getting stuck. Nails getting broken.

"You might want to try being a girl," Ellen Cottone, a make-up artist at Cablevision smirked the other day when I was making an appearance on a local talk show. She stopped spongeing make-up long enough to let me see that she was looking at my godawful fingernails.

"Windsurfing." Why is this embarrassing?

"Get a life, Laurie. At least, try acrylic tips."

At the rate they would break out here, it could cost me over one hundred dollars a month to maintain acrylic nails. After a year, I could have bought a new windsurfer with that $1200. On the other hand, orange acrylic nails would accessorize these orange and purple striped Okespor neoprene boots. "How would they go with my blue velvet evening gown?" I asked John when I tried them on last week. I can tell from his expression, that he's not one hundred percent sure I'm joking.

Sapphire ice is the color of this afternoon. Quietly,

evenly, moving each piece into position: sail onto mast, pulley hook into sail grommet, boom clamp to mast, out-haul line to clew. Dune brush, edged in subtle maroons and ochres, punctuates the shoreline. Air sparkles, breathing slows, unconsciously in rhythm with the sea. This morning's southeaster makes this one of the last "warm enough" days. Tomorrow, a cold front will ship down from Canada, bringing summer's curtain down. Next act: autumn.

A note on the kitchen counter for her to see, when she gets home from school: "Back at 3:30. Love U, Mommy."

Flags along the oceanfront: around 15 knots. Studying the water's surface: incoming chop. Nothing serious. Satisfaction. Knowing I can do this.

"It's all in the knots." Checking the 5.7 sail. Nice job. I can always come back in and rig down, to a 4.6 meter sail if I need to. Wetsuit. Orange and purple Okespor boots. Harness. After carrying the Xantos and the rig to the water's edge, I leave a mesh bag with a pair of shorts, my car keys, and Proventil inhaler (just in case), behind a stand of gold-enrod on a low dune.

Within seconds I'm hooked in, moving back on the board, noticing that there seems to be a lot more room to move around back here after a two-day clinic in Southampton with *Wind Surfing* magazine's technical editor, Alf Imperato. "To be a man of knowledge one needs to be light and fluid," say the Yaqui's of northern Mexico, who could have been describing Imperato. "Getting up speed on a windsurfer is like changing gears on a car," Alf says, shifting into third so that his superlight custom board stops in mid-air with a sound like a car transmission shifting gears, before repositioning itself like a hovercraft, horizontal to the water. Watching him in high gear makes me think he must be made of something between energy and matter. In my next life, I want to come back as Alf Imperato's biogenetic twin sister or brother so that I can work the wind like that!

Knees bent, easing one foot between the straps, arms

extended in a "starfish" position, the Xantos breaks through a line of foam, sparkly as Christmas tinsel. Half a mile from the beach, an ugly, white ship, with peeling paint, anchored here for no apparent reason looks mysteriously vacant, like something from a James Bond movie. A sleek pair of black cormorants dive across the bow, circle to port, and take off again in synch, like twin aircraft streaking in front of a peach-colored, three-quarter moon. The long, slow foghorn of Kismet lighthouse vibrates through the ocean air. Magic.

A roller, surfed at the wrong angle, flips me into the sea. Whitecaps and swells become less friendly. The windsurfer keeps pointing into the wind, and I keep repositioning the sail so that it doesn't hit me in the head. Struggling onto the board, I feel like an elephant trying to balance on a slippery ball, unable to hold still in time and space. Dumped again. Incoming tide swirls in from the ocean. Cold water. Very cold water, like a sharp knife cutting through this 3mm wetsuit. Lungs spasm. Can't breathe. Asthma.

"When you can do nothing, what can you do?" — Zen koan

There is a point, when your lungs start closing down, quickly, and you can't take in any air, that you understand that your life can go in one direction or another and that you have no control. Everyone I've ever spoken to who struggles with adult-onset asthma knows about this moment. In fact, there are two choices. Your first reaction, fear, is one. Fear causes the bronchial passages to constrict. So, if you give in to this one, it will kill you. The other choice is single-pointed focus. Get out of your own way. Observe. Surrender to whatever will happen. Turn it over to God. Step back from the outcome. Either way, it's not your call.

The cold is cutting through my chest. If I can't get back to land, it feels like I've got maybe ten minutes before I black out. Two flash frames: a Coast Guard cutter winching my body up to deck, on a giant hook. How many of those stories did I write over the years? The second: Mindy's face. *"Mommy!"* I can hear her...

Focus. Prioritize. Number one: Talk to the part of myself that knows how to do this. With my breathing shutting down, it's hard to concentrate. I keep sliding off the board. Humping back on. Telling my lungs to stay open.

Floundering out here, alone, these orange and purple booties make a sucking sound, grabbing onto the rough surface of the board. Never realized that traction like that could be a life saver. Finessing along the ridge of the chop, I fall in again. This time, it seems routine. No big deal. Like climbers in the death zone on the upper reaches of Everest, my brain is not getting enough oxygen. Somewhere, in the middle of my head, I know this is very dangerous. No, it's not "routine." It's getting harder to take in oxygen. In fact, it feels like my body is rejecting it.

A prayer from faraway: "Yemaya, Mother of the Sea, come in through my body."

Windsurfing for my life.

Another two hundred meters. Landfall.

My head is floating somewhere near Mars. Weighing in at three hundred pounds apiece, my feet ache with each step. A tall, lone figure with a long shadow, stalking the blazing white sand, scattered with low brush and goldenrod. I can't find the right dune. The one with the mesh bag that has the medication that can give me back my breathing.

An existential moment. Camus would be proud. Standing on the edge of life, calculating options before blacking out. Can I make it fifty yards up the sloping dunes to the car? If so, drinking water might help. If water doesn't work, I can flag the next car. Flash frame: *"Mommy's in the emergency room, honey".*

I mentally flog myself. *Whatever happened to that woman who swore she would be grateful if she could walk and talk and breathe again? Why wasn't that enough?*

Sitting down, hard, in the sand, I will myself to gulp air. *I can do this!*

Focus on the car. Reorient, the way my mom taught me

how to reconstruct looking for something that was lost. Slowly, in my head, I struggle to find some logic: *When you were standing at the car, where did you walk with the mesh bag?*

Staggering, like a drunk in a spaghetti western. Falling. Getting up. Falling. Got it. Inhale. Wait. Inhale. Wait. Hitching a ride on a few million oxygen molecules, the invisible spray penetrates through the clamped-down inner walls of the airways, expanding into a warm, safety foam. Inhale. Locked down bronchiae release themselves. Air, smelling of ocean and damp with tender mist, moves, coolly through those places that were constricted and blocked off, just seconds ago. *Oxygen!* Like the end of the first act in *The Miracle Worker*, where Helen Keller connects the touch of water with the sound, I can feel the cells absorbing every molecule of oxygen, as if remembering what it means to breath. *Oxygen! I can go home!* A fragile ecosystem, this respiratory apparatus.

Tonight, as the wind shifts to the northeast, we light the first fire of the season and I wonder about the thin edge that separates us from the other side. I'm angry and disappointed, since I thought I had won out against the "permanent, irreversible" diagnosis, that I had beaten the odds, instead of merely pushing back the line of remission. I'd forgotten how lungs can feel like balloons, with all the air getting squished out of them by a black hand, so maybe today was just a gentle reminder. Then I smile. Flash frame: A line of silver foam, laced with adrenaline, suspended between space and time, surfing along the edge of forever at warp speed. Or was that a crazed illusion of invincibility, taking me into a zone of energetic meltdown?

Sitting in front of the fireplace, the windsurfing trophy that my daughter won, in a children's event, on a lake, at the end of the summer, reflects a curve of flame. I hold her in my lap while she reads her composition for Spanish class:

"*Me gusta surfear en el viento*," she has written.

"I like to surf in the wind."

1 This quote comes from *The Birthday Boys*, Beryl Bainbridge's fictional account of Captain Robert Scott's failed expedition to the South Pole in 1912. (New York: Carroll and Graf, 1991), p. 60.

2 So begins *Justine*, the first book of The Alexandria Quartet.

3 Ming–Dao, Den, op. cit., p. 248. Yes, it does have a colon at the end of the first line!

4 Clarissa Pinkola Estes' metaphor of an archway symbolizes my entering a new stage of renewal here, in a new home. "No matter how old a woman becomes, no matter how many years pass, she has yet more ages, stages, and more 'first times' awaiting her. That is what initiation is all about: it creates an archway which one prpeares to pass through to a new manner of knowing and being." op. cit., p. 68.

5 Schiller, David, op. cit., p. 147.

6 I found Gaston Bachelard's classic meditative essay on how the architecture of a house becomes a blueprint for the minds and spirits of those who live in the house has captivated me since 1965 when I read *The Poetics of Space* for the first time. Bachelard's thesis, that houses with turrets and eccentric shaped rooms will inspire more imaginative thinking than boxlike homes, propelled me toward a feral quality in redesign and renovation. (Boston: Beacon Press Books, 1994) p. 17.

7 In *The Art of Dreaming*, Carlos Castaneda offers insight into such phenomena as lucid, precognitive, and telepathic dreams. (New York: HarperCollins, 1993) p. 73.

8 Castaneda, ibid, p. 79.

9 The vine of death, *ayahuasca*, was the tarlike potion I slugged down with Kitiar in 1994. Because certain parts of the vine are poisonous, the Shuar caution that taking *ayahuasca* in a ceremony will either kill you or you will be spiritually reborn. Hence, the term, "vine of death."

[10] Synchronicity is a physical event preceded by a mental event. (LN) Jungians define it as a "meaningful coincidence."

[11] Blaise Pascal was a French mathematician/philosopher who lived during the 17th century, known as the Golden Age of Reason.

[12] *Zen and the Art of Motorcycle Maintenance* by Robert Pirsig. (New York: Bantam Books, 1974.)

[13] One of the classic beginners' books on Zen. *Zen Mind, Beginner's Mind* by Sunryu Suzuki (New York: Weatherhill, 1970.) p. 21.

[14] Castaneda, op. cit., p. 81.

[15] Herrigel, op. cit., p. 35.

[16] Bainbridge, op. cit., p. 46.

[17] Schiller, op. cit., p. 225.

[18] Pirsig, op. cit., p. 284.

[19] Circa 1956.

[20] Jamling's account of how he lived his dream of following his father to the top of Mount Everest is explained in the excellent documentary *Everest* (MacGillivray Freeman, 1997).

[21] When I told a Buddhist monk that, as a mother, at times I feel like a rubber ball at the end of a rubber band attached to a paddle, the monk said, "You must become the paddle." Parenting gives so many opportunities to practice, as stated in this quotation from *The Heart of Being* by John Daido Loori (Boston: Charles E. Tuttle Co., Inc., 1996). In taking responsibility for losing the page reference, I apologize to my readers and copy editor.

[22] Deng Ming-Dao, op. cit., p. 344.

[23] Schiller, op. cit., p. 331.

[24] The guru of flow, Mihaly Czikszentmihalyi, Ph.D. describes the state of being "in the zone" in "Finding Flow," *Psychology Today*, July/August 1997 pp. 46–48, 70–71.

[25] Csikszentmihalyi, ibid., p. 46.

[26] Herrigel, op. cit., p. 70.

[27] *Sacred Hoops: Spiritual Lessons of a Hardwood Warrior* by Phil Jackson and Hugh Delahanty (New York: Hyperion, 1995), p. 216. At the time of publication, Jackson coached the Chicago Bulls.

[28] Suzuki, op. cit., p. 317.

[29] Deng Ming-Dao, op. cit., p. 160

[30] Deng Ming-Dao, ibid., p. 240.

[31] Herrigel, op. cit., p. 61.

[32] Deng Ming-Dao, op. cit., p. 360.

Part Four
1998–1999

The practice of Dharma,
real spiritual practice,
is in some sense like a voltage stabilizer.
The function of the stabilizer is to prevent
irregular power surges and instead
give you a stable and constant
source of power.

—HIS HOLINESS THE DALAI LAMA[1]

Moroccoy National Park, Venezuela
May 7, 1998

"Death is like a scene in a grainy, black and white movie where you are standing on the platform at night, in the fog, waiting for the train to come in. You don't know when it is coming or where it will take you. The only thing you know is that when that train arrives, you have to get on. But as it pulls in, you panic. In that moment, you remember that your bags are not packed. " Laughing at his own metaphor, Tibetan lama Sogyal Rinpoche smiles, "One of the secrets to living a good life is to always have your bags packed."[2]

Mine were not packed last October, when windsurfing shifted from recreation to survival. In the hierarchy of terror, nothing beats facing your own imminent death. Back from the edge, will you do it again?

In the words of Georgia O'Keefe, "I've been absolutely terrified every moment of my life. I've never let it keep me from doing a single thing I wanted to do."

The Travel Industry Association puts windsurfing in the same "hard adventure activity" category as mountain climbing, hangliding, and parasailing.[3] I'm not sure how I've landed in the same group with anti-gravity artists although there is probably a shared compulsion for the Edge. "Feeding the rat," climbers call it. "Being in peril sharpens your sense for life," says Stacy Allison, who, with Peggy Luce, became the first American women to reach the summit of Mount Everest in September 1988.[4] As the late Bruno Goovy, a snowboarder, put it, "Sure there is a risk I might be killed. But in exchange, I have such a powerful sense of being alive. It's a bargain. Without risk, the sun is just the sun, the grass is just the grass. With risk, common things have incredible freshness."[5]

One climber shrugs off danger, saying, "Sure, rock

climbing is dangerous. But I had a neighbor who choked to death on a hot dog."

Or, as a Hungarian proverb would have it: "If a bullet has your name on it, no knife can ever kill you."

Mistaking enthusiasm for skill, I overestimated my strength and underestimated the wind's. I like to believe it was simply miscalculation but I was hooked into a belief that through the right combination of positive mental attitude, exercise, and nutrition, I had somehow reengineered my DNA. Having beaten the odds, I deluded myself about the facts. I live with a crisis trajectory condition, defined as one "that could change at any moment, leading to a quick trajectory to death."[6] Still, don't we all living on the edge of a crisis trajectory? Just watch the news and the wisdom of Chairman Mao is in your face: "People die all the time." We live in this illusion that we can schedule predictability but that train can arrive at any time.

Perched on my shoulder like a parrot, a fragile understanding: 180. *One hundred eighty days.* Dr. George Solomon, the father of psychoneuroimmunology, tells cancer patients to put the number 180 on their refrigerators. If you were told you had 180 days, or six months, to live, what would you do? "Banish uncertainty. Affirm strength. Hold resolve. Expect death," says one Taoist meditation.[7] Live each day as if you had six months to go and even the air tastes different.

May 6: Scavenging a few days for myself while my daughter is away on a school trip, on the eve of becoming one of millions of baby boomers who turn fifty every eight seconds,[8] I want to get as far away, for as little money as possible: a $350 roundtrip ticket, crash budget, and a hit-and-run trip to the middle of nowhere so I can look at who I was, and at the woman whom I never expected to become.

Threatened by the prospect of raising a child on my own kept me married long after we were both unhappy. These past few years, raising multitasking to a fine art, I have become my own worst fear: a single mother in her forties, experiencing life in two gears, overdrive and collapse. You would think I would have developed a more effective strategy by now. Chasing the edge keeps me landing back in a psychospiritual twilight zone called burnout. It feels all-too-familiar, this frazzled workaholic DMZ. Didn't the Dalai Lama say something about a voltage regulator? "What would you do?" I ask my friends. In reply, someone e-mails an Ojibwa poem:

"Sometimes I go about in pity for myself
And all the while
A great wind is bearing me across the sky." [9]

First stop, Caracas. It makes no sense but when my suitcase fails to appear on the conveyor belt, I start to cry. God knows, I've lost suitcases in more desolate places than this. I know how to function. (*Se perdio la maleta mia. Me puede ayudar, por favor?* Trans: My suitcase has lost itself. Can you please help me?) At least the windsurfing equipment has made it safely off the aircraft. As a favor to my friend John, I agreed to courier an assortment of fin boxes, footstraps, neoprene headgear, and duct tape to the wilds of Venezuela.[10]

Q: How is duct tape like The Force?

A: It has a light side and a dark side and it holds the universe together.[11]

John has given me a repaired Neil Pryde XS 5.3 meter sail for his friend, Alex Hansmann, an agreeable thirtysomething German who owns Windsurf Adicora. Alex gave up a career as a computer scientist in Germany for a life in bump-and-jump heaven–constant, warm wind and whitecaps all year round, right outside his door. "No more drysuits!" he laughs.

Thirty-five miles across the water from Aruba, the Caribbean's most popular windsurfing destination, Adicora catches the same steady breeze on *Lonely Planet* prices. An oceanfront room with a few rolled-up sails and a mast or two in the corner runs around thirty dollars a night at Windsurf Adicora, Alex's white beach house that is home to windsurfers from all over the world. Everyone gathers on the wide porch strung with hammocks, windsurfing harnesses, and wetsuits to swap wind and wave stories at the end of the day. Compared to the other Caribbean windsurfing centers – Aruba, Bonaire, and the Dominican Republic – not much is known about Adicora, or the Venezuelan coast, for that matter, which the National Tourist Board calls "the best-kept secret in the Caribbean."

My affection for barren windswept places notwithstanding, until a planned "free trade zone" along the coast brings hotels and casinos, this stretch of Caribbean is likely to retain its position on the "best kept secrets" list. Nonetheless, after a few days of roughing it, I decide it's impossible not to like Alex. In addition to being laid-back, funny, bright, and looking sort of like Pierce Brosnan, Alex has the ingenuity and self-reliance of a frontiersman, which in a sense, he is, since the Paraguana peninsula looks like a set from a spaghetti western. People even ride bareback to the grocery store. A patient, experienced guide, Alex navigates unmarked dirt roads that snake through the endless candelabra cactus jungle in this forgotten, windswept corner of South America in a rusty 1983 Jeep Wagoneer that has already logged more than 281,000 dusty miles.

I can't help noticing that Alex has one of those empathic relationships that some men develop over years, with their cars. Even though the gas gauge hasn't worked in years, Alex's system ensures that he never gets stranded with an empty tank. Whenever he passes a gas station, he tops up the tank. His hearing is so finely tuned to the Jeep's internal sounds he can intuit when the shocks need adjusting, tossing a gallon of water against the windshield to wash it down before restarting the ignition.

After hiking through nature preserves, exploring bat caves piled with animal skeletons, climbing through colonial ruins, and circumnavigating salt ponds the unlikely color of Pepto-Bismol, something about this wild, unsettled countryside fuses with a wild, unsettled part of me. This feral, resistant-to-enculturation, gypsy part of me doesn't get much chance to explore the unknown anymore, so when I heard about a national park of tropical islands accessible only by boat from the mainland, I could hardly wait for this trip. Now, with my clothes and tripod heading for Buenos Aires, I'm not so sure.

"You're working too hard," Alex says, patting me on the shoulder the next day. "You need to windsurf more." Alex, his assistant Oscar, who looks like a cross between a Mayan statue and my ex-husband are sitting with me in a fifteen foot launch at nine AM, heading for Playuela, one of the fourteen islands that make up Morroccoy National Park. As sun burns through morning fog, the temperature climbs into the eighties and mist coming off the wake of the stern feels warm on the back of my arm. As the captain slows the engine, the boat maneuvers through a labyrinth of twisted, red mangrove roots. A scarlet ibis, its beak curved like a huge machete, observes our approach from an overhanging upper branch. Another two ibises are staked out on a stretch of silver sand next to a small wooden dock.

The fragrance of hibiscus blends with the sea's, blue and yellow butterfly clouds float in front of our heads, and bright geckos, the color of leprechauns, dance from tree to tree. When two pelicans walk over to inspect us, I imagine the startled face of a bearded conquistador and wonder how the first explorers must have felt upon facing similar inspection by the indigenous wildlife. Snorkeling over a reef alive with iridescent blue surgeon fish, schedules and laundry, bills and deadlines belong to another world. In this land that time forgot "if only" thoughts wriggle like those fish underneath: If only it was this easy. If only you could spend more time floating with rainbow colored fish and less time worrying. If only....

A few hours later, under the palms, I drift into sleep. Last night, a thunderstorm knocked out power for the city of Morroccoy. The air conditioner, as it was euphemistically called, died. As I lay sweating in the dark, something with squiggly legs walked across my face. Now, I'm not afraid of insects but I'm not exactly in love with them, either, so I did what any other red-blooded American woman would do under the circumstances: I shrieked, jumped out of bed and opened the door, thinking that I'd run down the hall to my friends' room. But the corridor was pitch black. The thought of possibly stepping on something furry, oozy, prickly, painful, or all of the above, made me scoot back inside where I remembered an emergency candle squirreled away in my backpack. Lighting it, I fumbled around the room looking for six-, eight-, or hundred-legged insects. Nothing on the floor. Nothing on the bed. Aah! The air conditioning vent, near the ceiling...swarming with orange salamanders!

A lizard walking across my face is less upsetting than a centipede but both are high on my personal list of Unacceptable Nocturnal Experiences. So unacceptable, in fact, that I couldn't fall asleep for the rest of the night. At breakfast, when I told my story to Submantour dive shop owner Mike Osborne, who also happens to be director of tourism for Morroccoy, he laughed and laughed, shaking his head from side to side. "Never stay in hotels," he sputtered when he finally stopped laughing enough to talk. "Next time, try one of the *posadas*, or government-approved inns. You'll find they are much better all around. I myself would never stay in a hotel in this town." *Now* he tells me.

"Santo Lepanta, levanta la pata, svelta el perro y traige el Viento!" ("Santa Lepanta, lift your paw, release the dog, and bring the Wind.")[12] Although this is a Puerto Rican wind chant, Santa Lepanta must have heard us just before sunset. Driving to a launch site facing the archipelago. A quick look in the Jeep's rearview mirror confirms what I sensed:

My hair is a lost cause. If only I'd had the guts to become that redheaded lady in the green sneakers. I'd be on my way to reinventing myself as one of those people Sal and I used to write about: the windsurfing granny, planing across Tampa Bay with Lights, Camera, and Action, the waterskiing squirrels.[13]

"Why do you think I keep mine so short?" Alex chuckles when he catches me making a face at myself in the mirror. "A few weeks around here and your hair turns to wood." Hair is a high-maintenance item back there, in my regular life. Here, sunburned, drinking a bottle of Coke with Caribbean wind blowing through the Jeep's open windows, admiring the tropical late afternoon sky, high maintenance hair has gone the way of cell phones and e-mail and lizardless air conditioners that don't break down.

Again we meet! That Neil Pryde XS 5.3 meter sail that I brought down from the States reappears, rigged on a Fiberspar mast whose universal is screwed to the base of an old Hi Fly 285. A clunker if there ever was one. If my Xantos 310 is a Porsche, this board must be the old school bus of windsurfers. With temperatures in the 80's and bathtub-warm water, there's no chance of any cold current's shutting down airways. Maybe I'm being overly cautious, but I'm not taking my breathing for granted any more. New strategy: Wedge an albuterol inhaler into a 2mm wetsuit. Just in case.

Hesitant in new water, I inch toward the footstraps, pulling on the boom until the board cuts a wake of turquoise foam to the edge of a coral reef. Planing back to the white beach, I head out again, to sea, until a quarter moon, clear against a darkening marine blue sky marks this end of day. Rushed thoughts become calm. Pauses between each breath lengthen. No thought. In and around me, softly, a clearing.

"Por una vieja, no soy tan mala." ("For an old lady, I'm not

doing too bad.")

"You were doing pretty good out there," Alex pats my shoulder.

Driving back to Adicora on a two-lane coastal road that cuts through miles and miles of empty, burnt orange fields stretching to hills of candelabra cactus, odd pairs of concrete huts occasionally punctuate this nothingness. They look like penal boxes the Japanese used for punishing American P.O.W.'s in World War II movies: unforgivingly, suffocatingly hot. There always seems to be a man in a white, sleeveless undershirt sitting on a cane chair in front of the pairs of huts, watching us pass. Is it the same guy? It's inconceivable that anyone would choose to suffer like this. "What do people do here?"

"Dairy and goat farmers, mainly. Some people own little roadside restaurants."

A mountain in the distance is consumed by yellow flame, a corona of light outlining its ridge.

"How can people live here?"

Alex laughs, gently patient with his American friend who doesn't get it. "Why not? They have their work, their friends."

A remembered image: a blind harpist in the Andes with a voice like Louis Armstrong. My only Quechua phrase means "kiss my ass" so I whisper to my friend, "Ask him if he knows who Louis Armstrong is." Words I don't understand are exchanged with the blind musician. My friend laughs.

"You know what he said? 'This Louis Armstrong...did he ever play Cuzco?'"

Maybe Alex is right.

As darkness spreads into forever, the ocean smell, misting from the other side of the hill, blends with gasoline vapors and dust.

Who would I be if I lived in the middle of nowhere?

Sagaponack, NY
June 30, 1998

The Zen masters were men of few words, but mature in insight and skilled in means.

—Irmgard Schloegl [14]

"I don't know anything about windsurfing, really," says the Zen master.

For a flash, I wonder if I've wasted two and a half hours driving eighty-seven miles in teeming rain to get to this interview. Hands clasped, the tall, intense man in blue jeans and a cambray work shirt leans back in his chair, thinking. Behind him, on the computer, shine words of his latest book. The ingrained instinct to snoop gets the better of me. I try to read what's on the screen without looking like I'm looking at it. There are a few lines that look like dialogue. Piled around the studio on desktops, bookshelves, and any flat surface are manuscripts, articles, and pictures. Years of ideas expressed and exchanged, gathered on expeditions, inner and outer.

Is it coincidence or synchronicity that brings me face-to-face with a Zen master who happens to live a few miles from Peconic Bay?

That the person in question also happens to be award-winning author-explorer-environmentalist Peter Matthiessen challenges presuppositions about random odds ruling events. If synchronicity is "a meaningful coincidence," this encounter weaves together a subtle pattern of personal events that have been affected by Matthiessen's work. In 1968, as a student in London, I read *At Play in the Fields of the Lord*, Matthiessen's novel about missionaries in Peru's Madre de Dios jungle. Four years later, I found myself working as a photojournalist in the same jungle, filing stories about *chiringeros* who milked rubber sap from one of the world's last remaining forests of natural rubber trees and photographed a gold rush in a jungle town named Quincemil–15,000–a sum which the town priest allegedly lost in a poker game. Without consciousness, I seem to have followed Matthiessen's journeys to the cloud forest that he explored eleven years earlier by boat. It has thrown me off guard that he has generously agreed to an interview. Is this an interview? Or is something else pulling me to this writing studio in a Sagaponack garden near the sea?

Like life, what first seemed simple is turning out to be more complex. I'm not sure whether that's because it is more complex or whether I tend to make things more complicated than they are. This started as a "Zen in the art..." journal.

Personal notes on trial and error. Efforts on effortlessness. Finding and not finding Flow. And along the way, life. Wild swings through a canopied forest: TV news, birth, disability, divorce, motherhood, and love. Loss and healing. Windsurfing teaching me Zen philosophy and more: It's okay to fall down, even in front of other people. The important thing is learning how to get back up. And never give up on your dreams. Like the story about a young Albert Einstein, daydreaming that he was riding on a beam of light and when he woke up, he had returned to his point of origin. He could have said, "Wild dream. Think I'll have a beer and watch the game." Instead, he took years to work the dream out mathematically until that intuitive skein of inner vision became the theory of relativity. An equally impossible daydream (with no comparable importance to humanity): What would it look and sound and feel like to merge between light and water?

From Zen to windsurfing and back to Zen.

Which brings me to why I'm here. It seems almost ludicrous to end at the beginning with an obvious question: "What is Zen, really?"

A fresh intensity of rain muffles the sound of classical music playing in the background. He is scribbling on a pad, apparently half-listening. "Didn't you get wet on your way in?"

"Quite."

"Your question...?"

"What is Zen?"

He nods as if he's been expecting this one. "What isn't Zen?"

"Isn't it a religion?"

"A religion before religion."

He continues, "The ground of all religion is certainly meditation and mystical experience. Zen is the ground of seeing more deeply. It's really an understanding of life, appreciating your life..." *Like that promise you made to be grateful if you could only walk and talk and breathe normally again. Remember?*

"When you eat, you eat. When you sleep, you sleep..." *Me? I could write 'The Hit and Run Cookbook—The Un-Zen Way': How to prepare a meal and eat while talking on the phone, writing, cleaning up, caring for a child, and driving a car.*

"I used to have a teacher who asked, 'When you vomit, do you think about it? No, you just vomit!' That's all. Paying attention to this moment."

As if sensing my question before I say it out loud, he responds with a koan: "'Rice in a bowl; water in a pail.'"[15]

We sit quietly. Physical details: He is in his mid–seventies, around six foot two, with gray hair, pale–blue eyes. Wicked smile. It's hard not to admire the stillness in his posture–the gift of a straight spine or years of meditation practice? And his eyes–can he really see me from the inside out as if I was transparent, or am I just insecure? Or both?

According to legend, Sakyamuni Buddha was asked, "Are you a saint? A prophet? A god?"

"I am awake," he answered.

Twenty years of reading Zen and I still have no idea

what that means. What does it mean to be awake? Not skimming the surface or rushing around, making excuses that there's no time when that's all there is. Awake: I might not know what it is but I sure know what it's not. Some say we are each of us born awake, and then over time we close down. Matthiessen writes, "Soon the child's clear eye is clouded over by ideas, ambition, preoccupations, opinions. Simple, free being becomes encrusted, year by year. The armor of the ego. Not until years later, an instinct comes that a vital sense of mystery has been withdrawn. The sun glints through the pines and the heart is pierced in a moment of beauty and strange pain, like a memory of paradise. And as of that moment, we become seekers."[16]

Living so much of the time on automatic pilot, how much of life gets missed along the way? I am about to ask a question on the art of paying attention when a fine silver-white mist forms around Matthiessen's head and shoulders.

"The aura is a luminous egg-shaped cloud of pulsing energy that surrounds the human body," writes the late Barbara Bowers in *What Color is Your Aura?* This electromagnetic field around humans, animals, plants, and minerals has flickering bands of very subtle color as well as size, depth, texture, movement, and vibrational pitch, which Bowers described as a "humming sound." An engineer, Dr. Bowers' vision was scientifically measured several times. Apparently, she could see fifty thousand hues, tints, and color values in contrast to most of us who can see only five thousand shades, give or take a few hues. Our paths crossed when she introduced herself to me after listening a talk on intuition I was giving in La Jolla. I had seen a few auras spontaneously. Could she teach me how to see them more consistently, I asked.

"Why would you want to?" Bowers asked.

"Good question." I stalled. "If it can help me understand how someone is thinking and feeling, then it could be another source of information." Later that evening, in a dimly lit basement den in La Jolla, Bowers sat me alone with a candle. About three hours later, she had me describe what I saw. Since that night, when there is subtle shadow in the room, as there is here, the aura is often visible. Maybe I should tell him but as a reporter I would feel foolish commenting on that luminous eggshaped light, the color of polished pewter. I don't know what to say. Why is my composure unraveling like transparent fishing line unwinding from a reel? This is not supposed to happen. I have prepped for this interview by rereading *Zen in the Art of Archery, Zen Philosophy, Zen Practice; Zen Mind, Beginner's Mind*, and Matthiessen's *The Snow Leopard*, in which he describes his own journey into Zen practice. *Where is that list of questions, anyway?*

"I s–seem to have an aversion to sitting down and meditating. *Where did that come from? Why am I stuttering?* "I started to meditate when I got sick with chronic fatigue. Now, it feels like if I let go, I'll be overwhelmed." I'm not telling him about the flashbacks. Waking up in the middle of the night, coughing. Looking at the wall, waiting for the black door to appear. Afraid it will come back when I'm alone in some hotel on the other side of the world. I tell myself this is P.T.S.D. That I'm not afraid. I'm not telling him.

"You don't know what's behind that door when it starts to open. The best way is to go through it." He speaks in a deep, thoughtful voice, tilting his head slightly to his right as if to study me with a hint of mischief in his eyes.

"What you look for in a really good teacher is that quality of rascalness," says Ram Dass.[17] A rascally teacher will find your weak spots and provoke you to reveal them, often using unorthodox teaching methods. He (or she) will test your strength, stretch your limits, and when you believe you can't go any further, lead you past the edge to new insight. A really great teacher keeps you on that edge until you find that place where the arrow releases itself. Or he might laugh.

Zen masters are respected not only for their scholarship and knowledge of Buddhist texts but also for their intuitive knowledge of human nature. Yes, I came as a journalist to interview Mathiessen but the questions which I won't admit I want to ask is whether Zen could help me become less anxious and reactive? Could it help me come to terms with the aftermath of a Near–Death Experience? Could meditation lead me into effortlessness and flow the way windsurfing can, especially when windsurfing is out of the question? As these questions take shape, I sense that if I have to ask, then that man sitting across the room cannot provide answers. To do so would deprive a student of doing her work.

What, exactly, is "the work?" Doing the work. Being on the path. Terms which describe a spiritual journey, regardless of denomination. But Zen has its own ritual and mystique. In *The Roots of Buddhist Psychology*, Jack Kornfield has an anecdote about a student who is given a basic Zen meditation assignment: Breathe to the count of ten without thinking of anything except your breathing. During *dokusan* (student–teacher interview), the student complains, "This meditation of counting ten breaths is boring. Don't you have anything more interesting?" Grabbing his student by the back of his neck like a kitten, the teacher takes him outside to a stream, where he pushes the student's head under the water, holding it down. When the student comes up sputtering, the teacher smiles,

"So. Is your breathing *interesting* enough for you now?" Not that Peter Matthiessen would hold my head under water as a teaching strategy; nonetheless, it feels like something rascally is getting ready to happen.

"You are welcome to join us," he says.

Quiet.

"All Buddhas throughout space and time..." The words of the Heart Sutra. All buddhas and an energetic contingent of

heavy hitters in the playing fields of the Lord have taken up presence in this room. To have earned the title of *roshi*, or senior teacher, Matthiessen received transmissions of the *dharma* through a lineage that extends back more than 2500 years, or eighty-two generations back to the Buddha.

The air feels warmer, heavier in texture. Time is taking on the consistency of warm Turkish taffy, folding over and stretching into a slower configuration. How did I get here? A series of hunches in three cities which prompted me to look for a book called *Tropical Classical* by *Time* essayist Pico Iyer? Having finally acquired it, this book turned out to have no apparent relevance to my work or life until a quiet inner voice–*Open the book!*–guided me to Iyer's essay, "Peter Matthiessen: In Search of the Crane."[18] Iyer writes, "an aristocratic, solitary, exacting, elegant discipline which prizes immediacy, irreverence, and unanalytical attention to the moment, Zen might almost have been made for this practical rebel."

"Thank you." Eventually, it seems, there are words.

The Zen master's blue eyes crinkle up at a private joke with himself. "You have to sit." He is smiling so hard that he is having a hard time not laughing. Locked in, like a laser. He's got my fear and he knows it. Rascalness. *What if I can't? What if my leg falls asleep?* I hate sitting still. I'm a squirmer. I tried Zen meditation at a weekend retreat a few years ago. I failed Zen 101 when my left leg fell asleep and I wriggled my foot and a monk led me out of the meditation hall. Do I confess up front or just show up and see what happens? It's not as if I have never meditated before. But Zen…? "In Tantric practice, the student may displace the ego by filling his whole being with the real or imagined object of his concentration; in Zen, one seeks to empty out the mind, to return it to the clear pure stillness of a seashell or a flower petal," Matthiessen writes in *The Snow Leopard*.[19]

The heart of Zen meditation practice is "the scientific method…we learn by doing, by our own experience," Thich

Thien–An writes in *Zen Philosophy, Zen Practice*. "Keeping the mind under control, concentrating on the object...seeking the significance of life in daily activity; that is the method of Zen."[20]

But the "experience" involves sitting cross-legged on a little black cushion, with your eyes open. Early in the morning. Sitting still. No twitching allowed. Breathing. No thinking allowed. Then a few minutes of *kinhin*, walking in formation, focusing on your breathing. Back to the cushion. More breathing. That's it. No bells and whistles. No colored wheels of light. No angels or spirit guides. No pretty rainbow bridges or power animals. "Zen is not some kind of excitement, but concentration on our usual everyday routine," Shunryu Suzuki writes in *Zen Mind, Beginner's Mind*.[21]

This is it: spiritual bootcamp. "No exit" meditation..."with no thought of achievement." It is not for nothing that in Japan, a Buddhist man is called *"un shui,"* or "cloud and water man." The paradox, like the tension of moment-to-moment balance between light and water, is that sitting still without expectation can lead to "...a sense of the all-embracing harmony of things...which reflects the stillness and emptiness that ever dwells in the middle of constant change."[22]

Sagaponack, NY
July 1, 1998

*To perform one's daily activities in the Zen spirit, one should
perform them as forms of meditation. We should not meditate only
when we sit in quiet but should apply the method of meditation to
our daily life. When we wash dishes, we must meditate. When we
work in the garden, meditate. When we drive, meditate. When we do
business, meditate. In other words, we must meditate at every
moment, in every activity of daily life.*

–Thich Thien-An[23]

To help with my research, Matthiessen suggests that I contact one of his monks, a woman who used to windsurf in
the Hamptons. "What you are doing is ambitious. *Zen in the
Art of Archery* is a classic," he says, adding, "The monk may
have more of a handle on the relationship between Zen
and windsurfing."

A windsurfing female Buddhist monk? In the
Hamptons? How progressive is that? As far as I can tell, religion seems to have been created by men, for men, and
about men, to keep women in their place. I tend to avoid
the subject after many years of getting caught in the cross-
fire between my father, an atheist, and my maternal grand-
father, a Jewish version of an ayatollah. While I don't know
very much about the role of women in a Zen world, I am
aware of innumerable references to Zen patriarchs. Where
are the matriarchs? Maybe I haven't read the right books.
In *Nine-Headed Dragon River*, Matthiessen remarks that there
are surprisingly few Zen nuns (or female monks) in Japan.
But American women are changing the way Buddhism is
practiced in this country. Several of the monks at the Ocean
Zendo in Sagaponack are women in their fifties and sixties–gutsy, educated, adventurous women at that, who

have knocked around the world and brought up children of their own.

From the special place in which we store our broken hearts, broken promises (real and imagined), and broken dreams, women seem to find their way to Buddhism when love or life breaks down and nothing else seems to help. Paradoxically, those spiritual emergencies become the critical turning points that made us look within ourselves for clarity or resolution. Pema Chodron, an American Buddhist monk and bestselling author says that the time her soul broke apart was the day her husband told her he was leaving her for another woman. Years later, she can point to that trauma as the entryway, a new beginning. Other women describe the death of someone close, a betrayal or profound loss as the point of impact which moved them through the door. One breath at a time.

Atlantic Point, NY
July 5, 1998

Some notes on Zen and windsurfing:

Similarities:

Windsurfing	Zen
Present focus/being in the moment	Present focus/being in the moment
Heightened awareness of environment	Heightened awareness
Focus and discipline essential	Focus and discipline essential
Posture important	Posture important
Concentration!	Concentration!
Practice necessary for improvement	Practice necessary for improvement
Attention to details	Attention to details
Physical and mental challenge	Physical and mental challenge
Can be frustrating	Can be frustrating

Differences:

Windsurfing	Zen
Equipment: complex	Equipment: simple
Young tradition	Ancient tradition
Movement	Stillness
Speed	Slowing down
Exhilaration	Tranquility

The monk does not wish to speak with me about comparisons between windsurfing and Zen or anything else. "Too busy," she says. People not wanting to talk to me has become something of an occupational hazard over the years. It's one of the similarities between being a journalist, and a therapist. It is a journalist's job to get people to talk about things they don't necessarily want to talk about. It's also the job of a therapist. I don't take it personally when she doesn't want to talk to me. Reading between the lines, my sense is that this female monk thinks my work will be superficial. Maybe that's my fault. I launch on an obvious tack, how windsurfing and Zen can lead to Flow, or at-one-ment.

"At-one-ment," the monk sniffs. "At-one-ment can come from anything we do."

"That's true." We are both quiet for a while.

"Peter has invited me to sit in the zendo," I tell her.

"Good." More quiet. The spaces between words feel waxy, as if initial resistance is softening. After awhile, she starts to talk about the tedium of rigging and de-rigging. "Oh yes," I agree, thinking of Jace's observation that rigging is what women hate most about windsurfing.

"One day, I focused on that tediousness and used it as my meditation," she remembers. "Instead of assembling everything and taking it apart as quickly as possible, I made myself do each step as carefully as I could. I turned it into a kind of tea ceremony. It became so absorbing that when I looked up, a small crowd was gathered, watching me."

"At a workshop for nurses at a hospital, recently, I suggested that we can find our most difficult, obstreperous patient and, for a day, treat him or her as we would our best friend. Paying attention to that person in the same way that you would pay attention to your best friend."

There is something to this: Choosing someone or something you dislike and treating him or her or it with patience and consideration. It doesn't matter whether it's rigging a sail or someone who complains too often or even a part of yourself. The exercise is the same.

Without my needing to spell it out, the monk gets it. On the other end of the phone, I can hear her smile, just a little. "Good luck with your book."

Sagaponack, NY
July 14, 1999

Why leave behind the seat that exists in your own house and go aimlessly off to the dusty realms of other lands?....Do not be afraid of the true dragon. Devote your energies to a way that directly indicates the absolute (and) gain accord with the enlightenment of the buddhas. [24]

With this quotation from 13th century Zen master Eihi Dogen, Peter Matthiessen begins *Nine-headed Dragon River: Zen Journals.*

As concentric circles ripple outward on the surface of a pond after someone tosses a stone into the water, this quote has a peculiar meaning as I leave home at first light. Why am I going off aimlessly, in pursuit of emptiness, when it exists in abundance all around me? For some reason, an early morning conversation with Neil replays itself:

"I need to go to the mountain. To the high places," he said.

"Why?"

"To find peace." He had looked at me with disappointment in his sea–colored eyes. "I thought you knew that."

For some reason, his reproach made me smile. "You won't necessarily find peace in the mountains. You find peace in yourself."

Where had that come from and why is that dialogue coming back right now? Is it because I'm driving into the dawn looking for something that won't necessarily be there? It's so easy to advise other people, isn't it? No use fooling myself or anyone else: This babe does not expect enlightenment of the buddhas to come near her anytime soon.

Today feels like a very long eighty–seven miles from my

world to the magical cut through the trees that opens into a rectangular garden with a gray stone Buddha in its southwest corner. Walking on silvery wet grass, unbelieving that windsurfing has brought me here, I remember Matthiessen's description of his introduction to Zen: "On an August day of 1968, returning home to Sagaponack, Long Island, after a seven-month absence in Africa, I was astonished by the presence in my driveway of three inscrutable small men who turned out to be Japanese Zen masters..."[25]

On that August day thirty years ago, one of those three Zen masters had spent the day, a few yards from here, standing on his head, waiting...

There is no one waiting for me except a black bird. Taking off from a low bush, he zooms low, in a straight line, to the top of the Buddha statue's head.

that stone Buddha deserves
all the birdshit it gets
I wave my skinny arms like
a tall flower in the wind

—Ikkyu [26]

The door to a small, gray wooden building at the eastern end of the garden opens. The former stable is so well hidden by trees that I am surprised to see a monk in a black robe, her head shaved, smiling at me from the entryway. Inside, we sit on a low wooden bench to the right of the door, where I remove my shoes while she whispers a few minutes of meditation instruction. Then she waves me into a plain room with eighteen sets of black meditation cushions lined up on two raised wooden platforms that extend along each wall. Looking around a foreign space for the first time, an obsession with facts takes over. *Count the pillows! Measure the mats!* Each position for a sitter holds a rectangular flat mat (*zabuton*), approximately 29" by 34". In the center of each *zabuton* is a circular cushion (*zafu*), with an approximate radius of about fourteen inches and a height of about eight inches. You are expected to sit cross-legged, without squirming, on the *zafu*.

"Expect nothing!" Rearranging my legs a few times, I face the wall. Matthiessen, who I am seeing for the second time, enters barefoot, wrapped in a black kimono. After stretching, face down on the mat, for three full bows in front of the altar, he sits, cross-legged, on the first *zafu* to the right of the altar. With no one to cue me, I observe the others, retrieving a black booklet from beneath the *zabuton*. Somewhere behind me, a woman announces, "Page three" and we begin to chant. Well, everyone else begins to chant. I'm attempting to sound out syllables, stuttering a few lines behind everyone else. It feels like the first day at a new aerobics class. When the chanting is over, it feels as if the room itself is breathing deeply. Now, all I have to do is breathe, counting silently to ten breaths.

Somewhere between two and three on the first round, I lose it. "Serenity now!" It's the voice of George's father on Seinfeld. "Serenity now!" I can hear him just as clearly as if I was home, watching the episode where George's manic father was learning to meditate by shouting "Serenity now!" at the top of his lungs. I want to giggle. *Shut up! What if you get thrown out for laughing? You're not cut out for this. It's too rigid. Everyone else seems to be getting it, like in aerobics class. Who are these people anyway?* My monkey mind is swinging from branch to branch. The last time I sat this close to a dozen people, we were in a loud, crazy newsroom. This is pretty weird. It's the opposite of a newsroom. You can feel that everybody's working only nobody's talking. *What are they doing? Have they been studying those inscrutable koans? Have they heard the sound of one hand? Have they seen their faces before their mothers and fathers were born? Do they know the color of wind? Well, at least they don't know what I'm thinking. They don't know that I'm not meditating. Or do they? Shit. What if they are all telepathic?*

A wide splash of sunlight. Back to zero. Focus on inhaling, exhaling, inhaling again. Last night, chasing a yellow band of fading sun across Napeague bay, listening to soft, curling wake. Breathe in. Floating now, no questions. A gong breaks the quiet. Stand up, just in time. My left leg has gone to sleep.

Sagaponack, NY
August 2, 1998

*Buddhism does not have the answers to your questions. I do
not have the answers to your questions. History does not have
the answers to your questions. You do. ONLY you do. The answer
and the question are the same thing. Zen is a process, not an
answering machine.*

–John Daido Loori[27]

References to Zen proliferate this summer. In windsurfing:
Zen wetsuits, Zen Flow, and "Zenning" the waves.

In basketball: Michael Jordan says he is using "a little
bit of the Zen Buddhism...instead of being frustrated, just
smile and flow naturally, channeling my thoughts and frustrations in a whole different form...This may be the last
time, the last dance, whatever. I should enjoy it."[28]

And in the news: "You have to take sort of a Zen atti-
tude," says former White House spokesman George
Stephanopoulos about the American public's distrust of
President Clinton's motives.

Kundun and *Seven Years in Tibet* have brought Tibetan
Buddhism to the big screen. *Everest*, an IMAX documentary,
shows Tenzing's son making offerings to the mountain spirits in a Buddhist temple. The news god and Hollywood
have "discovered" Buddhism. Zen is chic. And I'm not.

In keeping with that time-honored tradition of windsurfers around the world, I travel with a portable cabana: a
triangle of space formed by opening the driver's door at an
angle. Just the right size for a universal, one-armed ritual–
the pulling on and peeling off of wetsuits while wrapped in
a towel. Exploring the narrow, northern coastline of the
South Fork, I seek out those mysterious points where road-
lines on maps abruptly end.

Today, I am the proud possessor of one such map, on which Jace has marked several such points, winding roads which end abruptly at the water and where parking permits are not required during the crowded summer season. With hundreds of thousands of people descending on the Hamptons throughout July and August, it is something of a miracle to find hidden beaches that are practically empty, clean, and ideal for launching a windsurfer and kayak. Scheduling conflicts have made windsurfing lessons impossible this summer. Jace is modeling and writing for local papers and windsurfing magazines. He published a story about how he nearly got himself arrested for riding an Orca Landcruiser—a skateboard with a windsurfing rig—through midtown Manhattan. Swapping notes, each of us has had a close call in the water; his, while windsurfing along the crest of a crashing Hawaiian wave and mine, closer to home.

"Without weekly lessons, I'm holding my own but making no progress," I explain. After hooking into the harness lines and backing towards the footstraps, the next project is learning how to beach start, holding the rig up so that the wind flies the sail before stepping onto the board. One reason why the U.S. windsurfing population has remained stable at 1.2-million since the mid-1980s is because people get fed up with the equipment and they get exhausted pulling the sail out of the water again and again. In heavier winds, a windsurfer pitches so quickly that standing while pulling on the uphaul becomes impossible. You need to be able to launch from the water, positioning yourself so that the wind lifts you and the rig to an upright position.

The first step towards mastering this maneuver—the water start—is the beach start. So far, my attempts to learn have gotten me conked in the head. I tell myself that I should be realistic. Why not be satisfied with what you have already learned, improving your existing skills, instead of expecting the impossible? But the rat wants more wind.

Thinking it's way too early for anyone I know to be awake, I swing past Windsurfing Hamptons at 6:15 AM, ducking off route 27 at Water Mill, barrelling too quickly past homes whose average price ths season is around $1,950,000, according to those real estate booklets that are distributed, free, in the local 7-11. A summer rental can easily run you $100,000. Too many zeroes for me.

Parking on the grass alongside a handful of other cars, I sip coffee until five minutes to seven when I head inside, where the rhythm of morning Zen service is becoming more familiar. The senior monk, a woman in her sixties of impeccably still posture–she was a professional dancer in an earlier life–recommends that I sit every day even if it's only for five or ten minutes. "The important thing is that you practice every day. Every day," she says with a certain kindness and precision I wish I had. "When you sit on your cushion, you can say, 'I take refuge in the three treasures: the Buddha, the *dharma*, and the *sangha*.'" The *dharma*, to me, is how you walk your talk or how you put the Buddha's work into action. The *sangha* is the collective term for people who practice Buddhism. At first, it seemed odd to be meditating when I wasn't sick but, as when I faced the water again for the first time in eight years, I am approaching my morning sessions on the cushion with "great faith, great doubt, and great determination." Maybe that's how I should approach life. My conscious mind buys into the health benefits; my unconscious mind is...well, unconscious. As in not sure what I hope to get from this. Insight into Zen?

"Meditation has nothing to do with contemplation of eternal questions, or of one's own folly, or even of one's navel, although a clearer view on all these enigmas may result. It has nothing to do with thought of any kind–with anything at all, in fact, but intuiting the true nature of existence, which is why it has appeared, in one form or another, in almost every culture known to man."

–Peter Matthiessen, *The Snow Leopard* [29]

These first attempts to stop thinking for a count of ten breaths reminds me of trying to stand on a windsurfer. Like then, I seem to fall more than I succeed. But meditation isn't about winning or losing, nor is it a competition. Or so I'm told. Counting breaths is harder than focusing on an image or mantra. With no mental props to hold onto, my mind feels like a car going down a hill with no brakes. So far, the only insight that I've gotten is that I have absolutely no control over the incoming, random, runaway thought patterns that keep my mind racing on a course to nowhere. Maybe some "insight into Zen" will come in a flash—like the first time I grabbed onto the boom and windsurfed, without falling—when I can sit still for ten breaths.

Or perhaps it will come when I am working in the garden, washing dishes, or driving my daughter to school. "When you become you, Zen becomes Zen. When you are you, you see things as they are," writes Suzuki in *Zen Mind, Beginners Mind*. I'm just beginning to see that since "I" can observe my runaway thoughts, then "I" must be something other than the mind. How can that information be put to some practical use?

"When you study Buddhism, you should have a general housecleaning of your mind," writes Suzuki. Symbols of cleaning out attics, basements, and rooms often appear in our dreams when we are getting ready to make changes in our lives. If, as Jung believed, every symbol in a dream represents some aspect of a dreamer's self, then objects to be cleared away can represent unwanted habits, hidden fears, or unresolved feelings, including old hurts from the past. Or they may represent an issue, like procrastination, that the dreamer struggles with in her waking life. Those boxes in the corner, for example. Or that old chair. Housecleaning metaphors are the psyche's way of helping us get ready to release what we no longer need, to make room for growth and change. High on my "to do" list would be cleaning up my act in traffic. Two minutes in a traffic jam and I start cursing under my breath. I hate when anyone cuts me off or wheels into a parking place before me. What happens when a tire blows out and a Zen student's Star-Tac cell phone cannot connect to the A.A.A.'s emergency 800 number? After twenty minutes being routed through voicemail, I feel like a parody of George's father on *Seinfeld*. Serenity now? You must be joking!

"No blame," says the *I Ching*, but when did you ever see anyone consult the *I Ching* about a flat tire? If Dante was alive, the eighth circle of hell would be interminable voice-mail. My teeth are clenched, jaw tight, when a renegade question brings me back to Mental Housecleaning 101: What would the Dalai Lama do in this situation? Dissolve to: His Holiness, sitting in the back seat of a limousine, smiling, while a flurry of orange-robed monks scramble to fix the problem. Well, maybe it was an absurd comparison, but laughing quietly might be even more effective for "house-cleaning of the mind" than breathing to the count of ten.

Still, it wouldn't hurt to drive more mindfully along these back roads. In another fifty years, when more people live along the coastlines of this country than currently live in the entire world, what will this thirty-seven mile shore-line look like? [30] Will Hollywood-style bus tours take gawk-ers past the celebrities' homes? Or will security checkpoints, like sets from a Spielberg movie, keep civilians like me from wandering south of Montauk Highway? Speaking of Spielberg, who is that man in black sunglasses reading a newspaper in a black Chevy blazer parked against the director's high wall of hedges at 8:30 AM? A reporter from the *National Enquirer* on a celebrity stakeout? Why would anyone from the *National Enquirer* want to take my picture? He must think I didn't see him grab the camera as I drove by. Don't tell me he's a secret service agent, checking for ter-rorists. Not even a secret service agent could suspect a woman with a purple sailboard on top of a white Honda Civic for a would-be terrorist. Or could he?

North of Montauk Highway, at 69 North Main Street. A banner in the window of an antiques shop: "WELCOME MR. PRESIDENT," a natural cutaway shot for the evening news. As if on cue, a little old lady rushes out of the store, talking into an imaginary camera. "The President's staying down the road at the Spielberg compound. He would never venture here, to the bad part of town. I'll bet he won't be going over to the Baptist church in the poor black part of town, either," she says brightly, walking up to me as though she knows me.

"Poor black part of town?"

"Mount Morris, it's called. The media will never go there, either. By the way, my granddaughter has one of those things like you," she says, pointing to the Xantos. "Don't you worry about sharks?"

"That seems to be a popular question, ma'am. Thank you for asking. I only sail in bays and coves." *And the only sharks I worry about are wearing suits.*

Speaking of bays and coves, it's time to follow one of these squiggly lines on Jace's map all the way to the end. Today's road stops in tall, dune grass at the shore of Mecox Bay. A shimmer of a southwesterly is teasing the grass. Typical August afternoon.

Inner debate: *Not enough wind. Go out anyway. Too much trouble. It will be beautiful out there...go!* The part of me that's determined to windsurf today takes over from the part that thinks it's too much bother to put all the gear together in ultralight wind. Yes, the back of my eyes ache from haze off the water but I'm stubborn and this is research, so I rig in the heat out of sheer determination while simultaneously a sly cartoon of Holden Caufield on a date with MTV's depressive Daria plays in a subliminal control room somewhere in the back of my mind.

With so little wind, there's hardly any pull on the rig.

Stillness within movement.

Zazen on the surface of the sea.

Worth the effort, especially when a band of sunlight reminds me of an afternoon when I was too weak to get across the room and I think of my friend Mindy and the bus turning around at the end of the street and how many women and children and men are inside today, sick and scared and alone. In the middle of this dance between light and water and the inexpressible freedom of perfect health, I remember that helplessness and isolation and fear and I start to cry for every one forgotten in her illness.

For she and I are the same.

Old Greenwich, Connecticut
September 11, 1998

Achieving the summit of a mountain was tangible, immutable, concrete. The incumbent hazards lent the activity a seriousness of purpose that was sorely missing from the rest of my life. I thrilled in the fresh perspective that came from tipping the ordinary plane of existence on end.

—Jon Krakauer[31]

With swells of vicious black water the size of four-story buildings, and chilling, 30-knot winds, the North Atlantic Ocean is, to the vast majority of windsurfers, an option ruled out by common sense. To a very small contingent, however, it is the nautical equivalent of Everest.

In describing the world of Everest climbers as "a self-contained, rabidly idealistic society, largely unnoticed and surprisingly uncorrupted by the world at large," Krakauer observes that "prestige was earned by tackling the most unforgiving routes with minimal equipment, in the boldest style imaginable."[32] What could be more "minimal and unforgiving" than hurling yourself off the deck of a pitching ship into cold, gray water while pitting your strength against the Atlantic's, attached by a thin line to a few square meters of Mylar threaded onto a skinny carbon pole screwed into a thin, eight-foot plank of epoxy weighing about twelve pounds? Who but a tiny elite of a similarly "self-contained, rabidly idealistic society, largely unnoticed and surprisingly uncorrupted by the world at large" would even wish to attempt it?

Jace, for one. A total of thirteen sailors, including some of windsurfing's top athletes will compete in the world's first Trans-Atlantic Windsurf Race, from Newfoundland to England, starting tomorrow. Compared to attempting

Everest, which costs about $65,000 per climber, each participant will pay $8,000 to enter this event. Even with partial sponsorship from equipment and sail manufacturers, the price is high. No athlete earns big money on the pro windsurfing circuit, especially in comparison to the purses for tennis or golf. It's a chance to make history but there are solid reasons why barely a handful of people have crossed the ocean on a sailboard. I hate to ask him the obvious, but...

"Why?"

"Because it's there."

Mallory's classic comment about climbing Everest has been used endlessly by adventurers in pursuit of new frontiers. Since 1928, when Mallory attempted to summit the world's highest mountain, climbing Everest has become heavily commercialized. The mountain's south base camp in May is covered with so many tents, it looks more like a social function than a hazardous expedition to the death zone at the roof of the world. In contrast, windsurfing offers genuine opportunities to skilled explorers who want to set records as the first person to windsurf across a particular body of water. From time to time, I still dream about organizing a windsurfing trip to the world's highest lake. Fly into Lima with a few friends, emergency medical supplies, and equipment, rent a four-wheel drive, and head south on the Panamericana, driving slowly into the Andes to acclimate. Why would I want to do this, given my medical history?

"It's so hard to find things that no one has ever done before." Jace looks thoughtful. "The real motivation for me and probably the others is that windsurfing across the Atlantic is taking yourself beyond what you've done before."

Since windsurfing has been around for less than thirty years, it is still open to pioneers. To date, only four men have managed to windsurf across the Atlantic, all French: Christian Marty, in 1985; Stephane Peyrone and Alain

Pichavant, whom I interviewed after their arrival in New York harbor on their tandem board, in 1986. Peyrone successfully windsurfed across the Atlantic, solo, in 1992. Fred Bouchet made it across a year or two after Peyrone. The very idea of windsurfing across an ocean is so incomprehensibly, overwhelmingly dangerous that even the late Baron Arnaud de Rosnay, whose personal mission was to spread diplomacy by windsurfing, solo, from one country to another, never attempted an Atlantic crossing. De Rosnay, who disappeared in 1984, while windsurfing to mainland China, made windsurfing history in 1984, when he crossed the three-mile Bering Strait. De Rosnay windsurfed from the Aleutians to a Soviet military base on the Siberian coast, in 1983. I still have a picture of him, smiling, sitting next to his sailboard, on an otherwise empty Soviet military transport plane that was taking him to Moscow.

Even using my own, comparatively limited experience, as a guide, the essence of windsurfing is to challenge yourself physically and mentally against the unpredictable forces of wind and sea. Add a no-holds-barred determination to venture into new territory and you have a mythic theme, one that takes spectators beyond the mundane, into the extraordinary, high-stakes domain of the sailor's risk, disappointment, pain, and, accomplishment. A human spirit unafraid to face the unknown may, in the end, become heroic in the act of touching us where we, too, would like to feel less scared. Likewise, witnessing someone else triumph over forces greater than himself can free a primal longing to accomplish more, ourselves.

Not that athletes talk about this much. Most of them, windsurfers included, tend to be kinesthetic thinkers. In order to learn, they need physical experience—"just do it!"— so that information can be processed and memorized through movement. Dancers, mechanics, artists, sculptors, and anyone who works with his or her hands tends to think kinesthetically. Visual thinkers store information in the form of pictures, usually speaking quickly as they race to describe images flashing across their mind's eye. Auditory thinkers need to hear information in the form of words or music, pausing to listen internally before speaking. They tend to use language carefully, unlike the rapid free association style of visual thinkers. Kinesthetics are often stuck for words, communicating enthusiasm through body language and facial expression. As any sports reporter knows, eliciting comments from monosyllabic kinesthetic athletes can feel like a journalistic equivalent of inching up an unyielding rock face. It has been my experience that trying to get someone to really talk about the inner dimension of windsurfing can end up with both of us conversationally becalmed.

On the face of the planet, few men are more artful in the Zen of windsurfing than forty-three year old Ken Winner. A master inventor, designer, engineer, technical wizard, and technical editor of *American Windsurfer* magazine, Winner is a world-class pro, who has won races all over the world.

Put another way, Ken Winner is to windsurfing what the late Dr. Jonas Salk is to the polio vaccine, identities interchangeably linked so that you cannot think of one without immediately connecting the other. Like Dr. Salk, whom I interviewed for *Sixth Sense*, Winner can become either a dream or a nightmare as an interview subject. If he likes you, and feels like talking, it's great. If he doesn't like you, or shuts down, you can spend the rest of the time trying to cajole him into saying something, but you've pretty much lost your window of opportunity for life. Men like Salk and Winner do not suffer fools and they don't give second chances if they find you boring. On the up side, anything that happens–or fails to happen–can become your story. If he's terse, it's news. If he doesn't want to talk, it's also news. If he looks out the car window and comments on the ugliness of a Bronx housing project, that, too, makes print.[33]

That Ken Winner has agreed to let me meet him at La Guardia airport today and drive him and his custom gear to Old Greenwich, Connecticut, seems nothing short of extraordinary. Our succinct exchange of e-mail messages has given me an introductory sense of his highly compressed intelligence, as if Ken Winner's brain has a kind of super zip drive that stores a few million more gigabytes of information than the rest of us have. Another hunch: Winner's thinking style is critical to an exacting degree, a talent needed for the precision of nautical engineering but quite possibly hell on wheels for conversational flow. This guy is not going to be easy, especially considering that he's taken a red-eye flight from the west coast.

My nervousness builds when Winner is A.W.O.L. at the baggage claim area when two padded board bags, obviously his, clog the opening to the conveyor belt. Who knows how many thousands of dollars worth of custom windsurfing gear could be getting banged and scraped over there? Maneuvering both bags through the opening, I am guarding his bags with my life, when Ken Winner appears, rubbing his eyes. At least, I think it's him. After seeing his pictures in windsurfing magazines for the past twenty-odd years, I'm surprised that I'm not one hundred percent sure. The man coming towards me looks taller than I expected, about six foot two. His face is thinner than in most pictures, and his hair, brown in all the photographs, is really that surfer's blonde. His eyes, blue and observant, seem to look through me, a sailor's natural expression. I get a sense that he can take in 360 degrees worth of sensory data within seconds, while apparently looking straight ahead. He also has the Walk.

There's nothing like meeting a physical genius to get me in touch with my inner klutz. Here I am, fumbling with the lines that tie his gear to the roofrack. It has taken about twenty minutes to get my car and find the exit to the multilevel, indoor parking garage, because the old exits are blocked off due to construction. All I can think of is how impatient I would be after a red-eye flight. Imagining Winner fidgeting and looking at his watch all this time makes me anxious. It doesn't help, when traffic stops in the middle of the Bronx Whitestone Bridge, and I decide that this man is incredibly handsome. All of a sudden, it feels like I'm trying to uphaul in 25 knots of wind, determined to give it my best, although it's clear there is no way this is going to work. All I want is a few quotes. *Well, maybe a smile.* The point of any interview, after all, is getting quotes and Winner, like my other inscrutable nemesis, Dr. Jonas Salk, is not too interested in talking. He does express concern, though, about the possibility "that people may have to spend more time on the mother ship than sailing if the winds are blowing thirty to fifty miles an hour." The mere thought of a ship tossing in 50 knot winds makes me seasick, but this passes quickly. Sailors say that when you get seasick, "first you're afraid you're going to die, and then you're afraid you're not."

Dave Weiss, 28, an amateur windsurfer on Team USA, has e-mailed directions to his Greenwich home but when we arrive, the four members of Team USA are—what else?—windsurfing at Sound Beach. Winner navigates our way through Old Greenwich, where there are allegedly more Rockefellers per square mile than anywhere else in America. This piece of trivia seems to appeal to his sense of irony. *Is that a smile?*

I have one more topic, as we come to the guardhouse where, normally only residents with seasonal permits are allowed to enter. Having reached adolescence, my daughter says that windsurfing is a waste of time. As the father of two daughters, does Ken have any advice for me?

"I designed the new Mistral Windglider, an inflatable sailboard with a small rig, in part so that my daughters, ages nine and eleven, would get into windsurfing. But they seem to like to use the inflatable part as a float," he sighs.

"Hey, Ken, we have a compatibility problem!" It's Jace calling as we pull into the parking area. Compatibility among whom? The team hasn't even gotten aboard yet. But Winner gets it: technical compatibility, as in boom–mast and universal–mast base attachments. The thingies that hold the gear together. Very important since your life literally hangs on them. Winner is out of the car before I've put it in park. *Was my driving that bad?*

Watching him take center stage under the tree where the equipment is laid out on the grass, I expect to hear, "Steady, Number One..." and "Yes, Captain." A few yards away, a crew from *Hard Copy* is taping Dave Weiss, Eddy Patrocelli, 28, and Kiran Beyer, 27, the first woman to attempt mid–Atlantic windsurfing. In 1986, Carolyn Stivens, then 18, windsurfed from Miami to New York with Stephane Peyrone and Alain Pichavant, an impressive accomplishment on its own. She was not part of the trans-Atlantic expedition.

As the first and only woman to join the "rabidly idealistic society" of transoceanic windsurfing, Kiran must have extraordinary skill, stamina, and confidence. I have seen only one picture of her, on the *American Windsurfer* website, and there is no question about her ability to loop off the lip of a wave. The basic starting position in windsurfing requires maneuvering the sailboard so that it floats, perpendicular to the wind. In this image, Kiran's board is airborne, 90 degrees perpendicular to the water, with her legs, back, head, and arms forming a "U" in mid–air. You might expect an athlete who can defy gravity while configuring herself into an advanced yoga posture *and* hang onto her equipment to have quads like a track star and shoulders like a diathalon thrower, but Kiran, at 5 foot 4 inches, radiates grace, energy, and openness about the adventure ahead. Her windsurfing career started in Baja California, where she worked first as a cook, then as a wavesailing instructor.

Following the wind, she toured the instruction circuit from Baja, to Maui, to the Gorge in Oregon, as well as the California coast. In the months before starting med school at Georgetown University in Washington, D.C., she is presently employed as a bilingual counselor for Planned Parenthood in Washington, D.C., competing in triathalons in her free time. Clearly a young lady who can hold her own, Kiran laughs when I ask her whether she thinks she's strong enough for this event. "Men, especially, think that windsurfing requires lots of muscle. They don't understand that it's a dance, like ballet," she grins, shaking water from her hair. Patty Hazen, owner of The Sailboard School in Sebastian, Florida, has a similar take: "When God created women to windsurf, She knew damn well what she was doing. It's not about muscle. It's all about finessing the wind."

Under normal conditions, perhaps. But who ever said the north Atlantic was a normal place to windsurf? Jason Upright, writing in the current issue of *Wind Surfing* magazine, cautions that even pros like Anders Bringdal and Micah Buzianis may be out of their league in the middle of the ocean because "World Cup sailors train for short and intense slalom events and wave riding, a far cry from racing across the ocean...Those guys are fast and big, but they're not necessarily used to sailing in a straight line forever." Noting the dangers posed by no landmarks or horizon for navigation, uninterrupted gray sky and sea, unpredictable swell patterns, gales, and an occasional passing whale, Upright notes that, "After an hour of sailing like that, even the World Cup guys may lose their focus and go down."

What happens then? "It's a logistical nightmare," confides John Chao, 45, publisher of *American Windsurfer* magazine. Chao, who windsurfed on the Taiwan team in the 1984 Olympics, is promoting TAWR98 in the United States. He will manage Team USA onboard the 330-foot Russian ship, the Kapitan Khlebnikov. "Our biggest fear, obviously, is losing someone. However, our technical support team has had experience with the Whitbread Round the World Yacht Race, the Virgin Atlantic Crossing, and the America's Cup. We're raising crisis management to an art form." State of the art safety gear given to the four windsurfers participating in each three and a half hour leg of mid-ocean racing will include a special flotation jacket containing an emergency beacon and bottle of water, and a two-way headset, so that he or she can radio for help, if needed. Every participant will have an inflatable rescue boat (R.I.B.) with trained technical support crew assigned to follow and assist, as needed. The R.I.B. will also pick up each racer at the end of a leg and bring him and his gear back to the mothership. "At least, that's the plan," says Chao, adding, "When you are dealing with a force of nature that is much more powerful than you, tactical plans and flexibility become more important than strategic planning." Planned or unplanned, the special events at sea this coming week will affect the course of windsurfing in the twenty-first century says Louie Hubbard, the 26-year old Englishman who is organizing this event. Louie's firsthand experience with ocean sailing included a brush with death when lightning and a force 12 gale struck his yacht, the Ocean Vagabond, in March 1993. With the yacht pitching heavily in 35-foot waves, Hubbard was nearly thrown into churning seas while climbing the mast to deal with a rebellious headsail. "I thought we had been through the worst when our yacht hit a submerged container and we were sinking!" Hubbard recalls. "I radioed for help and fortunately, we were rescued in a storm that claimed eight lives and the Ocean Vagabond, which was never found."[34] Returning to England, Hubbard concedes, "I never thought the sinking of the boat had affected me, but it actually twisted me inside. The idea of a Trans-Atlantic wWindsurf Race was born out of my confusion during this time." He believes the TAWR will become an important regatta like the Whitbread 'Round the World Yacht Race which, he says, started six years ago, with only three yachts. Hubbard says, "It is now one of the most televised sporting events in the world. Our plans for TAWR are no less ambitious."

That's if they get there. As I'm preparing to leave, having given Kiran a white rose to place in the sea for good luck, there's some heated discussion about whether all the equipment will fit in the luggage compartment of the bus. I'd love to see how they work it out but my other, "mommy life" calls. Checking my watch, I'll make it back to the middle school just in time. If I leave now...

Atlantic Point, NY
September 20, 1999

Does a wave leave a trace in the ocean?

−Zen koan

Like the art of finessing the wind, the art of finessing the written word requires that the practitioner, be she sailing or writing, practice an economy of energy. Too much movement or verbiage can cause one to flail, on a rather unstable platform. Other difficulties can arise from inadequate energy, equipment, ideas, or information.

Which brings me to the assignment at hand, writing about the world's first transatlantic windsurfing race without physically seeing it.

This is not the first time I've had this type of problem. When I interviewed Tenzing, among my assorted underpaid job functions was editing a newsletter for a company that specialized in adventure travel for the wealthy. Every month, I created a ship's log about the day-to-day activities of the company ship, and its various birdwatching cruises to Alaska, Baja, and Antarctica. This "log" was not the nautical record kept by the ship's captain; rather, it was a sketchy notebook of sorts, containing entries by the ship's onboard ornithologist or marine biologist, recording sightings of petrels, penguins, dolphins, and walruses.

Writing the ship's log required working with minimal facts, filling in key descriptions by tracking down a peripatetic ornithologist or two for phone interviews, and rewriting descriptions from travel guides. This is a trade secret: Travel guide editors do not leave their desks except to go to the bathroom. They spend most of their time rewriting material submitted by reporters in the field, checking facts over the phone, fleshing out paragraphs with

ideas and descriptions filched from other travel guides, edited by other editors who never leave their desks except...
This is how I managed to misplace a cathedral in Mexico
City, alleging it to be on the northwest corner of the *zocalo*
when, in fact, it stands cattycorner, on the southeastern tip
of that particular plaza. Our Mexico City–based reporter,
having filed his copy without mentioning the cathedral's
precise location, had been unreachable by phone the week
I was editing his chapter.

"What's the big deal?" my editor-in-chief shrugged after
the Mexico City–based writer complained about the mistake. "How many cathedrals can there be in that goddamn
zocalo, anyway? If a reader can find the *zocalo*, he would
have to be pretty fucking stupid to miss the cathedral!"
Details, details. Little did he realize that the "Get 'em and Go"
travel guides that bore his imprint were so notorious for
directional inaccuracies that they were jokingly known as
"The Get 'em and Get Lost" travel guides. Which is just as
well. In addition to his commanding persona, this seriously rotund fellow lacked a certain sense of humor when it
came to his formidable reputation as the media king of
travel publishing. Enthroned in his corner office like the
Emperor in the Tarot, he intimidated his minions, myself
included, with pragmatic intelligence and quick sarcasm. At
least I was intimidated when I found myself in his office,
like Oliver Twist asking for "more food, please." It seems
that, on the company ship's inaugural visit to China, not
one person had kept a notebook or ship's log.

"Please, sir, can we get some facts? I can't write this
month's log without facts."

"Facts?" he glared. "Any writer can write a ship's log with
facts. It takes real talent to write one without facts."

"I don't think I'm that talented, sir."

He dismissed me. "Nonsense. I have faith in you."

It occurred to me, then, as it does now, that the young
woman in the tale of Rumpelstisken had it easy. All she had

to do was sit in a tower and spin straw into gold.

Like a wave that leaves no trace, the drama at sea has gone unreported this week. Like scientists in Berkeley, California, who are using their computers to scan the galaxy for a radio signal from a distant planet, I log on to www.americanwindsurfer.com every morning. Nancy Roach and John Chao are doing an admirable job of filing dispatches, considering that the seas have been so rough that Jace was thrown from his bunk when the icebreaker rolled, and barf bags are hanging all over the Russian ship. Recovering the two-ton chase boats (R.I.B.'s) from the ocean is turning out to be a nightmare. A 900-pound swivel and hook has to be lowered from a crane on deck to a chase boat. One of the crewmen has to grab it quickly, hooking it so that the chase boat can be winched up to the pitching deck. In rough seas, the hook swings back and forth like a wrecking ball, making thousands of dollars worth of gear fly around. Two rescue boat crewmen have been hurt; one, whacked by sailboards being winched up to deck. The other crewman was knocked over by ocean swells.

On the morning of September 16, with winds blowing more than 40 knots and increasing swells, racing was canceled because it was too dangerous to launch and retrieve the chase boats. In the afternoon, the race committee ruled that only pro sailors from each team would be allowed to windsurf. Four of the world's strongest sailors–Micah Buzianis, Anders Bringdal, Robert Territheau, and Ken Winner–plunged into the ocean for a three-hour leg, during which they jumped the wake of the mothership and bombed down the sides of fifteen foot swells. A chase boat crewman said the seas were so rough that they could see the propeller and keel, as the icebreaker tossed around. After two hours of intense windsurfing, Winner's board cracked in half. "The ship was a mile away when it happened, so after that, I sailed very carefully. Just a little nerve wracking," he commented.

Team USA has been having a frustrating time. Dave Weiss has struggled with seasickness and broken gear. Kiran Beyer, overrigged on a 7.4 meter sail, found it hard to read the "bizarre, evil swell" on her first leg. Accustomed to reading sets of waves, she got disoriented. When the ocean sucked down the clew of her sail, it was impossible for her to relaunch, and she came back to the ship, disappointed. Eddy and Jace have had better luck on the water, although the team has consistently finished in last place. "I must be coaching the Bad News Bears," Winner reportedly grumbled one evening, but no one else seems to mind. As Jace said, before leaving, "We didn't come to win. We came to experience windsurfing in the North Atlantic and to work as a team."

But windsurfing is not basketball. In fact, a windsurfing team could almost be a contradiction of terms. Unlike climbers, who are roped together for survival, each member of a windsurfing team faces the ocean, winds, and his own strength, alone. "In climbing, having confidence in your partners is no small concern. One climber's actions can affect the welfare of the entire team...Hence it's not surprising that climbers are typically wary of joining forces with those whose bona fides are unknown to them," Krakauer notes.[35] Jim Gavin, Ph.D., an exercise psychologist in Montreal who has done extensive research into personality traits and sports, shows there is a correlation between sociability, spontaneity, risk-taking, discipline, competitiveness, and mental focus and certain sports. Tennis, golf, and downhill skiing, for example, rate high on the sociability scale. They appeal more to sociable types than to those who need more solitude. In contrast, yoga and running rate lower on the sociability scale and higher, in the focus category. While Gavin has not done any formal research on windsurfing and sailing, mental focus, risk-taking, spontaneity, and independence would probably top the personality trait chart.[36] As for competitiveness, Anders Bringdal,

Robert Territheau, and Micah Buzianis are among the most competitive pros in the world, but there is a common culture among sailors that helping a competitor in trouble is more important than a win. "If one of us doesn't come back, we've all lost," French sailor Isabelle Autissier, 42, said, after her boat was crushed by waves described as "the size of a four-story building" during the *Around Alone* solo, global sailing race. Since Autissier is the most popular female athlete in France, there's hope that sailing and windsurfing events, like T.A.W.R., will eventually capture the hearts and imagination of Americans, as well.

Today, having picked up speed to 14 knots yesterday to make up for the time lost at sea, the thirteen adventurers will make landfall at Weymouth, England. Team Liberty (Bringdal, Territheau, and Olausson) has won first place; Greece (Buzianis, Adamidis, and Fantis), second; Europe (Gilbert, Matin, and Pechere), third; and Team USA (Patricelli, Weiss, Beyer, and Panebianco), fourth. Having collectively windsurfed more than 450 dangerous nautical miles, they deserve all the champagne and television coverage they can get.

Southampton, NY
September 30, 1998

I have always known that at last I would take this road
But yesterday I did not know
It would be today.

−Narihara[37]

"What's taking you so long?" Kneeling, Jace watches me thread the black Fiberspar 3000 carbon mast through the sail's orange sleeve, making sure that the plastic pin locks into the hollow tip of the mast. If it doesn't lock in, the first downhaul will cause the entire sail to bunch around the mast. Most of the time, I get it right. Today is not one of them.

"We've been out twice since you got here," he grins.

"You just gotta keep going till you get it right." Leg extended, foot braced against the bottom of the mast foot, a sharp pull on the downhaul line and the tip snaps. "No way," I mutter. A few months ago I would be fuming at my own mistake. Could it be that daily Zen practice is having a calming effect? Working my way towards breathing to 100, spaces between thoughts are getting longer. Even mechanical problems such as this don't upset me as easily.

Now, start over: Release the downhaul. Walk fifteen feet to the tip of the mast. Pull the sail toward the mast tip, hand over hand. Quietly. Maybe I am learning something, after all.

"If I'm angry when I rig, I'll be angry when I sail."

"True," he agrees. When I look up a few seconds later, he is chasing the wind through a gathering, fine mist with his father and their friend. The three men look as natural as dolphins riding the surface of the sea.

Finally rigged, I stand near the back of the board, letting the wind "fly" the sail. When US 57 gets close enough to see, I step onto the board, pushing the rig forward, balancing behind the mast, and sheeting in. The 310 cruises into the water–a beach start!

"Beautiful! When did you learn that?" Sailing side by side, we resume last season's dialogue as if there had been no interruption. John and Maureen Ford of Windsurfing Hamptons host an annual clinic every September. Total immersion, small group work, simulators, and video playback create an accelerated learning environment where you can improve very quickly. The clinic is also building community among local windsurfers. Charles Dasher of Vela Windsurfing in Aruba, one of the world's instructional gurus who is also a talented filmmaker was here last week. During those two days of intensive retraining, Dasher, Donny, and Mark coached me past years of saying, "I can't."

"Something about seeing you guys off inspired me."

Carving a jibe, he calls out, across the water, "Next time, muscle the sail!"

The instinct to teach, like the instinct to dream and to risk, must be in his cells. Whether he sticks with pro windsurfing, or changes careers, Jace is one of those people who will need to keep challenging himself to take on the impossible and make it real for himself, and others. Now, if only I can catch up with him.

"What was it really like, windsurfing across the Atlantic?"

"The explorers must have been out of their minds!" he laughs.

"How so?"

"It's endless, the ocean. In seven days at sea, we never saw another ship. Imagine what it must have been like on a wooden boat with two masts. With no landmarks on the horizon." Maintaining a conversation while windsurfing is something of an art in itself. Standing on water requires one hundred percent concentration. Neither of us has said anything for a while. I'm about to ask a question, when Jace continues, "With no landmarks, it's easy to lose it out there. To keep myself from getting disoriented, I forced myself to zero in on little things, focusing just a couple of feet around me, so that I kept making a microcosm of my own little world at sea."

"What was your first impression?"

"Standing on the stern, rocking up and down. We needed to throw our rigs into the sea, then jump off the heaving deck, about twenty feet into the sea, then swim to our gear. I was asking myself if I could do it. Then, before I could answer, I jumped."

"I've seen the picture." Jace in mid-air, flashing a smile and thumb's up at the camera on the way down, has debuted on the web and will reappear in windsurfing mags around the world.

Naturally, conducting an interview from a moving windsurfer poses definite challenges. How do you take notes with both hands on the boom? I could have packed a tape recorder in a ziplock bag, strapped it to my wetsuit, and hoped for the best. Instead, I default to the "mental tape recorder" strategy that Francis Ford Coppola explained to me. The director was in his car one day, and wanted to dictate some notes, when he realized that he didn't have a tape recorder. "I was angry at first. Then I took an imaginary tape recorder and went through the process of loading it with fresh tape. Then, I began to push the button and speak. Later, I could sit down and type everything out just by activating that system."[38]

"For you, what was the most important part of the trans-Atlantic race?"

"From the time that you left us in Greenwich, it was pure adventure. When the bus arrived to pick us up, around eight o' clock PM, we couldn't fit all our gear into the luggage compartment! We called around, but no one would rent a van for a twenty-four hour drive to Newfoundland. We had a thirty hour window to make it to the ship. It was looking pretty grim when Dave Weiss pulled out his cell phone and eventually got a truck to bring our gear to St. Johns. He really made the event happen. Some people thought he wasn't experienced enough for the team, but without Dave, we would still be sitting on that sidewalk in Greenwich," he smiles, adding, "When we got into Canada, the truck drivers hijacked us. Basically, they refused to keep driving unless we gave them more money, then and there. If we left the main road to hunt for an ATM, we would lose time, and if we missed the ferry, the ship would be leaving without us. John Chao asked everyone on the bus to pull out their wallets. We raised $3,000 and got to the ferry with just ten minutes to spare."

"One last question: How did Kiran do?"

"It was mentally grueling for everyone. Kiran, especially, was pretty upset by the last day. She'd had major equipment problems throughout the race. I'm not religious, but I said a little prayer as she collected her gear and jumped off the ship about twelve miles offshore. I think she got lost and was floundering, underpowered, when Eddy Patricelli caught up with her. Even though Eddy wanted to be one of the finalists coming into England, he did something unbelievable. He gave her his own board, rigged with a 6.3 meter sail so she could be the one to windsurf the last few miles for Team USA. We were all waiting for her on the beach with champagne. When I ran over to her, mushing wet sand in her hair, I was about as happy and content as I've ever been." With that, the teacher throws the formless form of a jellyfish at me.

I know how hard everyone involved has worked to pull off this event, against considerable odds. Although he hasn't said so, I would imagine that, having invested his life's savings to enter a race that got hardly any media attention, Jace might be feeling just a little disappointed. I know I would. But in the big picture, history is a long-term proposition. Its current popularity notwithstanding, mountaineering has been around for centuries, and building, or changing a culture takes generations. The world may not yet notice the pioneers and adventurers emerging from this young, one-on-one type of sailing. But I have no doubt that the windsurfing chronicles of the future are holding a place for them.

Epilogue

Oak Beach, NY
October 28, 1998

Even the shriveled branch grows again,
And the sunken moon returns.
Wise ones who ponder this
Are not troubled in adversity.

—Bhartrhari[39]

A love affair should be like your relationship with a temperamental, adorable car—not necessarily good for you, but so engaging on an emotional level that you keep getting surprised by your own feelings. My love affair with windsurfing meets those criteria.

Then there's Neil.

Like an unexpected gust of wind that catapults you into the air, he has found his way back, after years of silence that seemed like the best course for both of us. His marriage having ended in the interim, we felt curious about what would happen, now. "Nothing that ends in hurt or anger is ever really complete," he tells me. And I agree. Years later, a jagged ending leaves the heart a little torn. At least, I think, we can say goodbye more quietly. That's what I was telling myself for the past month. Then, the night before his arrival, like a bungee jumper contemplating an illicit plunge from a suspension bridge in the middle of the night, I ran through hundreds of jump-cut scenarios at high speed, in bright color, till I couldn't sleep. Flashbacks and flash forwards. Night sweats. Adrenaline. Emotional bungee jumping.

A part of me was hoping that those "imponderables in

the chemistry of human transactions"[40] would simply not be there anymore. *Hi. Nice to see you. Thanks. Bye.* Or that psychological Gardol, the "invisible, protective shield" from those 1950s' black-and-white toothpaste commercials, would form a barrier between the clean, shiny surfaces of our respective personas. The truth is, I had no idea how, or even if, I would feel if I saw him again, and yes, it would be safer not to go there. But, as the man said, "I had a neighbor who choked to death on a hot dog." And Neil had a daughter who was killed in a car accident. We never know…

Despite whatever fears he may be feeling, it requires considerable courage for him to retrace such precarious steps of the heart. Who knows, this psychological terrain could turn out to have more hidden land mines than a wheatfield in Albania. How do you navigate under these conditions?

Gently, as it happens: driving through autumn-colored mountains, picnicking next to northern sapphire lakes, and hiking around white cliffs laced with webs of climbing ropes and human spiders. Searching for wind. Ever hopeful, I look out for activity in the upper branches of trees. Or non-activity. It would be elegant to end the season on a high lake. But it doesn't matter that much, now. The core of what was comfortable for us before is rediscovering its own sustaining rhythm. On this road trip, we also journey through several distinct regions of time, as mapped by Edward T. Hall. First, physical time, observable and digital, gives way to so-called biological time, the cadence of nature, marked off through rhythms of seasons, winds, and tides. Then sync time sets in.

"One of the first things that happens in life is for newborn infants to synchronize their movements to the human voice," says Hall, adding that "when people interact, they synchronize their motions in a truly remarkable way." Perhaps it's an empathic mirroring of gesture, voice tone, and facial expression that lets us drift in and out of talking and silence, picking up where we left off last time, as though there had been just a few songs in between, and neither one of us, changed. Which brings us, now, to mythic time, where "people do not age, for they are magic." Notes Hall, "This kind of time is like a story; it is not supposed to be like ordinary time...if the dance is successful, all awareness of the universe outside is obliterated. The world collapses and is contained in this one event."[41]

But haunting landmarks that code personal time often have a way of breaking into private, mythic zones, reminding us of places we would rather not remember. Just yesterday, when he admired a rundown, gray, stone building on a two-lane road, transparencies from my marriage, stored in a barricaded archive, flashed in front of me. Between jobs (or was it lifetimes?) my ex-husband and I had inspected that same building with a realtor, arguing outside about the money needed to turn it into a viable bed and breakfast.

"Too much," I remember saying.

To which he answered, "You never support my dreams."

There were years like that, sitting in cars, looking at properties we could not afford, in places we would never live. Exhausted from trying to make everything right, I lived in fear of provoking yet another quarrel. Wanting to be a good wife. Afraid to acknowledge the part of me that wanted out. Not wanting to rock the boat, mine or his. Weakened by two serious illnesses, afraid I couldn't make it on my own and support a child.

Pulling off the road, into a field stacked with wheat bales streaked white from the high sun, I reviewed some of those scenes for him. "If it weren't for you, I would still be in that car, driving around in the dark, looking to move my unhappiness to a new house." Even as I was saying this, an old disappointment broke free, like a plane streaking through the clouds.

"Our notions of happiness can be very dangerous," cautions Thich Nhat Hanh. How dangerous is wishful thinking that someone else should make up for what has not worked out? Or that it's possible to escape from the debris of a long marriage by falling in love? Yes, for a long time I blamed him for backing out, but it was not his job to put my soul together. The person I needed to become could only emerge, like learning to windsurf, again, by falling down and pulling myself up, over and over. "The truth is not what we expected," I had to laugh. "If you had come, then...if we had started living together, I would have recreated her. It would have been a disaster."

And so, back to rigging. "When listening not with the ear but with the spirit, one can perceive the subtle sound," says the Tao.[42] Threading the mast through the sleeve, determined to get out this afternoon, is that a thin, cold whistle hidden in the flapping of wind, sail, and asphalt? Behind the ears, a sliver–sharp reminder. Whitecaps. Zoom into a year ago.

"I got in trouble, there," I point.

His eyes track to the channel where the southwest wind funnels in from the Atlantic.

"When it comes to the sea, if you're in doubt, it's better not to go," he says, gently.

It's warmer sitting here, with my head on his shoulder, watching the last of the orange sun, listening to the ocean and its gulls. "Highly unlikely," I would have said a year ago, had anyone suggested that these two souls in transit would be here, at the beach, on a Tuesday afternoon, having carved out just enough time to reopen a careful affection. Tomorrow, we go back to the digital world of schedules and deadlines. Flying from different airports into opposite skies, he will head east, to complete a documentary on imagery with cancer patients; I will fly to the west coast, to finish a five–city, seven–seminar, three–week tour.

No time to think or feel sad. That's good. Meetings and partings, exhilaration and poignance, enhance each other.

Without them, it would be easy to slip into old habits, like believing that romance and security must coexist, or the illusion that planning the future will make it happen. Perhaps while chasing time down an airport corridor, or waking up in another hotel, one of us may question why this had to slip away. There will also be times when we forget to remember that yesterday is purely a memory and tomorrow, nonexistent; that life and love exist only in the *"O"* of *now*, a meditation on impermanence; and that trying to hold onto happiness, forever, is like trying to catch the wind.

1 *The Art of Happiness,* His Holiness the Dalai Lama with Howard Cutler, M.D. (New York: Riverhead Books, 1998), p. 195.

2 Lecture in Washington, DC. May 1996

3 Statistics on "hard adventure vacations" from 1992 to 1997 appeared in "Working Vacations," *American Demographics Book Store* publication, Cowles Business Media, NY, 1997, p. 10.

4 *Time,* March 6, 1989.

5 "The shaman of shred," Dana Miller, has numerous quotes about windsurfing, Zen, and life hand-written on his white Astro van.

6 The three death trajectories are described in *Working with Seriously Ill and Dying Patients,* a manual for a one-day seminar presented by Judith A. Skretny, M.A. (The American Academy of Bereavement, Carondelet Health Care, Tucson, AZ.)

7 365 *Tao Daily Meditations* by Deng Ming-Dao (New York: HarperCollins Publishers, 1992), p. 125

8 Statistics published in "Booming Business" by Lambeth Hochwald, *American Demographics,* December 1998, p. 32.

9 *The Little Zen Companion,* ibid., p. 43

10 After reading John du Quette's *Adicora, Venezuela: The Gringo's Windsurfing Map and Guide* (www.adicora.com), I went to Adicora in search of stories for *Wind Tracks Journal* and *Boards* (U.K.).

11 From a refrigerator magnet in a Disneyworld souvenir store.

12 Thanks to Dana Miller for sharing this Puerto Rican fishermen's equivalent of a Native American rain dance.

13 The waterskiing squirrels of St. Petersburg, Lights, Camera, and Action debuted on the CBS Morning News. Later in the day, they landed on my desk, to be rewritten for CBS affiliates and foreign markets.

[14] *The Wisdom of the Zen Masters* by Irmgard Schloegl (New York: New Directions, 1975), p. 16.

[15] Case 99 from the Zen text *Shoyroku* (Book of Equanimity): *"A monk asked Unmon, 'What about the 'speck of dust' samadhi?' Unmon said, 'Rice in the bowl; water in the pail.'"*
A deep bow to Lou Misunen Nordstrom, Sensei for his help in locating this reference via email, 8/19/00.

[16] Schiller, D., op cit, p. 16.

[17] Grof, S. and Grof, C., op cit, pp.

[18] *Tropical Classical: Essays in Several Directions* by Pico Iyer (New York: Alfred A. Knopf, 1997), pp. 110–119.

[19] *The Snow Leopard*, by Peter Matthiessen. (New York: Penguin books, 1978), p. 91.

[20] Thich Thien–An, op. cit., pp. 11 and 115.

[21] *Zen Mind, Beginner's Mind* by Shunryu Suzuki. (New York: Weatherhill, Inc., 1970), p. 57.

[22] Thich Thien–An, op. cit., The reference to *"un shui"* or "cloud and water man" occurs on page 108. The final passage quoted occurs on p.33.

[23] Thich Tien–An, ibid., p. 66.

[24] *Nine-Headed Dragon River: Zen Journals* by Peter Matthiessen (Boston: Shambhala, 1998), p.3.

[25] Matthiessen, ibid, p.3.

[26] Schiller, op. cit., p. 117.

[27] *The Heart of Being* by John Daido Loori (Boston: Charles E. Tuttle Co., Inc., 1996), p. 182.

[28] Michael Jordan's comments on Zen appear in *USA Today*, June 8 1998, p. 6C.

[29] The Snow Leopard by Peter Matthiessen (New York: Penguin Books, 1996), p. 90.

[30] Demographic projection of population density along the coast in fifty years comes from the Center for Marine Conservation. Members' talk. New York Yacht Club. March 1999.

[31] Jon Krakauer, *Into Thin Air* (New York: Anchor Books, 1998), p. 23.

[32] Krakauer, op. cit. p. 23.

[33] Interview with Ken Winner en route to Old Greenwich, CT, Sept. 11, 1998.

[34] Hubbard's account of his 1993 sailing accident was first printed in *American Windsurfer*, Vol. 7, Issue 3/4, 2000, "The Trans-Atlantic Misadventure" by Laurie Nadel, p. 79.

[35] Krakauer, op. cit., p. 47.

[36] Interview with James Gavin, Ph.D., 1993.

[37] With apologies to the reader, the source for this quote has disappeared into a pile of books and papers.

[38] Interview with Francis Ford Coppela, 1998.

[39] *Springs of Indian Wisdom* (New York: Herder and Herder, 1965), p. 1.

[40] Edward T. Hall, *The Dance of Life: The Other Dimension of Time*, Anchor Boooks, 1983, p. 47.

[41] Edward T. Hall, op. cit., p. 38.

[42] Deng Ming Dao, *356 Tao Daily Meditations*, p. 5.

Appendix

The Holmes and Rahe Social Readjustment Scale

The *Holmes and Rahe Social Readjustment Scale* is a list of stressful events which have been shown to have a cumulative impact on an individual's health and wellbeing. Each event has a rating of Life Changing Units, or L.C.U.'s.

To calculate your L.C.U. score, check off each event which applies to your life within the past two years and write the numerical rating in the SCORE column. Total your SCORE. You will find the explanation box at the end of this survey.

RANK	EVENT	POINTS	SCORE
1.	Death of spouse	100	_____
2.	Divorce	73	_____
3.	Marital problems	65	_____
4.	Jail term	63	_____
5.	Death of close family member	45	_____
6.	Personal injury or illness	53	_____
7.	Marriage	50	_____
8.	Fired from work	47	_____

RANK	EVENT	POINTS	SCORE
9.	Marital reconciliation	45	_____
10.	Retirement	45	_____
11.	Change in family member's health	44	_____
12.	Pregnancy	40	_____
13.	Sexual difficulties	39	_____
14.	Addition to family	39	_____
15.	Business readjustments	39	_____
16.	Change in financial status	38	_____
17.	Death of close friend	37	_____
18.	Change to different line of work	36	_____
19.	Change in # of marital arguments	35	_____
20.	Mortgage or loan over $15,000	31	_____
21.	Foreclosure of mortgage/loan	30	_____
22.	Change in work responsibilities	29	_____
23.	Son or daughter leaving home	29	_____
24.	Trouble with in-laws	29	_____
25.	Outstanding personal achievement	28	_____

RANK	EVENT	POINTS	SCORE
26.	Spouse begins or stops work	26	_____
27.	Starting or finishing school	26	_____
28.	Change in living conditions	25	_____
29.	Revision of personal habits	24	_____
30.	Trouble with boss	23	_____
31.	Change in work hours/conditions	20	_____
32.	Change in residence	20	_____
33.	Change in schools	20	_____
34.	Change in recreational habits	19	_____
35.	Change in Church activities	19	_____
36.	Change in social activities	19	_____
37.	Mortgage or loan under $15,000	17	_____
38.	Change in sleeping habits	16	_____
39.	Change in # of family gatherings	15	_____
40.	Change in eating habits	15	_____
41.	Vacation	13	_____
42.	Christmas season	12	_____

RANK	EVENT	POINTS	SCORE
43.	*Minor violation of the law*	11	_____
		TOTAL:	_____

How To Interpret Your Score:

Total score of less than 150 = 37 % chance of illness during the next two years

Total score of 150 – 300 = 51% chance of illness during the next two years

Total score of more than 300 = 80 % chance of serious illness during the next two years

Acknowledgements

A lifetime of friends and family, too numerous to mention by name, have helped me navigate through the crossings, crises, and adventures in these journals.

Dancing with the Wind owes special thanks to Dan Rather, who told me, in 1997, that I needed to start writing again. I would not have had the guts to start the difficult process of reworking the chaos of my handwritten notes without his giving me a push to launch myself. Dan's behind-the-scenes encouragement over the years has helped me stay focused and keep my eye on the ball. I also thank Claire Fletcher and Sakura Komiyama for their help.

Although our original newsroom tribe has scattered throughout the broadcast industry, our friendships have stayed intact and continued to grow. Special thanks to Sal Messina (my Siamese twin), Robin Skeete, Jack Smith, Sam Shirakawa, Bill Jones, Stephanie Abarbanel, Megan Marshack, Nell Donovan, Mary Jane Clark, Linda Karas, Andi Augenblick, Ted Data, Art Patterson, Bob Little, John Frazee, Marcy McGinnis, Laurie Singer, Nann Goplerud, Dan Meltzer, Harris Salomon, Rhonda and Al Lowe, and Keiji Imai.

For their friendship, mentoring, and encouragement in my second career as an author and psychotherapist, my deep gratitude to Dr. Edith Jurka, Dr. Sherman Schachter, PJ and Dr. Michael Dempsey, Dr. Michael Cindrich, Dr. Gideon Panter, Dr. Ramona Craniotes, Dr. Gary Leeds, Dr. Richard Goldberg, Madeleine Lloyd, Peg Baim, Dr. Ellen Slawsby, Bob and Rosalind Brigham, Ken Frey, Carol Feinhage, Maurice and Kathi Kougell, Dr. Al Siebert, Dr. Jeffrey Mishlove, Dr. Ronna Kabatznick, and Dr. Theresa de Luca.

John Chao, publisher of *American Windsurfer*, has been instrumental in bringing this book to readers. Part One of

Dancing with the Wind was first published on www.american-windsurfer.com, an award-winning site that gets more than five-million visitors each year. John's vision for *Dancing with the Wind* as a source of inspiration is unsurpassed. His optimism, drive, and friendship are an ongoing source of strength.

Deep thanks to Jon, Maureen and Nicolas Ford of Windsurfing Hamptons for their enthusiasm and expertise, and to my coach, Jace Panebianco, who further challenged me to get the book out of my head and onto paper. Among the worldwide family of windsurfers, my special thanks to Bonnie Pfeiffer for her great spirit, Suzy Chaffee (another great spirit), Raphaela le Gouvello, Joanie Graham, Annabella Claudia Hoffmann, Rafael Bach, Martin and Kristen Trees, Todd and Pam McCarthy, Warren Oakley, Ben Nathan, John du Quette, Alex Hanssmann, Gerhard Lattiner, and Tim Taggard, one of the gentlemen of windsurfing. To Tony Cirrincione, Karen Kaul, Phillip Hill, David and Adrienne Levine and Johannes Lourens for reading the entire manuscript pre-publication, deep thanks. Claudia Ghiringelli, who translated Part One into Italian for her master's thesis, has won my heart!

To Peter Muryo Matthiessen, who generously agreed to an interview and who invited me into the sangha so that I could become a beginner again after twenty years of studying Zen, a deep bow. I am especially grateful to the Ocean Zendo women's group and the monks–Dorothy Dai-en Friedman, Kendall Jishin Hoffmann, and Katri Kuge Kepponen, for their straightforward, warm, and humourous approach to life, love, and the dharma. To my dharma friends Joan Zandell, Linda Coleman, Jane Barton, Meghan and Scott Chasky, and Gudrun Gyo-ji Hoerig, and Hilda Hoerig, I could not have made it without you.

I cannot begin to thank my family for bearing with me: Mom, Mindy, Karl, Eric, Jeannie, Lucky and Bogart and to Santiago Aguinaga, who bravely soldiered through the bibliography. To my exteneded family, a bear hug: the Nadel–Eisman–Mordkoff–Glass–Matthias–Fink–de Chacon–Diamond–VanDijk–Hable clans.

To Murray Radzanower, the Computer King, and Sir John of Technoland, there are not enough brownies, cookies, or cartoon neckties for you guys! I'm a tech support nightmare.

Special gratitude to Lisa Hagen, for believing in me and the manuscript through several rounds of rejections and to Sandra Martin, Patrick Huyghe, Erika Lieberman, Mary Huff, Patty Conklin, Marie Birnbaum, Maddy Epstein, Geert Ekking and Nicoline, Jane, Tom, and Sean Finnegan, Charlene Harrington, Naima Rauam, Nancy Quade, Mike Greco, Agapi Stassinopoulos, Carol and Sandy Denicker, Pam Hrubey, Sandra Bower, Cherisa Burke, Martin Brecht, Steve Whitehouse, Saul Bickman, Liz and Dick Turner, Craig Diamond, Eric Stutt, Gayil Greene, Marilyn, Cindy, and Alda Bruno, Amy Haddon, Alice Bray, Pat Weiss, Marta, Carlos, Roger Pratt, Bill Barbanes, Linda and Ryan Pelerin, Ross Gilligan, Jacqui Lait and Peter Jones, Maureen Spires, Suzan Lang, Nancy Quade, Diane Kitchen, and Marina Nelson. For his shoulder to lean on, thank you, John.

When my daughter was four, she asked me if we were poor. I told her that if you don't have friends, no matter how much money you have, you will always be poor. And if you have great friends, you will always be rich—even if you don't have much money. As Albert Einstein is alleged to have said, "Many of the things you can count, don't count; many of the things you can't count, really count." Each of you who has touched, listened to, walked, or sat with us along the way has given us a measure of wealth that cannot be counted.

Glossary

Boom: a wishbone-shaped bar which attaches to the mast. sailor holds onto the boom to brace herself and steer.

Clew: the widest point of a sail

Daggerboard: a centerboard that runs vertically through the center of the windsurfer into the water to stabilize it.

Hobie Cat: a catamaran, meaning a sailboat with two hulls. Hobie Cats have no cabins or engines and are designed for flat-out speed in high-wind conditions.

Jibe: to change course by heading downwind.

Knots: Wind speed. Knots equals nautical miles per hour. A light breeze would be 3 - 5 knots; moderate 5 - 15; strong 15 and above.

Mast: looks like a flagpole. the sail is threaded onto the mast which is then attached to the windsurfer.

Port: directional–to the left

Reach: sailing at a wide angle to the wind.

Rig (v): to rig means to set up the sail so that can be used for windsurfing

Rig (n): a rig means a complete set of windsurfing gear (sail-boom-mast, etc.)

Starboard: directional–to the right

Tack: to change course by heading into the wind.

Universal joint: attaches the base of the sail to the windsurfer, enabling the mast to rotate.

Uphaul: a rope or line attached to the boom which lifts the sail out of the water

Wake: the path of water displaced by a moving craft, i.e., windsurfer or boat.

Bibliography

Adler, Allan J, M.D. and Christine Archambault. *Divorce Recovery*. New York: Bantam Books, 1992

Bachelard, Gaston. *The Poetics of Space*. Massachusets: Beacon Press books, 1969

Bainbridge, Beryl. *The Birthday Boys*. New York: Carroll and Graf, 1998.

Bandler, Richard. *Using Your Brain—for a CHANGE*. Utah: Real People Press, 1985

Batchelor, Stephen. *Buddhism Without Beliefs*. New York: Berkley Publishing Group, 1997

Bauby, Jean-Dominique. *The Diving Bell and the Butterfly*. New York: Alfred A. Knopf, 1997

Baynes, Carey F. *The I Ching* New York: Princeton University Press, 1967.

Benson, Herbert, M.D. *Timeless Healing* New York: Scribner, 1996.

Blachman, Sushila. *Graceful Exits*. New York: Weatherhill, 1997.

Bowers, Barbara, Ph.D. *What Color Is Your Aura*. New York: Pocket Books, 1989.

Brice, Jan. *The Secrets of Consciousness*. New York: Elzikior Publications, 1992.

Brigham, Deirdre Davis. *Imagery for Getting Well.* New York: W.W. Norton and Company, Inc., 1995.

Bucke, Richard Maurice, M.D. *Cosmic Consciousness.* New York: Arkana-Penguin, 1991.

Camus, Albert. *American Journals.* New York: Paragon House Publishers,1987.

Camus, Albert. *The Myth of Sisyphus.* New York: Vintage Books,1955.

Castaneda, Carlos. *The Art of Dreaming.* New York: HarperPerennial, 1994.

Chitrabhanu, Gurudev Shree. *The Psychology of Enlightenment.* New York: Dodd, Mead and Company, 1979.

Cooper, Andrew. *Playing in the Zone.* Boston: Shambhala, 1998.

Collins, Sean, Dr. *Tipping the Scales.* Dublin: DigiSource Limited, 1997.

Deng Ming-Dao. *365 Tao.* New York: Harper Collins, 1992.

Durrell, Lawrence. *Justine.* New York: Pocket Books, Inc., 1957.

Estés, Clarissa Pinkola, Ph.D. *Women Who Run With the Wolves.* New York: Ballantine Books, 1995.

Evans-Wentz, W.Y. *The Tibetan Book of the Dead.* London: Oxford University Press, 1980.

Gerber, Richard, M.D. *Vibrational Medicine*. Santa Fe: Bear and Company, 1988.

Gersten, Dennis, M.D. *Are You Getting Enlightened or Loosing Your Mind?* New York: Harmony Books, 1997.

Glaser, Barney G. and Strauss, Anselm L. *Awareness Of Dying*. New York: Aldine Publishing Company, 1980.

Goleman, Daniel. *Emotional Intelligence*. New York: Bantam Books, 1995.

Goleman, Daniel. *Healing Emotions*. Boston: Shambhala, 1997.

Grof, Stanislav, M.D. and Grof, Christina. *Spiritual Emergency* New York: Penguin Putnam Inc.,1989.

Hall, Edward T. *The Dance of Life* New York: Anchor Books, 1983.

Hall, Edward T. and Mildred R. Hall. *Hidden Differences*. New York: Anchor Books, 1987.

Hall, Edward T. *The Hidden Dimension*. New York: Anchor Books, 1982.

Hall, Edward T. *The Silent Language*. New York: Anchor Books, 1981.

Harner, Michael J. *The Jívaro* Berkeley: University of California Press, 1984.

Herrigel, Eugene. *Zen in the Art of Archery*. New York: Vintage Books, 1971.

His Holiness The Dalai Lama and Cutler, Howard C. M.D., *The Art of Happiness*. New York: Riverhead Books, 1998.

Holmes, Ernest. *The Science of Mind*. New York: Dodd, Mead and Company, 1938.

Iyer, Pico. *Tropical Classical*. New York: Alfred A. Knopf, 1997.

Jaworski, Joseph. *Synchronicity: The Inner Path of Leadership*. San Fransisco: Berrett-Koehler Publishers, 1996.

Jackson, Phil and Delehanty, Hugh. *Sacred Hoops*. New York: Hyperion, 1995.

Kharitidi, Olga, M.D. *Entering the Circle*. New York: Harper Collins, 1996.

Krakauer, Jon. *Into Thin Air*. New York: Anchor Books, 1997.

Krieger, Dolores, Ph.D, R.N. *The Therapeutic Touch: How to Use Your Hands to Help or to Heal*. Englewood Cliffs: Prentice-Hall, 1979.

Lawrence, Gordon. *People Types and Tiger Stripes*. Gainesville: Center for Applications of Psychological Type, 1979.

Loori, John Daido. *The Heart of Being*. Boston: Charles E. Tuttle Co., Inc., 1996.

Martin, Philip. *The Zen Path through Depression*. New York: Harper Sanfrancisco, 1999.

Matthiessen, Peter. *At Play in the Fields of the Lord*. New York: Vintage Books, 1991.

Matthiessen, Peter. *The Cloud Forest* New York: Penguin Books, 1997.

Matthiessen, Peter. *Nine-Headed Dragon River.* Boston: Shambhala, 1998.

Matthiessen, Peter. *The Snow Leopard.* New York: Penguin Books, 1996.

Mindell, Arnold. *The Shaman's Body.* New York: Harper Collins, 1993.

Morgan, Marlo. *Mutant Message Down Under.* New York: Harper Perennail, 1995.

Nadel, Laurie. *Sixth Sense.* New York: Prentice Hall Press, 1990.

Neruda, Pablo. *Twenty Love Poems* London: Grossman, 1969.

O'shea, Farrel. *An Introduction to Windsurfing.* New York: Gallery Books, 1987.

Perkins, John. *PsychoNavigation.* Rochester: Destiny Books, 1990.

Perkins, John. *The Stress-Free Habit.* Healing Arts Press, Rochester,1989.

Perkins, John. *The World Is As You Dream It.* Rochester: Destiny Press, 1994.

Pert, Candace B., Ph.D., *Molecules of Emotion.* New York: Touchstone, 1997.

Pirsig, Robert M. *Zen and the Art of Motorcycle Maintenance.* New York: Bantam Books, 1975.

Rabbin, Robert. *The Sacred Hub.* San Francisco: New Leaders Press, 1995.

Remarque, Erich Maria. *Arch of Triumph.* New York: Appleton–Century Co., 1945.

Rinpoche, Sogyal. *The Tibetan Book of Living and Dying.* New York: Harper Collins, 1993.

Rossi, Earnest Lawrence. *The Psychobiology of Mind-Body Healing.* New York: Norton and Co., 1986.

Salajan, Ioanna. *Zen Comics.* Rutland: Tuttle Co., 1974.

Schloegl, Irmgard. *The Wisdom of the Zen Masters.* London: New Directions, 1976.

Siebert, Al, Ph.D. *The Survivor Personality.* New York: Perigee Books, 1996.

Siegel, Bernie S., M.D. *Love, Medicine and Miracles.* New York: Harper and Row, 1986.

Smith, Jean. *Everyday Mind.* New York: Riverhead Books, 1997.

Schiller, David. *The Little Zen Companion.* New York: Workman Publishing, 1994.

Suzuki, Shunryu. *Zen Mind, Beginner's Mind.* New York: Weatherhill, 1998.

Thich Thien-An. *Zen Philosophy, Zen Practice*. Berkley: Dharma Publishing, 1975.

Todd, Olivier. *Albert Camus*. New York: Alfred A. Knopf, 1997.

Various. *Springs of Indian Wisdom*. New York: Herder and Herder, 1965.

Weiss, Brian L., M.D. *Many Lives, Many Masters*. New York: Fireside Book, 1988.

Whitaker, David. *The Gospel According to Phil* Chicago: Bonus Books, 1997.

Winner, Ken. *Windsurfing with Ken Winner*. Toronto: Personal Library Publishers, 1980.

Wolinsky, Stephen, Ph.D. *Trances People Live*. Connecticut: The Bramble Company, 1991.

Yalom, Irvin D., M.D. *Love's Executioner*. New York: Harper Perennial, 1989.

Zadra, Dan with Susan Carlson. *Brilliance*. Edmonds: Compendium Inc., 1995.

Audio and Videotapes

Video

Judson, Stephen and Lorimore, Alec, and Macgillivary, Greg.(producers) *Everest* Burbank, Miramax productions,1997.

Audio

Chodron, Pema *Noble Heart*. Boulder: Sounds True, 1998.

Dass, Ram. *Spiritual Practices and Perspectives* Boulder: Sounds True, 1992.

Grof, Stanislav, M.D. *The Transpersonal Vision*. Boulder: Sounds True, 1998.

Hanh, Thich Nhat. *The Present Moment*. Boulder: Sounds True, 1993.

Kornfield, Jack. *The Roots of Buddhist Psychology*. Boulder: Sounds True, 1995.

For more information about Laurie Nadel, PhD., and "How To Be Your Own Coach," a companion series of individual workshops on enhanced CD and cassettees containing exercises for stress reduction, accelerated healing, the science of peak performance, and the science of dreams, go to *www.laurienadel.com*.

Printed in the United Kingdom
by Lightning Source UK Ltd.
591